THE GREAT ENGLISH FINAL

DAVID TOSSELL

THE GREAT ENGLISH FINAL

1953: CUP, CORONATION & STANLEY MATTHEWS

Pitch Publishing Ltd
A2 Yeoman Gate
Yeoman Way
Durrington
BN13 3QZ
Email: info@pitchpublishing.co.uk
Web: www.pitchpublishing.co.uk

First published in the UK by Pitch Publishing, 2013
Text © 2013 David Tossell

A CIP catalogue record for this book is available from the British Library.

ISBN: 978-1-90917-844-1

Cover design by Brilliant Orange Creative Services.

Typesetting by Pitch Publishing.

Printed and bound by CPI Group (UK) Ltd, Croydon, CR0 4YY.

CONTENTS

ACKNOWLEDGEMENTS

PROJECTS OF this nature rely heavily on the cooperation of many people and I am indebted in particular to those people who shared memories of the events and the era captured in this book. Their assistance is apparent throughout the text, although some who do not appear are also deserving of thanks: Andrew Dean and Gareth Moores at Bolton Wanderers FC, Frank Buckley, Mike Davage, Lynne Mollard, Haydn Parry, Richard Whitehead, the staffs at the British Newspaper Library, Colindale, and Blackpool Central Library and the various eBay sellers from whom I have purchased all manner of obscure items.

I owe enormous gratitude to the authors and editors of all the written material that has been the cornerstone of my research. I hope I have captured everything in this book's bibliography, but my apologies for any inadvertent omissions. Additionally, I would like to thank Martin Johnes for permission to reproduce an extract from *The 1953 FA Cup Final: Modernity and Tradition in British Culture*, Aurum Press for use of an extract from Arthur Hopcraft's *The Football Man,* and David Goldblatt for allowing me to quote from his seminal work, *The Ball is Round*. Attempts to contact the excellent but now closed Bolton Revisited website proved fruitless, but I thank them nevertheless for the extract from Brian Farris's *Cottontown Biography*.

Thanks to Paul and Jane Camillin and Duncan Olner at Pitch Publishing, and Laura Wagg at the Press Association for help in sourcing photographs.

My family continues to be as supportive as ever and my wife, Sara, deserves special praise for barely raising an eyebrow when another box-load of vital 'research material' appears in our spare room.

INTRODUCTION

"The climax to the 1953 final may have been dramatic but there were more skilful Cup Finals in that era that are largely forgotten. It was the combination of different narratives that were not centred upon the actual play in the 1953 final that have ensured the game's place in popular memory." – Martin Johnes and Gavin Mellor, *The 1953 FA Cup Final: Modernity and Tradition in British Culture.*

I WENT there in search of ghosts, but the few I found were in unlikely places. I'm not sure exactly what I expected to encounter on a bitterly cold November day at Bolton's Reebok Stadium that would hark back to a sunny afternoon in May 1953, when Blackpool's orange-jerseyed heroes had scored three times in the final 20 minutes at Wembley to fulfil the burning ambition of Stanley Matthews, the country's most-famous and most-loved player. I certainly wasn't harbouring notions of seeing the spectre of the great winger materialise among the burly athleticism of a modern Premier League match. And no one had turned up expecting drama and excitement to match that 4-3 epic almost six decades earlier. I just knew that

Bolton Wanderers' home game against Blackpool, the clubs' first meeting in England's top division since 1968 – 42 years earlier – had exerted a magnetism over someone studying the most famous of all matches between these teams.

Blackpool's fans arrived dressed in orange, just as the famously flamboyant Atomic Boys had done at their club's biggest matches in the years after the Second World War. Yet where once this band of brothers had worn colourful tailored suits, even oriental outfits with turbans, and had carried an orange-dyed duck as a mascot, their 21st century ancestors were more predictably attired in polyester replica jerseys emblazoned with the kind of commercial messaging unthinkable in the 1950s. With 90 minutes to go before kick-off, however, a frisson of nudges and nods outside the stadium's main entrance revealed that the sartorial spirit of the old-school fan was still alive. Barely a head remained unturned as BBC radio reporter and *It's A Knockout* legend Stuart Hall, a man synonymous with a more uncomplicated age, strode jovially through the glass doors wearing a thigh-length fur coat over mustard-coloured trousers. No duck, though.

Nor, on this day, was there anyone to remotely challenge the popularity of Matthews, the acclaimed "Wizard of the Dribble", whose quest to claim a winner's medal at Wembley at the third attempt had diverted the watching nation from its anticipation of the Coronation of Queen Elizabeth II a month later. Charlie Adam, a skilful Scottish midfielder who in bygone days could have been a devastating foil for Matthews as an old-fashioned wing-half or inside-forward, was the best Blackpool could offer. Appropriately he was the first man to step off the team coach, acknowledging the cheers as he walked briskly towards the players' entrance.

Once the article in the matchday programme about the famous final had been absorbed, the contemporary football on display served to delete my black and white images of

1953 as effectively as if I had hit the off button on my DVD player while viewing the often-blurry BBC footage and been assaulted by MTV instead. It did seem appropriate, at least, to discover via an advertising hoarding that Bolton's current full-backs – heirs to the legacy of uncomplicated muscle men such as Tommy and Ralph Banks, Roy Hartle and Johnny Ball – were sponsored by a tattoo parlour.

And there was a late comeback, although this time it was Bolton who scored twice in the final 15 minutes to achieve a draw against a visiting team who had no intention of sitting on a 2-0 lead away from home even when it would have been advisable and excusable. Quite right, the Blackpool of Mortensen and Matthews and skipper Harry Johnston would have said.

When, six months later, the teams reconvened at Bloomfield Road for the Seasiders' last home game during their brief reacquaintance with English football's top level it was on FA Cup Final day no less. The estimated 1953 final audience of ten million had been enough to finally convince the football authorities to move the sport's biggest showpiece away from the concluding weekend of the League schedule. Yet now, for the first time since Matthews's finest hour, the Cup finalists would have to share their day, victims of the demands placed upon Wembley by the UEFA Champions League, the monolith of modern club football. As if to remind everyone of how things once were, the fates, the gods and some sub-standard defending contrived to produce a final score of Blackpool 4 Bolton Wanderers 3. Those ghosts had finally turned up.

* * * * *

TWO MILLION more people watched the 1953 FA Cup Final – many on friends' and neighbours' sets – than tuned in for the Manchester City–Stoke City final of 2011, which

11

kicked off just as the Blackpool and Bolton players were arriving back in the Bloomfield Road dressing room. Such figures say much about the position of the competition in football's 21st century priority list, but also about its place in the country's consciousness almost six decades earlier.

Although not the first Wembley final to be televised live, the 1953 showpiece was the first to achieve a significant audience. On top of the viewing public, almost as many again listened to it on the radio. And it was a shared experience for most, with the ten million who watched on BBC sitting around the fewer than five million televisions in British homes at the time. Many of those sets, nine-inch screens set in teak or walnut cabinets, were recent additions as electrical stores enjoyed a rush of people eager to purchase prior to the planned live broadcast of the Coronation ceremonies.

Author and sports sociologist Garry Whannel would state that the events at Wembley on 2nd May 1953 constituted, after Roger Bannister's first sub four-minute mile and the 1966 World Cup Final, "probably the most mythologised moment in British sporting history". The reasons it has endured over six decades, why modern fans whose fathers were born years after the game know the narrative details of "The Matthews Final", are manifold.

Not least in importance is the fact that the Coronation-induced television boom contrived to take the Cup Final to the masses in exactly the year that many more casual fans had found a reason to follow the game – in one Stanley Matthews, whose England debut had been almost two decades earlier, who was the first-ever Footballer of the Year and who, as he approached the end of his fourth decade, was assumed to be on the verge of leaving the sport he had graced. The manner in which his storyline captivated a wider audience beyond the traditional working-class followers of the sport made it one of the most significant moments in the widening of football's social boundaries.

It is easy to see a comparison with the way that, in 1990, a British public disaffected with the national game after Heysel, Hillsborough and countless hooliganism-related problems rekindled its old passion via another humanitarian tale, Paul Gascoigne's tears at the World Cup semi-final. Just as the affair with Gazza was to be almost instantly consummated by the glossy arrival of Sky Sports and the cash-rich Premier League, the Matthews love story was nurtured – albeit in a more reserved, front-parlour manner – by the sport's steadily escalating courtship with the media over the next decade, culminating in the arrival of *Match of the Day* in 1964.

As Dave Russell notes when discussing the 1953 final in his social history of the sport, *Football and the English*: "That so many, even those who were not close followers of the sport, experienced the novelty of watching a national hero win an honour which had previously eluded him not only gave this game in particular a privileged place in football history, but gave the sport in general an enhanced status."

Neville Cardus, the doyen of cricket writers, was even moved to write to *The Times* after the game suggesting that football was usurping his favoured sport as the game of the British people. It is no coincidence that the inevitable shallowing of football's post-war attendance figures since the high-water mark of the 1948/49 season was momentarily reversed in the season that immediately followed such a captivating Wembley final.

It is possible, too, to look back now and see the game as being indicative of Britain standing at an important crossroads in its recent history, as endorsed by Martin Johnes and Gavin Mellor in their 2006 article, *The 1953 FA Cup Final: Modernity and Tradition in British Culture*. In it, they contend:

> It was also a match that was intertwined with the ideas of modernity and tradition that ran through British culture

in the early 1950s. The new Queen, present at the game, represented optimism in the future, an optimism closely linked with a technological progress that was epitomised by television… Yet, as the loyalty towards the monarchy and the celebration of a respectable working-class hero like Matthews showed, British culture also remained profoundly attached to older traditions.

The wholehearted, cynicism-free embrace of Matthews's search for the Cup winner's medal that had eluded him in two previous finals was in some ways a mirror of the country's conservative – and Conservative – reinstallation of the old warhorse Sir Winston Churchill as Prime Minister in 1951. It was Britain's way of placing its very own old-fashioned heroes up on pedestals at a time when the country itself had been slipping down the pecking order of the world's most powerful nations.

That combined mood of national chest-beating and lauding of have-a-go heroes would continue on into the summer. First, a British-led Everest expedition under the guidance of John Hunt became the first to successfully climb the world's highest mountain – never mind that it was a New Zealander, Edmund Hillary, and Sherpa companion Tenzing Norgay who actually stood on the summit. The sporting arena saw 49-year-old Gordon Richards, the nation's most popular jockey, win his first Derby after 32 years in the saddle, before Len Hutton's England cricket team beat Australia in the fifth Test at The Oval to regain the Ashes for the first time since 1934. The Coronation honours list would even bestow cricket's first knighthood on Jack Hobbs, rewarded for a remarkable three-decade career in which he had broken all the game's batting records.

The support for men such as Matthews, Hobbs and Richards both reinforced and reflected the spirit of social unity that existed in the country. The shared experience of six years of conflict was still a powerful force and it was a period of political consensus. The post-war Labour government of Clement Attlee had managed to demonstrate concern for the underprivileged without alienating the middle and upper classes, and all parties – despite the recent change of government – remained committed to the development of the welfare state.[1] Although many effects of post-war austerity still lingered by the time Blackpool were embarking on their journey to Wembley in the first weeks of 1953, there was an undoubted improvement in the economics and comforts of most people's everyday lives. It was, according to historian David Kynaston, "the breakthrough year in terms of moving away from austerity and towards improved living standards and even a measure of affluence". One effect was to make the population more enamoured of their country's figureheads, more ready to embrace the monarchy. In particular they were in thrall to their glamorous new Queen and excited at the prospect of celebrating her big day.

According to Johnes and Mellor: "This was all more than mere symbolism. The 1953 Cup Final was reported and constructed by the press in line with these other cultural currents, helping shape how people thought about the Britain in which they lived."

Significantly, *The Times* led its matchday preview with the presence of the Queen at Wembley, while the *Sunday Times* followed up with the headline "QUEEN SEES BLACKPOOL WIN 4-3". Even in the wake of its local team's victory, the press in Blackpool made much of the Mayor's reaction to meeting Elizabeth, who he described as "just wonderful – a charming person".

. . . .

1 When the Conservative party regained power in 1951, it kept intact the National Health Service unveiled by Labour's health minister Aneurin Bevan three years earlier and made no attempt to tear up the Attlee government's plans for the nationalisation of industries.

It was little wonder then that 20.5 million people in Britain, including 56 per cent of all adults, eventually watched live TV coverage of the Coronation, approximately 12 million of them doing so in pubs, cinemas or the homes of others. A further 11.7 million were estimated to have listened to the ceremony on the radio. The loveable, youthful Elizabeth, and the inclusive nature of her Coronation, went a long way towards re-establishing the reputation of the monarchy, which had suffered through the pre-war abdication of Edward VIII. The wave of goodwill she rode to the throne was evidenced by the outrage caused when the *Manchester Guardian* described the Coronation as "a £100,000 spree".

American sociologist Edward Shills called the Coronation "an act of national communion", adding that "one family was knit together with another in one great national family through identification with the monarchy". Change Coronation to Cup Final and monarchy to Matthews and he could have been talking about the climax of the football season.

As early as the following day, *The Times* was putting forward a prescient explanation about why the game would continue to occupy a prominent place in the public memory, beyond just the excitement of the action: "It will largely because here in the presence of the Queen and the Duke of Edinburgh the game of football, the game of the people, was crowned with all felicity in this year of Coronation and national rejoicing."

Put simply, the same game played a year earlier or later, while dramatic, would not have acquired the same almost-mythical status. It benefits from the veneer that other events, sporting and cultural, have layered upon the perception of the year of 1953. As Johnes and Mellor contend: "The links to the Coronation, with all its connotations of a reverent, unified and optimistic Britain, enhanced such memories."

When it comes to the football itself, the game was also to become viewed as the glorious last stand of the traditional 'British' style of football; all tricky wingers, bulldozing centre-forwards and uncompromising whack-it-anywhere defenders. Even here, though, there are comparisons with the wider historical narrative of the country. "The mood of pride and optimism that the Cup Final caught proved to be short-lived," write Johnes and Mellor. "By the end of the decade, the Suez crisis had shattered any sense of national confidence and revealed the major fissures in the political consensus."

On the field, things fell apart even more quickly. Barely had the sport finished congratulating itself on being able to serve up such excitement and human drama than the Hungarian national team turned up on the same Wembley turf and broke down English football's walls of self-satisfaction with a stunning 6-3 victory. The flaws laid bare by Ferenc Puskas and his colleagues were exposed even more savagely the following year when Hungary won the return game 7-1 on their own soil.

As author and football historian Jonathan Wilson points out: "The golden age, if not of any great success, then at least of the old, winger-oriented style of English football was at an end… That final stands as its apogee."

It is easy to pick fault with the football in that year's Cup Final; not for its lack of red-blooded excitement but for the kind of naivety that would soon be exposed on the international stage. Yet few were aware of such things as Matthews was being feted for his achievement. Even fewer would have cared. Just as British industry in the 1950s was content with its complacency and unaware of the impending challenge of rapidly-modernising foreign competition, so football was happy to revel in the popular theatre of the domestic game. Who is to say they were wrong?

As the country watched and listened on the first Saturday in May, tactical nuances and the state of the national game were an irrelevance, incapable of impinging on the day's significance. Rather, the merging of historical, cultural and personal narratives – allied to a bloody exciting game of football – made the FA Cup Final of 1953 an iconic and enduring moment in the history of English sport. This is the story of that remarkable event.

CAST OF CHARACTERS

THE FOLLOWING biographies are extracted from the *Charles Buchan's Football Monthly Who's Who in the Football League* for 1952/53. Where no entry existed for certain players or where the author has added additional comment, this is written in italics.

BLACKPOOL FOOTBALL CLUB

George Farm (goalkeeper): Capped by Scotland. Joined Blackpool from Hibernian in 1948. Diligent practice allied to his courage have made a cool, fine keeper with an unusual style – deceptively nonchalant. Played in the '51 final. Height 5-11. Weight 12-10.

Eddie Shimwell (right-back): A tall, hefty full-back who played for England v Sweden in 1949. Rose to fame with Sheffield United. Joined Blackpool in December, 1946. Strong kick with either foot, he scored from the spot in the 1948 final and was at Wembley again in 1951. Height 5-11. Weight 12-0.

Tommy Garrett (left-back): Made an outstanding international debut for England against Scotland at Hampden in April 1952. Durham-born, he cost Blackpool only £10 from junior football. Shows dash and strength, combined with a cool head. Height 5-10½. Weight 12-10.

Ewan Fenton (right-half): A promising young half-back, Blackpool developed, who played for the Army while serving in the Hussars. Height 5-7½. Weight 11-0.

Harry Johnston (centre-half): Deservedly Footballer of the Year for 1951. A magnificent wing-half; strong in the tackle, splendidly artistic; constructive and cool. Has several England caps. Born by the Manchester City ground, but Blackpool signed him from Droylsden Athletic. He skippered them in the 1948 and 1951 finals. Height 5-11. Weight 12-8.

Cyril Robinson (left-half): *Limited chances at Blackpool but injuries to team-mates saw him picked for Wembley, the youngest and last-surviving member of his club's Wembley line-up.*

Stanley Matthews (outside-right): Probably the finest outside-right of all-time. Born at Hanley in February, 1915. Was taken on the Stoke City ground staff and remained with the club until Blackpool signed him in 1947 for £11,000. As a schoolboy he once scored ten from centre-half, but in 1929 appeared for England schoolboys on the right wing. The first of his England caps was won at 19. Height 5-8½. Weight 11-0.

Ernie Taylor (inside-right): A little inside-forward with speed, ball control and a quick eye for the open space. Did much to help Newcastle win the 1951 Cup, then went to Blackpool later that year. Ernie was born at Sunderland, shone with the local school's side, and was snapped up by Newcastle. Served with submarines during the war. Shoots with surprising power. Height 5-4. Weight 10-8.

Stan Mortensen (centre-forward): A dashing, courageous, raiding inside or centre-forward, was born in County Durham. Signed by Blackpool before the war while a lad. Was nearly discarded then for being too slow. Shone with Bath City and the RAF during the war. Played in the Cup Finals of 1948 and 1951. Height 5-9½. Weight 11-8.

Jackie Mudie (inside-left): A house painter, he joined 'Pool from Lochee Harp, Dundee, as a centre-forward. Played in the 1951 final when 21. Born Dundee. Height 5-6½. Weight 11-0.

Bill Perry (outside-left): Had a good game in the 1951 final. A South African outside-left, recommended to Blackpool by the old Bolton winger, Billy Butler, and signed from Johannesburg Rangers in 1949, when 19. Fast, persistent and a snatcher of scoring opportunities. Height 5-8½. Weight 11-10.

Joe Smith (manager): *Would spend 23 years as Blackpool manager, having scored for Bolton in the first Wembley final in 1923 and captained them to two FA Cup successes.*

Allan Brown: Inside-forward. Allan was originally a wing-half and has been picked for Scotland in both positions. A fine ball player and opportunist. Left East Fife for Blackpool in 1950/51 after a long dispute which kept him out of the game several months. First capped for Scotland 1950, v Switzerland. Height 5-10. Weight 11-6.

Hugh Kelly: Was given his first Scottish cap against the USA in May 1952. A strong-tackling courageous, skilful left-half who joined Blackpool from Jeanfield Swifts in 1943, playing for Blackpool in the 1948 and 1951 finals. His friendship caused Allan Brown to join Blackpool. Height 5-10. Weight 11-10.

John Crosland: A centre-half who became an emergency left-back for the 1948 Cup Final. Played for England B in 1950. Height 5-11. Weight 11-4.

BOLTON WANDERERS FOOTBALL CLUB

Stan Hanson (goalkeeper): A fine goalkeeper; unspectacular but an excellent positional player. Never flurried, with very safe hands. Born Bootle. Liverpool gave him trials but didn't sign him. Joined Bolton, August 1935. Height 5-9½. Weight 13-4.

John Ball (right-back): A Manchester United product, and caught the eye by his cool display on his debut in a 1949 Cup tie at Hull. Joined Bolton 1950. Has played for the Football League. Height 5-8½. Weight 11-0.

Ralph Banks (left-back): *Older brother of reserve defender Tommy; would leave Bolton soon after the 1953 final.*

Johnny Wheeler (right-half): Strongly-built Liverpool-born right-half. Can also play inside-right. Cost Bolton a forward and a fee when he joined them from Tranmere Rovers in 1950/51. Has played for England B. Height 5-8½. Weight 12-1½.

Malcolm Barrass (centre-half): Won a Victory England cap against Wales at inside-left in 1945. His next appearance for England was at centre-half! In the interim, he had rather faded from the picture, becoming a left-half and then re-emerged as a pivot. A big fellow with good positional sense who never takes unfair advantage of his size. Born Blackpool. Height 5-10½. Weight 13-4.

Eric Bell (left-half): *Wing-half who spent all of his eight years as a professional at Bolton and whose injury would be a pivotal moment in the 1953 Cup Final.*

Doug Holden (outside-right): A young outside-right whom Bolton brought into their First Division side in 1951/52. Born in Manchester, he joined the Trotters from Manchester YMCA. Height 5-7. Weight 10-0.

Willie Moir (inside-right): Dark, curly hair. Topped the First Division goalscorers with 25 goals in 1948/49. Played for Scotland v England at Hampden in 1950. Born Bucksburn. Height 5-7½. Weight 9-13.

Nat Lofthouse (centre-forward): Began to play for the Wanderers side when 15. A very strong player, immensely courageous. Powerful with head and foot. Works hard and most intelligently. First of his England caps came against Yugoslavia in 1950, when he scored two goals. Height 5-9½. Weight 11-13.

Harold Hassall (inside-left): Shining new inside-forward, star of season 1950/51, his first as a Huddersfield Town regular. Born 1929 and a qualified physiotherapist who intends to become a PT schoolmaster. He first shone in the Army representative side. A surprise choice for England v Scotland, April 1951, he scored a terrific goal. Tall, powerful, long-striding and a fine shot. Height 5-11. Weight 11-8. To Bolton in season 1951/52.

Bobby Langton (outside-left): One of the cleverest left wingers in the League. Has a powerful left-foot shot. Originally a Blackburn Rover. Born at Burscough, he moved to Preston (1948) and to Bolton for £20,000 in 1949. Has many England caps. Height 5-7½. Weight 11-0.

Bill Ridding (manager): *Former player and physiotherapist; in the second full season of a managerial reign that would last 17 years.*

Tommy Banks: Like his brother, Tommy is a full-back born at Farnworth, who has been developed by Bolton. Height 5-7½. Weight 12-6.

Roy Hartle: *Another physical player who became a Bolton stalwart at full-back after missing out on the 1953 final, having played in every game before Wembley.*

George Higgins: A Blackburn Rovers product, albeit he was born at Dundee. A full-back, standing 5-7½ and weighing 9-12. In early season 1951/52 he moved to Bolton.

Vince Pilling: *Winger who was officially the Bolton 12th man at Wembley.*

Ray Parry: Made his debut at inside-left for Bolton at the early age of 15 in season 1951/52. Outstanding as a schoolboy international. Brother of Jack Parry of Derby County. Height: 5-8½. Weight 11-2.

OTHERS

Queen Elizabeth II: *In the second year of her reign after acceding to the throne following the death of her father King George VI early in 1952. Her Coronation in 1953, one month after she attended the FA Cup Final, was to symbolise her country's passage from post-war austerity into a new age of optimism and prosperity.*

Kenneth Wolstenholme: *A boyhood Bolton fan and wartime RAF bomber pilot who progressed from print journalism and radio to become the voice of the BBC's televised football for two decades, enjoying his finest moment during the 1966 World Cup Final.*

1

CAPTAIN, MY CAPTAIN

"I'm sorry we couldn't bring you the Cup, but we'll go back. We'll go back and win the Cup yet." – skipper Harry Johnston to Blackpool fans after the 1951 FA Cup Final.

THE VOICES can be heard in spite of the distance and the concrete; their song muffled yet unmistakable: *Abide with Me*, the hymn of the FA Cup Final. Harry Johnston, centre-half and captain of Blackpool, takes it as his cue to pick up a football from the floor of Wembley's north dressing room, running his hands over the polished leather and fingering the laces.

Outside, clasping their *Daily Express*-sponsored lyrics sheets, the crowd have been filling time before the entrance of the two teams by engaging enthusiastically in the 'Community Singing', accompanied by the band of the Coldstream Guards and conducted from his raised podium by Arthur Caiger, the white-suited and bespectacled London headmaster who has been waving his arms around at English football's showpiece ever since the war. As the final notes fade, song sheets are tucked into jacket pockets to be kept as souvenirs and eyes turn excitedly towards the east end of the stadium. Not long now.

Blackpool manager Joe Smith, buttoned snugly into his new three-piece suit, has given his final instructions. Never one for elaborate game plans it could hardly be described as a tactical briefing. "Don't be put off by the occasion," he warned his men, "or by the fact that we've lost two previous finals. Go out and play your natural game. Just try to be your own normal selves. Be the players I know you are and we'll be all right. Whatever happens, remember you're my boys and I'm proud of every damn one of you."

He had then paused, letting the painful memories of the team's two Wembley defeats hang in the air. "And let's win this one."

At ten minutes to three, the match referee, Mervyn Griffiths, a schoolteacher from Abertillery, orders the sounding of the buzzer that beckons the teams from their dressing rooms. Johnston opens the door and leads his players into the corridor, waiting for Smith to place his trilby on his head and take his place at the head of the line, giving one final rallying cry: "We dream brave dreams, eh? So be brave, lads."

The white-shirted players of Bolton Wanderers line up on Blackpool's left. The man with whom Johnston will be occupied for most of the afternoon, Bolton centre-forward Nat Lofthouse, has prior Wembley experience yet even he is unprepared for the heightened anxiety that grips him; unlike anything he has experienced in his four appearances there for England. "When you stand in the tunnel at Wembley you might be in another world," he explains many years later. "All you can see of the stadium is a small square of light some 20 or 30 yards ahead. The other side lines up alongside you. There will be a joke and a laugh but the tension is there. Then you start the long walk towards that square of light."

Behind Lofthouse is left-back Ralph Banks, a relative veteran at the age of 33, but still five years younger than the man he will be marking and at whom he can't resist throwing a glance. Having fought throughout the Second World War, Banks has seen enough of life – and death – not to be intimidated by the threat posed by the great Stanley Matthews, the man with more knowledge of Wembley's pitch than anyone on either side and who has, it seems, the whole country willing him to win an FA Cup winner's medal. Even he is being tormented by the occasion, admitting later that he "never felt worse in my life before a match".

Banks had at last come up against England's most renowned footballer for the first time in his career earlier in the season and felt he had acquitted himself well. Of greater concern than his esteemed opponent is his own fitness over the course of 90 minutes. Fearing that his shins will be susceptible to cramp on the testing Wembley pitch, he has been assiduously massaging oil into them in the dressing room. If he knew how events will play out, he might still be in there working on his limbs.

Johnston, Matthews, Lofthouse, Banks and their team-mates clack their boots along the players' tunnel, the upward incline meaning that blue sky is all that is visible at the end of their journey. Suddenly, spring sunshine dazzles Johnston's sight after the gloom of the stadium's bowels and the paint-stripper roar of 100,000 voices almost stops him in his tracks. According to team-mate Ewan Fenton: "When you walk down the tunnel at Wembley, it is very, very quiet. Then as you approach the pitch and hear 100,000 people cheering, you think this is what it must have been like for the Christians at the Coliseum."

Two years earlier, Johnston had been through this same routine; making the identical walk and finding himself waiting, as now, to introduce his colleagues to a member of the royal family. One thought dominated his mind on that occasion. "This time it's got to be us," he had repeated to himself over and over, unable to clear his mind of his team's defeat to Manchester United three years previously. Now he has a second Wembley defeat, to Newcastle, to dismiss from his thoughts.

At 33 years old, he is determined to remain more at ease in his third FA Cup Final for his only professional team, taking in the surroundings on what he knows might be his last appearance on such a stage. Dry-mouthed, he looks towards the sideline and sees injured team-mates Allan Brown and Hugh Kelly taking their seats on the bench. Alongside them is team trainer John Lynas, attired in a smart blazer, sharply creased flannels, tie and sweater, his football boots being the only clue to the role he expects to play in the course of the afternoon.

Behind the goal, the orange scarves, hats and favours worn by the Blackpool fans punctuate the terraces like splashes of paint. Johnston searches for relatives, but amid the more uniform grey of the stands, where the predominantly male gathering sits soberly in jackets and ties, it is hard to distinguish individuals. Instead, what catches his eye are the dresses in which the small number of female spectators have decked themselves out. The warmth of early May seems to have brought out the frocks that they'll likely be wearing again in a month's time at the street parties to celebrate the Coronation of the new young Queen, Elizabeth II. Johnston can't help thinking that, placed alongside the explosion of colour in the pitch-side flower beds below the Royal Box, it appears as though the entire playing area is flanked by a magnificent extended herbaceous border. Funny what your mind comes up with at moments of high tension, he notes.

Prince Philip, the Duke of Edinburgh, performs the pre-game ceremonial duties on behalf of his wife of five and a half years, who is attending her first football match as reigning monarch and from whom Johnston hopes to be receiving the famous trophy in a couple of hours. The Duke is guided along the line of players, receiving bare-arm handshakes from men who have rolled up their sleeves in the hope of making their heavy cotton shirts more comfortable in the heat. Johnston is impressed by the royal guest's apparent interest in all the players and unsurprised when he pauses for a longer word with Matthews. Even Lofthouse notices it, accepting the situation: "Everybody in England, except the people of Bolton, wanted Stanley to get his medal. We had a huge emotional barrier to break down."

The winning of a Football League championship may be the truest testament of a team's ability, but in 1953 it is still the FA Cup that shines most gloriously in the vision of the population. Winning it now, before the Queen and with more people than ever watching the whole game live on television, will be the most fitting climax to a career that is widely assumed to be approaching its conclusion.

Unknown to Johnston, he and Matthews share a secret that has intensified their ambition. Just as Johnston has promised his mother, before her death four months earlier, that he will win the FA Cup, so Matthews made the same pledge as his father lay dying eight years earlier. It is an oath he will keep private until shortly before his own death more than 50 years later.

Above dark blue socks topped by long orange turnovers, Blackpool might be wearing the most spacious shorts in Cup Final history – making them look more like circus clowns than professional sportsmen. But it is Bolton's shiny satin navy britches that catch the eye of the Duke as he makes his way down their line-up. "You all look like a bunch of pansies," is his appraisal, overheard by Banks.

Formalities over, Johnston has a moment of panic when he realises he has forgotten to take out the dental plate containing his two false teeth. Usually he slips it into the pocket of his suit jacket, but now he has to dash to the touchline, where Blackpool's 12th man,[2] Johnny Crosland, is the lucky recipient of the captain's choppers. Johnston trots back to the centre circle, shakes hands with opposite number Willie Moir, wins the toss and elects to kick off. The teams swap ends so that Bolton have their backs to the tunnel and Blackpool's inside-right, Ernie Taylor, kneels to give his bootlace one last tie before kick-off. As he makes to rise, he hears the voice of the match official hissing at him.

"Ernie, undo it and do it up again, would you?" urges Griffiths. "I can't start the game until bang on three o'clock and we're a minute early."

Once the game has made its punctual start, Taylor sets off on an attempted foray into the Bolton half. Lacking in real intent, it is more of a boxer's range-finding jab than anything else, but he does beat one white shirt before losing control and allowing Lofthouse to play the ball safely to Banks. A pass forward to Harold Hassall results in Blackpool regaining possession just inside Bolton territory and Stan Mortensen advances, head down as though deep in concentration, before delivering to the right wing to offer Matthews his first touch.

Matthews gives the crowd little time to anticipate any trickery. Instead, he quickly controls and crosses without taking on his opponent, only for the ball to be headed behind by Bolton's Eric Bell. His corner fares no better, cleared to the edge of the box where Jackie Mudie's efforts to create some space are closed down.

Now Bolton launch their first attack, Lofthouse spreading the ball to the right and seeing it ricochet off the back of a team-mate. A further Bolton attempt to get across the halfway line goes only as far as an orange shirt before

. . . .

2 Substitutes were not introduced in English football until 1965, but teams did habitually nominate an official 12th man in case of a late emergency.

outside-right Doug Holden finally advances the ball and then sets off down the right wing in anticipation of a return pass. It takes Moir, his inside-forward, two attempts to get the ball back to Holden, who pulls it back across the face of the Blackpool box. Moir misses it completely and Hassall's failure to control cleanly gives him no option but to return the ball to the winger. This time Holden lays it gently first time to his left, where Lofthouse is waiting with a massive swing of his right leg.

"I think the shot took everyone by surprise," he explains later, noting his fear that Moir might have been caught offside if he had attempted to pass the ball into the box. He even apologises to Johnston. "There wasn't much else I could do, Harry. So I shot."

The ball barely rises above shin height but bounces in front of George Farm as he dives to his right, slipping through the Blackpool keeper's arms and into the net. "What seemed to be the sound of thunder swept down from the terraces alive with blue and white," according to Matthews.

"No one was more surprised than me when it went in," Lofthouse admits subsequently. "I didn't hit the shot properly and it must have bounced three times before it got to Farm. But George made a complete mess of it. Whether he dived too early or took his eye off the ball I don't know. But it hit him on the shoulder and bounced into the net."

Fewer than 80 seconds have been played.

Reminding viewers that he used to be a goalkeeper, BBC TV commentator Kenneth Wolstenholme ventures that Farm should indeed have stopped the shot, but adds in mitigation: "This Wembley pitch is like no other. I walked on it this morning and it's a bit skiddy."

One writer, Ivan Sharpe of the *Sunday Chronicle*, had warned of such an occurrence a week earlier, noting that the law of averages indicated a likely individual blunder because there had been none in the final since Charlton's Bert Turner scored an own goal in 1946.

As Lofthouse accepts hugs and manly back-pats from his team-mates, Johnston turns towards his keeper and slaps his hands together in a mixture of admonishment and defiance, his disappointment clearly visible. In a second or two, though, he gathers himself, turning to all parts of the field with clenched fists and loud yells. He claps his hands in encouragement. "Let's get those heads up!"

This time, he vows, his Wembley outcome will be different.

* * * * *

THE SLENDER, flinty figure of Harry Johnston had become as much a part of the Blackpool landscape over the previous two decades as the Tower itself. Eighteen years had passed since he first arrived at Bloomfield Road, during which time he had witnessed and played no small part in the elevation of the club into the elite level of English football. Like most footballers of his era, he looked older than his actual age; but that was down to his prematurely thinning hairline and the attritional effects of the war years and the austerity that followed – not to mention the styles of the day, which made little distinction between young adults and their ageing fathers. It certainly owed little to the stresses of his employment. Blackpool, as one would expect from a town specialising in the provision of fun, was mostly a happy football club.

Johnston had found his way there from his birthplace of Manchester, where he grew up as a United fan, even though his home in Moss Side was only a short walk from City's Maine Road ground. After leaving school, he worked in a millinery firm, sorting out hats in the basement, while playing for Droylsden in the Manchester League. Early in 1935, a Blackpool director went to take a look at one of the team's strikers but was taken with the 15-year-old left-half, signing him for the club as an amateur. Johnston was less enamoured with his first look at the town, but was assured by his father: "Harry, if you don't make the grade as a footballer, son, you can always come in with me in the haulage business."

In the summer, he signed as a member of the Blackpool ground staff, earning £2 and ten shillings (£2.50) per week. Training as a footballer was something he got to do only after the completion of the daily chores foisted upon those of his lowly status. There were boots to be cleaned and polished, dressing rooms to be tidied and washed down, and terraces to be cleared of litter and debris after home matches. "A youngster has to take this sort of thing in his stride. It deflates his airy-fairy approach to the game," was his pragmatic view; one shared by just about every prospective professional of the time. Pre-war Britain was no place for rebellious youth, especially when the alternative was life in a factory, down a mine or on the dole. "Picking up bits of paper and cigarette-ends is one of the best things I know to cure the swelled head of some budding genius who thinks the whole football world should bow down and acclaim him as soon as he arrives on the ground," Johnston would write.

His first-team debut was made against local rivals Preston at Deepdale in November 1937, a few months after Blackpool had achieved promotion to the First Division in their second season under new manager Joe Smith. Other than through the intervention of war or injury, his place was secure for the best part of the next two decades.

Once Matthews had been signed in the early years after the war, it was the superstar winger who became the public face of the Blackpool team; his fancy footwork and personification of English sportsmanship and good humour having crowds queuing up and down the country for a chance to see the Seasiders in action. Yet, in many ways, it was Johnston who best characterised the style of football that managed to earn Blackpool a vast numbers of friends, as well as a more than satisfactory amount of victories, in the ten years following the hostilities in Europe.

Composed and quietly determined, he favoured the thoughtful pass over the bludgeoning boot when it came to advancing play from deep positions. In his autobiography, written in the mid-1950s, he condemned teams who thumped the ball forward in the hope that a lumbering centre-forward would win a knockdown for a team-mate, describing it as "spiv soccer". As someone who spent most of his career at wing-half, inter-play with the inside-forwards was, he believed, the key to attractive football and the method that ensured wide men such as Matthews were brought into the game as frequently and effectively as possible. While regular left-half Hugh Kelly would adopt a more defensive function, Johnston took a greater attacking role, launching his forwards at the opposition whenever possible. He did so with such effect that *Charles Buchan's Football Monthly* described him as "one of the greatest attacking wing-halves ever".

Long, direct passes were employed only as a method of putting forwards Stan Mortensen or Allan Brown in the clear against unsuspecting defences. "We in the Blackpool team set out to try to play pure football," Johnston explained, arguing that their best results were achieved by "a mixture of the long and short passing game".

After moving to centre-half for the latter stages of his career, Johnston admitted to feeling "shackled" and missed the attacking involvement that his preferred position afforded him. "I used to play hard," was his own assessment of his game to author Robin Daniels in the 1972 book *Blackpool Football*. "I used to tackle hard. I used to try to play good constructive football when I was in possession. But I never played dirty."

Even in the number five shirt he was more than a mere stopper, ensuring that those flanking him in the half-back line reflected his philosophy on how the game should be played. Bill Holden, the Burnley centre-forward, was one of many players who cited Johnston as his toughest opponent, noting his "ability to anticipate a move in advance" and his "good distribution of the ball".

Blackpool's position within the English football hier-archy and consciousness had changed considerably due to the war. From being an unregarded team that had spent only three years in the top flight of English football before winning another promotion to the First Division in 1937, they became the glamour side of the sport's makeshift, regionally-based structure between 1939 and 1945. In the club's favour was its seaside location, which offered plenty of accommodation and made it an ideal home for the Royal Air Force's wartime training base. Among the many buildings requisitioned was Bloomfield Road, which was used as military offices – providing the club with a windfall that enabled them to clear their £33,000 debt. Their own team office shifted, meanwhile, to an accountant's office in Birley Street. Colonel William Parkinson, the club secretary, acted as liaison with the RAF – a relationship that helped Blackpool make the most of the football talent it suddenly found on its doorstep.

The nature of wartime football was that clubs were able to take advantage of players based locally. It meant that military men unable to get the leave required to return to their home clubs were frequently available to turn out in tangerine instead. While some teams were unable to name their sides until they saw which players were able to make it to the ground for kick-off, Blackpool were frequently in the position of having more men to select from than they had open slots. The football authorities, meanwhile, were understandingly indulgent when it came to the formalities of acquiring permission from clubs who owned those players' registrations.

It meant that men such as Matthews of Stoke, Ronnie Dix of Tottenham and William Burbanks, an FA Cup Final goalscorer for Sunderland, regularly featured in the Blackpool forward line. Spearheading the attack was Jock Dodds, who had joined the club from Sheffield United in March 1939 and, according to Johnston, "moved like a ballet dancer despite his bulk". He would score more than 200 goals during his wartime posting as an RAF physical training instructor before moving via Shamrock Rovers to Everton when League football returned. By that time he had helped Blackpool become a dominant force, going unbeaten at home for two years and winning the northern regional league three years in succession. As is the English way, even in times when the country was unified as never before, success bred some resentment, with Blackpool attracting censure for borrowing players in order to boost ticket sales. They were even criticised on one occasion for using a coach to get to a game in Manchester, although they had also had to withdraw from cup competition one year because of a ban on servicemen travelling.

In 1943, Blackpool won the War Cup North and came from two goals down to beat southern victors Arsenal 4-2 at Stamford Bridge in a game billed as the "Championship of England". Skippering the side that day was Johnston, who had become a corporal physical training instructor and would be posted to Kasfareet in Egypt the following year.

Aged 26 when the war ended and married with a son, Johnston was more fortunate than many pre-war footballers in that he still had the prime years of his career ahead of him. Few in the football world, however, felt the same could be said of Blackpool. They were generally expected to slip back into the sport's other ranks once they were denied the personnel advantages they had enjoyed for six years. Yet the permanent signing of Matthews – who had already settled in Blackpool – for £11,500 in 1947 helped change the perception many had of a supposedly friendly, non-threatening club.

They breezed through the early rounds of the 1947/48 FA Cup, beating Leeds, Chester, Colchester, the season's giant-killers, and Fulham without conceding a goal. In the semi-final, a Stan Mortensen hat-trick saw off Tottenham, taking the club to their first Wembley final. Their opponents were a Manchester United side led by young Scottish manager Matt Busby, a three-time Cup Finalist as a player with Manchester City and part of the generation whose careers had been sawn in half by Hitler.

The Seasiders took the lead when Eddie Shimwell converted a penalty following a foul on Mortensen, becoming the first full-back to score in a Wembley final, but a defensive mix-up allowed United to equalise through the prolific Jack Rowley. Mortensen scored by shooting home on the turn and Blackpool entered the final 20 minutes with the advantage, only for Rowley to equalise after a free-kick. United's pressure proved too much for Blackpool, goals by Stan Pearson and John Anderson inside the final ten minutes giving them a 4-2 victory. Johnston demonstrated the tactical simplicity of the age by putting much of United's success down to goalkeeper Jack Crompton being instructed to direct his clearances away from Matthews's side of the field. "It is the sort of deep thought Matt puts into the game," he said of United's manager.

Less risible were Johnston's painful recollections of the maelstrom in which the losing Cup Final team feels trapped once the last whistle has sounded. "It is very lonely standing below the Royal Box at Wembley at the head of a defeated team. They have given their best, and in the heat and excitement of the game, they have had no time to think about what will happen after the match. Once the final whistle has blown, the handshakes with the victors follow. It's all goodwill and backslaps – then the reaction! You watch the winning skipper lead the way up to the Royal Box, while the losers stand sheepishly around awaiting their turn." Then, Johnston concluded, "the losers shamble off".

It was a torture that he would have to endure again three years later. And then it was even more painful. At least in 1948, Blackpool had the quaint – but in those days apparently genuine – consolation of having played a full part in a great game against a great team. In 1951, having been challengers for the League championship, they were expected to do better against a Newcastle side that had been struggling for form since reaching the final. Blackpool played poorly and deserved to lose, making it a miserable end to a season in which Johnston had been named Footballer of the Year.

Johnston felt, with hindsight, that "we lost the Cup at Huddersfield several weeks before the great day", referring to a knee injury suffered by forward Allan Brown. The constant – if unsophisticated compared to current times – attention of trainer John Lynas was unable to provide a remedy and Blackpool lined up with an amateur, Bill Slater, at inside-forward. Johnston and Joe Smith felt that using the offside trap to contain Newcastle and England centre-forward Jackie Milburn was the key to their chances as they doubted that the opposition defence could contain the skill of their attack.

Without playing particularly well, Blackpool were holding their own in an even game when Matthews worked some of his magic, beating defenders and clipping the ball towards Mortensen, who had advanced into a threatening position. A perfect delivery could have set up a goal, but the ball went astray by a few inches, allowing Ted Robledo to clear to his brother George. The older of the Chilean-born siblings pushed the ball through for Milburn, the speed of Newcastle's switch from defence to attack preventing the Blackpool defence executing their offside tactics. Milburn tore clear and beat Farm to give Newcastle the lead. He doubled the advantage after a couple of feints and a back-heel created the opportunity to fire in from the edge of the penalty area. The Cup was heading to Newcastle, where it would remain the next year after victory over Arsenal.

Returning home, Johnston found himself once more addressing disappointed Blackpool fans outside the Town Hall, promising them that the Cup was destined eventually to find its way to their stretch of coastline. He might have been speaking more in hope than expectation, but in Johnston the club had a reliable figure as its captain; composed and credible, a good head for a crisis. He had shown his patience after winning his first England cap in an 8-2 victory against Holland in 1946. With opportunities limited by the presence of Wolverhampton Wanderers' Billy Wright, he'd played only twice more by the time of the 1953 final – on his way to an eventual career tally of ten international appearances. He said of his calm personality: "It's not something I've tried to cultivate. It's something I was born with," and stressed its importance to the performance of his duties. "You can't be a manager or a leader or a captain if you are continually losing your temper," he said.

He had become captain of a side that included many older players, whose respect, he felt, he could earn more effectively through example than through shouting and yelling. "I used to say: 'Look, I'm doing this; running about, struggling like hell to help. You can do it, and you will do it.'"

It was an approach that worked, according to team-mate Eddie Shimwell. "The captain has got to be a consistently good player, which Harry was," he said. "He was a very nice chap, on the field and off the field. He was a hard driver. But he was always driving himself as well."

Bill Perry said: "Harry was a very good skipper, forceful but very fair. He played hard and expected everyone else to do the same thing. Harry led by example."

Cyril Robinson, the youngest member of Blackpool's 1953 Wembley line-up and another member of the half-back line, recalled: "Harry was a good footballer and a good captain and he used that position. He would shout to you: 'Come back, quick, watch him.' He had played wing-half and when he wasn't so quick he went centre-half and was as good there. He could head a ball and he could kick with two feet. I always tried to copy Harry because he was good in the air and he was a good passer of the ball. I always thought I would like to be a similar player to him."

Unlike the modern day, captaincy of a football club in the Johnston era involved a lot more than tossing the coin and placing an elasticated armband on one's sleeve. Many teams still acted more like their cricketing counterparts, with the captain directing tactics on the field. At Blackpool, Smith happily ceded such responsibility to his captain, who was thereby able to ensure that his team employed his own preferred method of thoughtful, creative attack. Besides, Johnston had little trouble anticipating Smith's own desires. It was the captain's duty to maintain a close working relationship with his manager and Johnston took the opportunity to get to know Smith better by driving him to work. Smith would walk down Palantine Road and wait at the bus stop at around quarter to ten, in time to catch the bus that would deposit him at Bloomfield Road for training. Most mornings, Johnston would be leaving the newsagent shop he had bought, having supervised delivery of the morning papers, and would offer his boss a lift. Their conversation would contain "nothing serious" but was important in forging a closer bond between the men.

Johnston identified strong personal relationships throughout the team as an important part of its success. As captain, he sometimes felt a little removed from the banter and bonding, torn between being unofficial assistant manager and one of the lads. But he also understood how vital it was for him to know the different personalities inside the jerseys, noting: "One man you can really get into and rollock, whereas with another player you've got to get at him in a different way altogether. You pat him on the back and say: 'Well, come on. You can do better than this.'"

In the days before players had agents to represent their interests, the captain also had to tread a delicate path between the changing room and the manager's office. Former Blackburn Rovers and England captain Ronnie Clayton, who made his League debut in 1950, recalled: "If any of the lads were unhappy or had a bit of an argument about money, then they came to me and had a bit of a word. Then I would try and do something."

Likewise, it was Johnston who would accompany aggrieved Blackpool players on their visits to see Smith, although he applied his own judgement first, withholding his support if he felt they were in the wrong or putting ego ahead of the team. "If I felt a player was right, and that he had a rightful grumble, I would support him all the way," he explained.

Johnston was certainly no revolutionary when it came to the issue of wages. In his autobiography he wrote far more passionately about the need for footballers to equip themselves with an alternate trade and to arm themselves for life beyond the game than he did about the question of whether they were being rewarded enough in the post-war attendance boom that saw money pouring into clubs' coffers. And he remained an advocate for a uniform ceiling on players' salaries, which at the time of the 1953 FA Cup Final was £12 per week. "If there had been no maximum wage in my playing days and one man was getting £40 a week and one was getting £80, there would have been a right shemozzle among some players because they were both in the same team."

* * * * *

IT IS that all-for-one spirit, coupled with the adherence to constructive football, that Johnston is looking for as Blackpool set about recovering from falling behind inside two minutes against Bolton. "I don't have to tell the lads what to do," he tells himself. "They know there is only one answer to a blow like this. There's no use in banging the ball hopefully upfield."

Their first attempt to clear the deficit ends after Bill Perry chips an aimless ball forward from his left-wing position when he has time for greater thought. In the common style of the era, although somewhat contradictory to Johnston's preferences, right-back Shimwell drives his boot through the ball to launch the first of a series of downfield hoofs. "Full-backs gave it the old boot mostly," according to Robinson. "They never helped the wing-halves with the way they played. They would kick it long a lot. Then they thought they had done their job."

Malcolm Barrass recalled the approach of Bolton's defenders being no different. "When we got the ball it was 'bang' down to the other end of the field. We got the ball forward to Nat and he held it up."

This time Shimwell's long ball is punched clear by Stan Hanson, who has been performing such acts in Bolton's goal for the past 17 years. Then Perry again finds himself in a position to attempt a foray into the area, but is outnumbered on this occasion.

After a few more aimless punts up and down the field, a header by Blackpool left-back Tommy Garrett falls at the feet of Bolton winger Holden, who combines with Lofthouse and Moir before finding the ball being clipped back to him further down the line. Twice he fails to get past Garrett on the edge of the box and when Blackpool work the ball away towards the halfway line, Wolstenholme can barely contain his laughter in declaring excitedly: "Matthews in the inside-left position. Good gracious."

These are days long before the idea of giving anyone a free role is considered prudent. Wingers rarely venture in from the touchline without the ball already at their feet, although Matthews's status and skill make him one of the few able to get away with it. Without a full-back to shimmy past on this occasion, he drives the ball optimistically into no man's land and sees it run into Bolton's area. "Stanley's obviously decided that to win his Cup winner's medal at the third attempt he has got to wander and roam," says the reverential commentator, ignoring the wastefulness of his pass.

Wing-half and inside-right, Ewan Fenton and Ernie Taylor, combine through the middle to give Jackie Mudie the ball on the edge of the Bolton box, but he is unable to beat the attentions of Johnny Wheeler. Then Matthews and Perry try to burrow their way into dangerous territory from their respective positions on the flanks and, at last, Mudie manages to deliver low into the penalty area. Barrass has ample time to usher the ball away.

Five minutes have been played when Robinson commits the first foul of the game on Holden on the right corner of the Blackpool area. Wheeler's misdirected free-kick is typical of the ungainly play thus far, as is keeper Farm's decision to flap the ball over the bar when it drifts innocuously towards him. Langton swings Bolton's first corner in the direction of the penalty spot, where Hassall heads on and Blackpool clear. "We were excited from the word go," Barrass remembered. "We chased the ball everywhere."

In explaining the mistakes being made on the field, Wolstenholme describes the swirling wind in the stadium and notes the lushness of the pitch in contrast to the muddy or dry, bumpy pitches the players have been playing on in League games. No sooner have the words travelled the short distance from mouth to microphone than a wild clearance from Garrett hits Holden, who is able to advance into the box. Instead of bearing down on goal he pulls the ball back and Lofthouse has to dig it out from under his feet in order to deliver a shot that drifts harmlessly over the bar.

Seven and a half minutes have been played, and the 1953 FA Cup Final shows little sign of going down in history.

2

NEW ADVANCES, TRUSTED METHODS

"One may wonder why there was no mass orgy of hedonism after World War II as there was after the first. The Fifties were nothing like the Twenties… The reason surely was that with the explosion of the hydrogen bomb the world suddenly grew old, too old for parties." – Peter Lewis, *The Fifties* (1978).

A S THE last day of 1952 ticked towards its final minutes, the thick rain clouds over Blackpool began to drift away like disinterested window shoppers, vacating the midnight air for an impatient winter frost. In Talbot Square, the civic and symbolic centre of the town, more than 3,000 stood clustered below two 30ft Christmas trees, the North Pier extending its cast-iron welcome to the Irish Sea behind them.

Most eyes were turned east towards the illuminated Jacobean masonry of the Town Hall. Councillor Peter Fairhurst, the town's avuncular Mayor, was due to emerge shortly before midnight from the tall windows of the council chambers, which sat above the pillars of the ground-level entry porch and beneath the clock tower with its stone belfry.

Elsewhere, more than 20,000 partygoers were spending the evening inside the town's various dance halls. As many as 7,000 of them were in the Empress Ballroom at the Winter Gardens, where the polished parquet flooring, set below ornate balconies and chandeliers, offered more secure footing than the quickly freezing pavements.

As those outside stamped feet in an effort to maintain a warming flow of blood, Councillor Fairhurst, short and bald with dark-rimmed spectacles, appeared from his parlour. He approached the microphone stand. Earlier, he had told the town's hoteliers and landladies: "What a fine job you are doing."

Addressing 250 members of the Blackpool Hotel and Boarding House Association, he had promised: "We can face the 1953 season with confidence." Fears that the crowning of a new Queen in the summer would draw people to London rather than Blackpool were countered by an expectation that some of the increased numbers of overseas visitors to Britain would find their way to the north-west coast. By the end of January, airlines and shipping companies would be reporting "heavy bookings" by foreign tourists. Meanwhile, the British Travel and Holiday Association had just reported that more people than ever had taken holidays away from home in the past year and that most resorts were exceeding their projections.

Taking up that optimistic theme, Councillor Fairhurst spoke to his shivering townspeople. "Locally, 1952 has been a successful year," he announced through clouds of icy breath. "And we look forward with enthusiasm to 1953, Coronation year, and to the Royal Show which is to be held in Blackpool in July."

Once the clock had ticked over into a date that would forever be synonymous with the town, the crowd was led in a rendition of *Auld Lang Syne* by tenor Josef Locke, who had driven from Oldham Theatre to fulfil a promise he had made to the Mayor.

The Blackpool British Legion Silver Band played on for a further half-hour and, a few miles out of town in the village of Thornton Cleveleys, two mortar-fired rockets were launched joyously into the night sky from outside the Savoy Ballroom. Similar celebrations were still going on all over the country by the time Prime Minister Winston Churchill, in mid-Atlantic, was seeing in the New Year in the first-class lounge of the *Queen Mary*, bound for New York, where he would meet with US President-elect General Dwight D Eisenhower.

Less than 30 miles south-east from Blackpool, almost on a direct path towards Manchester, the less hedonistic town of Bolton had staged somewhat more sober celebrations, although its Empress Hall had been packed with enthusiastic revellers. The New Year event that attracted more attention than any of the midnight parties was the traditional Bolton Canine Society annual show at the Drill Hall, Silverwell Street, where more than 3,600 people turned up to see the 450 dogs being shown.

Giving his New Year message to the town, Bolton Mayor James Vickers expressed his hope that the town's Hospital Management Committee would go ahead with programmes aimed to offer additional care to the chronic sick. He also wanted "a measure of stability for the cotton industry", adding: "I would also like to see the town do everything within its power to attract other industries so as to increase the diversity of trade."

He had begun his comments by looking beyond his own constituency. "My most earnest hope is that it might be possible to end the Korean war," he said of the conflict that had begun in 1950 between the Republic of Korea in the south, supported by the United Nations, and North Korea, backed by China and offered military aid by the Soviet Union.[3] Despite its geographical distance, the war had become a constant, unwanted companion to British life thanks to the threat of escalation into a nuclear encounter.

Author Peter Hennessey recalls in *Having It So Good: Britain in the Fifties*: "For those in my generation and older who spent the bulk of their lives in the shadow of the bomb, that the Cold War ended at all is probably the greatest shared boon of our lifetime."

Britain's politicians, meanwhile, saw the development of their own nuclear armoury as a sign of national rebirth rather than a harbinger of death. The country's first nuclear test in October 1952 was greeted as a sign that it was back in the global first division. "Today Britain is GREAT BRITAIN again – in the eyes of the world", announced the *Daily Express*, with the *Daily Mirror* claiming: "It signalled the undisputed return of Britain to her historic position as one of the great world powers."

The threat of nuclear obliteration notwithstanding, there was a general air of excitement among the people of Britain as 1953 began. In part at least, it was reflective of the way that, over the previous two years, there had been a gradual lifting of the gloom that had blanketed the country during its period of immediate post-war austerity. Having stood firm against tyranny, oppression and a crazed dictator bent on genocide, the reward for many British citizens had been poverty and starvation as their country sold off foreign assets and found itself heavily in debt to the United States. There was little evidence of the culture of the "Bright

. . . .

3   The war would end in August 1953 after the estimated death of four million, civilian and military, more than 1,000 of them British lives.

49

Young People" that had emerged in the wake of the First World War.[4] A significant landmark in the re-emergence from those dark days had come in 1951. Five days after witnessing Blackpool's FA Cup Final defeat against Newcastle, King George VI launched the Festival of Britain – a series of events and exhibitions centred mostly around London, where the newly built Festival Hall was opened on the South Bank, the first major public building to have been constructed since the war. Over the space of four months, 8.5 million visitors were attracted to the South Bank alone, although response to the Festival's content proved somewhat mixed. Symbolically, though, its importance was generally recognised; being both a celebration of having got through six tough years since the end of hostilities and a statement to the people of Britain and beyond that the country was in the midst of revival; on the threshold of an advance into a more modern way of life.

The mood for change was reflected in that October's General Election, which the Conservatives, under the old war hero Churchill, won on the promise of being able to "set the people free from controls". Eighteen months earlier, the Labour party had won a narrow victory, seeing its overall majority in the House of Commons slashed to a barely workable five seats, and had gone to the country in the hope of padding its lead. Yet the Tories' promise of a new, prosperous future with more choice and fewer restrictions on what they could do and buy had returned them to power.[5]

. . . .

4 The exploits of these socialites, a group of costume-wearing, drug-taking partygoers, had fascinated the media in the manner of the modern preoccupation with *Big Brother* contestants, although without the cynicism and super-injunctions. They were offered amused tolerance until the economic realities of the latter half of the 1920s made them an anachronism. There was less appetite for such indulgence in the late 1940s.

5 Labour actually gained more overall votes than the Conservatives and more than they had achieved in the 1950 election, but a decreased number of Liberal candidates gave the Tories a clear run towards victory.

Comedian Alexe Sayle comments in his memoir of child-hood in the 1950s: "There still seemed to be something dreary, life-denying and over-zealous about food, drink and clothes being so severely rationed up to a decade after the conflict ended."

Many Britons were seeing little evidence that they had actually won the war and, summing up the mood that cost his party, MP Peter Parker commented: "Labour was seen to be the party of boring rationing and planning regulation."

Historian David Kynaston notes in *Family Britain, 1951-57*: "The Tories before and after the 1951 election did not disguise their desire to dismantle, as soon as economic dictates allowed, the elaborate wartime apparatus of rationing and ensuing austerity."

This is not to say that, by early 1953, the entire population was giddy with dreams of a brighter tomorrow. Even allowing for the growing anticipation of the Coronation's uplifting pageantry and the sense that the country was entering a new era under its young monarch, the concerns of day-to-day life continued to weigh heavy upon some. A survey in 1952 had even revealed that more people (40 per cent) felt that their standard of living was decreasing than improving (29 per cent).[6]

Tea had been taken off rationing in October 1952 and, a few months later, sweets would follow. Yet basic items such as sugar, butter, cheese, eggs and meat were still restricted. One newsreel clip of the time shows a mother of 16 children in Liverpool, including four sets of twins, fanning out her multiple ration books like a bridge hand and detailing the household's daily entitlement of ten pints of milk, eight loaves and 15lb of potatoes.

Also in Liverpool, Sayle recalls the view held by him and his parents, well-travelled, committed Communists, of

. . . .

6 A survey conducted in York in 1950 had previously discovered that only 12 per cent of working class households were living at poverty levels, compared with 33 per cent in 1936.

the British diet. "One area where we were convinced our life was superior to anybody else's in the street was in the food we ate," he writes in *Stalin Ate My Homework*. "The taste buds of most British people had been destroyed by six years of war and another eight years of rationing, so to the neighbours food had become fuel, pure and simple, to be shovelled down the gullet without ever being tasted."

Hennessey records that developments in rationing were followed as closely as the football results, noting: "Some consumption benchmarks, such as the final ending of the sweet ration in February 1953 will, I suspect, be remembered by readers over 60 almost as vividly as the Stanley Matthews Cup Final, the Coronation and the scaling of Mount Everest in the same year." There was even the promise later in the year of "Coronation food bonuses" on each rationing book, plus further concessions for organisations staging celebrations for pensioners and children on the big day. The government planned to ensure that there would be a treat on the party tables by removing all control on the pricing and manufacture of cream between early May and late June.

By the end of March, the government's annual economic survey would earmark 1953 as a year for a "new advance", which it would achieve by prioritising a stable balance of payments and achieving victories in the export market. Recording that 1952 had seen a restoration of international confidence in sterling, the report called for less rigid control of agriculture and greater availability of building material for private manufacturing in order to assist "the new industries and techniques" needed to secure exports. "We must continue to concentrate on increasing exports and saving imports," it said simplistically. Even though 1952 had seen a balance of payments surplus of £291m, compared to a £400m deficit in 1951, the report warned of keen competition in the exports market from Germany, the United States and Japan.

For those with little interest in, or understanding of, such publications, the condition of the stomachs of Britain's citizens was seen as being symbolic of the state of the nation. One of the New Year's Day headlines pointed to greater health by noting: "Meat Outlook Best Since War", with 1.8 million tonnes expected to be available to British consumers during the year. Although still well below pre-war levels, it beat the previous highest post-war figure of 1.783 tonnes in 1946. However, looking beyond mere weight, TG Noble, re-elected as chairman of the Blackpool and Lytham St Annes Joint Food Control Committee, complained about the quality of imported meat. "Even dogs have been turning their noses up at it," he sneered.

* * * * *

THE TOWNS of Blackpool and Bolton would become inextricably linked later in the year, therefore it was appropriate that the first *West Lancashire Evening Gazette* of 1953 should be advertising a train excursion departing Blackpool's Central and North stations on the morning of Saturday 3rd January, bound for the Seasiders' First Division game against Wanderers at Burnden Park.

Before that, Blackpool's players faced an 11am kick-off at Preston on New Year's Day, a fixture that had curtailed their revelry the previous evening. Don Creedy of the *Gazette* would describe the game as being played in a "cup-tie atmosphere", for which he gave this definition: "Hand bells were rung, rattles twirled and there were splashes of tangerine and white among the crowd." Many Pool fans had been up early to catch buses to the town of their nearest rivals, while others had cycled the 17 or so miles and left their bikes in the gardens of accommodating locals.

One Blackpool supporter, 49-year-old Herbert Hatfield from Eden Street, had a day he would rather forget. First, he got hit by a car on the way to the match and was taken to Preston Royal Infirmary with an arm injury rather than joining the 35,000 inside the Deepdale ground. Then he was told his condition was not serious enough for him to be detained, meaning that he missed the chance to follow the live commentary of the game as part of the hospital radio station's brand new football service. The *Gazette*'s Clifford Greenwood was soon urging Blackpool to team up with Victoria Hospital in a similar fashion, with momentum building through the Blackpool Supporters Club's offer to sponsor the broadcasts.

For all the good the Blackpool players' early night had done them, they might as well have danced until dawn. After 68 minutes, they were four down. A pair of late goals were mere consolation, causing the *Gazette* to say: "Their football, until late in the game, was ragged and had little purpose behind it."

The following day, as the first meeting of the year with Bolton approached, Creedy's assessment was: "It seems unbelievable that a team which was Cock o' the North a few weeks ago could fall away so quickly as Blackpool have done." Typically of the time, he accused Blackpool of having forsaken the "long, devastating pass" for a short passing game that was "pretty to watch but profitless". Blackpool had posted seven wins and a draw in their first nine games of the season, including putting five past Aston Villa and Wolves on the road and then winning an astonishing home game 8-4 against Charlton. The defeat at Preston meant they had now won only three of their last 13 games.

Bolton, meanwhile, were hardly setting the First Division alight, reaching the halfway point of the season with only seven victories to their name. In their final two games of 1952, they had shipped ten goals in defeats to Derby and Arsenal and then begun the New Year by losing at home to Charlton. It was no wonder that Charles Buchan, previewing the season in his eponymous magazine, had identified Bolton, along with Sunderland, as teams with "powerful attacks and rather shaky defences, especially in away games". In forecasting the FA Cup at the start of the season Buchan had also written: "First to Blackpool. With the two great Stanleys, Matthews and Mortensen, back on duty, they will take a lot of beating in any conditions."

The first Saturday of 1953 saw Bolton comfortably beat Blackpool 4-0 on, as the *Gazette* put it, "one of the blackest days in Blackpool's post-war football history". What compounded the result for the visiting team was the incident after three minutes when Mortensen slipped on the icy surface, his feet going in one direction and his body another. The result was that the striker would need the second cartilage operation of his career. Such surgery was far from the simple and swift procedure it would become in later years, its victim usually immobilised in plaster for around six weeks. Doubts were expressed over whether Mortensen would return before the end of the season.

"There seems to be a hoodoo on us," complained manager Joe Smith, who had been without Matthews and Hugh Kelly for a long period, full-back Jackie Wright for the entire season due to a back injury, and was now thinking ahead to the following week's FA Cup game against Sheffield Wednesday. "This is the bitterest blow of all. Now we shall have to take the field at Sheffield without a centre-forward who has made a habit of winning Cup ties since the war."

No one in the Blackpool camp had much reason to remember the day fondly. Centre-half Jack Ainscough, in only his third game of the season, was given a torrid time by Johnny Wheeler, who scored a hat-trick within 12 minutes. Wheeler also benefited from a couple of misjudgements by goalkeeper George Farm, a portent of the unhappy time the Scot was to have in the final.

The following Tuesday morning found Blackpool's players gathering for the journey to the Derbyshire spa town of Buxton, where they would stay at the Palace Hotel and train at the local Cheshire League club. It had been a retreat for Smith's team for several seasons since their former player, Frank O'Donnell, had become Buxton's manager in 1947. This time, however, O'Donnell would not be there to meet them, having died in September at the young age of 41.

Mortensen was left behind in a nursing home in Manchester to have the cartilage taken out of his right knee. "If he played in less than eight weeks it would be a faster cure than average," club trainer John Lynas warned. Under the same roof as Mortensen was Matthews, being treated for a thigh injury that had sidelined him for three months. "The odds against his playing are obviously high," Smith reported. "But there is a prospect that he might be in the forward line at Hillsborough."

Matthews's injury had been something of a mystery, so much so that newspapers were able only to refer to a "muscular ailment", without even specifying which part of the body was affected. He had, in fact, pulled a muscle at the back of the thigh. "They thought I was kidding but I was not fit," he would record later. His visit to Manchester, however, finally brought him some relief. "It seemed on the Monday before the match that my chances of being in were nil. As a last hope, however, I went next day to hospital for treatment and when I returned a few hours later I felt so much better that I began thinking seriously about the Cup tie." In the book *Cup Kings* he would explain: "I was there one night; they stretched it and broke down the adhesions."

With defender Johnny Crosland also remaining at home because of his brother's illness and Jackie Mudie not released by the Royal Air Force, the 12 players who boarded the train to the countryside included several who were far from being first-choice players: winger Albert Hobson, who had been trying to fill Matthews's jersey; George McKnight, a wing-half who had not played a first-team game for 17 months because of injury; young forward David Durie, yet to play during the season; and reserve wing-half Cyril Robinson, an emergency left-back in Blackpool's second match of the season and forgotten since. "We drew against Preston at home and I played reasonably well against Tom Finney," Robinson recalled. "One of the lads said 'you will be in on Saturday', but I wasn't."

Before the trip to Buxton, Robinson had been singled out for praise by the *Gazette* as the reserves had beaten Bolton 1-0 to remain top of the Central League. "Robinson revealed himself again as the man who will fight for a ball as a bull terrier for a bone and these days, too, he is learning to give the correct pass," reported Clifford Greenwood.

In the days before wall-to-wall coverage of every breath taken by a football club, Blackpool's country retreat meant that there was very little news coming from the camp as the game against Wednesday approached. Not that there was much going on that was any different from usual. The setting might have been a welcome change from Bloomfield Road, where Blackpool had to train as well as play matches,[7] but the weekly pattern for the players was too well established to be altered. The typical routine, assuming there was no midweek match, saw the players taking Monday off and then reporting back on Tuesday to begin their work at around 10.15am under the guidance of Lynas. After some sprinting and seemingly interminable lapping, a ball would appear for the first time and a full-scale practice match would take place, usually the first team against the reserves.

. . . .

7 Even in the 1950s, most top teams had either a separate field or gymnasium in which to conduct training, although Blackpool were far from being alone in having to use their main pitch – a contributory factor to the poor playing surfaces of the era.

Wednesday followed a similar pattern – laps of the pitch followed by some work with the ball and games of five-a-side – and Thursday was a slightly shorter version. Friday consisted of a few more laps, some sprints and a massage. The ball was kept locked up, Blackpool being followers of the popular theory that denying the players the ball before a game would make them hungry for it on Saturday. Besides, physical strength and fitness were still valued more highly than close ball skills, especially during an English winter that traditionally made the heavy grounds more a test of endurance than technique.

Full-back Eddie Shimwell's view of training was a typical one for the time. "The basic training in the Third or Second Division club was similar to that in a First Division club. After all, the only goal is peak fitness. Football comes through your natural instincts." Even at Manchester United, where manager Matt Busby was building the team that would take the country by storm, there was nothing innovative to be found. When a young Johnny Giles signed for the team in the middle of the decade he found that the Busby Babes prepared for games no differently to the youth teams he had played for in Dublin.

Robinson, a regular in Blackpool's reserve team, explained: "We had two dressing rooms. If you got into the first-team regular you got moved from one dressing room to the other. There were certain areas where the first team and reserves mixed, running round and round. If a ball suddenly came out it was 'great we are going to kick a ball'. But the reserves had to keep on running and the first team got the ball. The only time the reserves went on was when we played the practice match on Tuesday morning. Definitely, the first team got the treatment over the reserves. We might get the ball later in the week. Perhaps they didn't want us to kick anybody."

If there was to be any discussion of the upcoming game and opponents it usually took place during training on

Tuesdays. Rarely did the team sit down as a group away from the field and go over the previous match or plans for the next. When they did, the boardroom was called into use. On most days, the players were finished by noon, at which time they would gather around the tea bar – often chatting with fans. Then it was off home or to the snooker hall or, in the case of men such as Johnston, Mortensen and Matthews, to devote a few hours to various business interests.

Robinson recalled: "It did get boring. We did quite a bit of running and although there was a small gymnasium at the ground, there wasn't a lot of variation like they have these days. We did a bit of head tennis inside maybe, but we never went swimming or anything – although we went golfing once. On Fridays you would get there for ten o'clock and do a few sprints and then wait for the team sheets to go up in the first-team dressing room. That was how you found out if you were in. There were just a couple of times when Joe Smith would actually say to someone 'I am putting you in tomorrow' – that was to give them a bit of a kick."

On Saturday, it was simply a case of turning up and getting changed for the game. There was no question of loosening up prior to taking the field at five minutes to three. "There was a massage for some if they wanted it," added Robinson, who also suggested: "You never know exactly how other teams trained."

In most cases, however, it was pretty easy to guess and the Bolton routine described by Nat Lofthouse has a familiar look to it. Having caught the bus to arrive at training by 10am – "It was a long time before I could afford a little car" – he would take part in half an hour's worth of running around the pitch, followed by a similar period throwing and catching a medicine ball. After a few more exercises, a five-a-side game might be staged, but Lofthouse admitted: "We were usually too knackered to do very much by then."

Doug Holden found it ironic that he played less football in adult life than ever. "You grew up playing with the ball the whole time, then as a professional you didn't get much chance," he said. Malcolm Barrass added: "We came off the field when we were told to. We finished training well before midday, went in the dressing room and had a cup of tea." After lunch was served, the players would disperse, with Lofthouse usually going home to do odd jobs or gardening.

As Arthur Barnard, a reserve goalkeeper at Bolton, put it: "Two hours a day doing something you love, and all that spare time in the afternoons. A great life, eh?"

Holden expressed surprise at the club culture he discovered after joining Bolton following his National Service, where he felt the levels of fitness and discipline had been higher. "It was an eye-opener. You think as a kid that the players are all going to be super fit and professional but they all drank their pints and liked a smoke. That is how they lived. Having been in the army, perhaps I expected it to be different."

On this particular week, with Blackpool's players having been on retreat, there was a buzz of excitement at Bloomfield Road on Friday lunchtime when Matthews showed up in a blue tracksuit and went through a fitness test. "I couldn't expect to be fitter in the circumstances," he declared. "I am 50 per cent better than I was a week ago. I'll play if Mr Smith is prepared to take a chance on it." With that, Smith was on the phone with instructions for Matthews to take a taxi to Buxton, from where the team would travel to Sheffield the following morning.

The ability of Matthews to take his place meant Smith's main concern now was combating the biggest threat posed by their opponents, centre-forward Derek Dooley. A year earlier, Wednesday had been lying 17th in the Second Division table when they introduced Dooley, born a few miles from Hillsborough, into their team, watching him score 19 goals in his first ten games. By the end of the season, Wednesday had been crowned champions and Dooley was the Football League's top scorer with 46 goals. "Dooley plays football with the approach of a boy who has not been spoilt by the current cult of over-coaching and the endless tactical chatter," wrote John Thompson in *Charles Buchan's Football Monthly*, even though there was little evidence of such a cult at most clubs. "He is employed to score goals. That is his job. It is as simple as that."

Harry Johnston had carried out an effective marking job on Dooley in a League game earlier in the season and was to wear the number five shirt in the Cup tie. Replacing him at right-half was McKnight, who had almost played in the 1951 final as a replacement for injured forward Allan Brown but had himself damaged a knee in a try-out against Sheffield Wednesday. McKnight's selection against those same opponents was now at the expense of Robinson, who could conceivably have come in at left-half with Ewan Fenton moving to the right, but instead had to rue the loss of the opportunity of a rare start.

"To get into the first team was hard," said Robinson. "In the old days they didn't transfer players – you just couldn't get in. The only way you could get in was every now and again when a first-team player got injured and if you were playing reasonably well you might get a go."

When Saturday dawned in Blackpool it brought with it, according to the *Gazette*, the "quietest Cup-tie morning since the war". A lower than expected total of three supporters' trains left for Sheffield, an indication perhaps that Blackpool fans had unfinished business with the FA Cup; that the third round was merely a necessary hurdle to be cleared and less of an event in itself. As well as the 1,500 travelling by rail as many again were in cars and coaches, many of which were last-minute bookings after the announcement of Matthews's participation.

The Blackpool team bus was escorted to Hillsborough by police cars to guard against congestion on the roads. Two years earlier, they had arrived late after making the same journey for a replayed semi-final, having been caught up in slow-moving traffic heading towards Sheffield. On this occasion their progress was smoother, although it still involved a battle to get through the packed neighbourhood streets close to the stadium. Queues had been forming outside the ground since early morning in anticipation of the gates opening at noon and the terraces were almost filled half an hour before kick-off. Blackpool's most colourful and famous fans, the Atomic Boys, paraded around the track and, as the *Gazette*'s Don Creedy reported, "bells rang and rattles twirled", once again meeting his criteria for a "cup-tie atmosphere".

The 60,199 who had squeezed inside the ground saw a cracking contest, with chances at either end and the winning goal scored only two minutes from time. Blackpool played with a confidence that had been missing from their game in prior weeks, which would be too easy to put down solely to the return of Matthews but was certainly an indication of the talismanic effect he had on his colleagues.

Further back, Johnston again prevented Dooley from having a major impact, while McKnight made a surprisingly effortless return to top-level football, helping Fenton close down Wednesday's playmakers. The home wingers were offered space by full-backs Eddie Shimwell and Tommy Garrett only in non-threatening positions close to the corner flags. Whenever they looked to venture into more dangerous locations they found their paths barred.

Blackpool's performance justified the confidence of their manager, who was convinced that poor officiating had been to blame when his team suffered their first home defeat for 13 months against Wednesday in October. "Give us a good referee – a referee who will protect the footballer – and we can win," he said before the trip to Sheffield. "We are better footballers and with a square deal we can win this time."

Dooley was denied by Farm's courageous save after carving out the first chance of the game after ten minutes and soon found himself in a scuffle with Shimwell in the Blackpool area. As a thick fog began to descend upon Hillsborough, some in the crowd began calling for a white ball to be introduced. The change was made after half an hour and Shimwell struck the new ball fiercely from a free-kick, seeing it deflect for a corner. Keepers Farm and Ron Capewell saved well from Jackie Sewell and Brown respectively before the first goal of the game arrived two minutes before half-time. After Blackpool won a free-kick, it took Taylor two attempts to lob it into the Wednesday box and Capewell's fisted clearance landed at the feet of Matthews. With barely a glance up, he lobbed delicately over the crowd of defenders and into the net. "Brilliantly conceived and cheekily executed," was the *Gazette*'s description of what was a rare goal by a man known more for setting up others.

Matthews had, in fact, scored four times in the first six weeks of the season after managing only one League goal in the previous three seasons. This one helped ease any remaining uncertainty he might have had about his fitness, a doubt that had led to a piece of pre-match kidology. Chatting in the dressing room area before kick-off, Johnston had whispered conspiratorially to Wednesday left-back Norman Curtis that Matthews should not have been playing. "Well, Curtis left me alone," Matthews reported. "He gave me a yard start and that was it."

Looking back on the season's Cup run, Matthews highlighted the personal importance of his performance.

"It pleased me to know I was 'on the map' when many had predicted I was getting past it. Fortunately I find that, unlike some players, I do not require two or three games to reach full match fitness."

Discussions were held during half-time about the wisdom of continuing the game in the worsening conditions, but the action went ahead, with Brown miskicking the ball after Matthews created an opening. It was an uncharacteristic blunder by the Scot, leading the line energetically, and he was soon forcing Capewell to turn his shot away for a corner.

It was then Farm's turn to spring into action, twice denying Cyril Turton.

When Wednesday won a corner after 74 minutes, 19-year-old inside-forward Albert Quixall lined up to take it. Described by *Football Monthly* as "small, flaxen-haired imaginative and courageous", Quixall would become a key part of Manchester United's rebuilding programme after the Munich air crash when signing for a British record £45,000 in September 1958. For now, two years after his League debut, he was an integral component of Wednesday's attacking threat and his delivery was met by a Dooley header that rebounded off the bar for Sewell to net the equaliser. It was another instalment in Sewell's repaying of the British record £34,000 Wednesday had paid in 1951 when they signed him from Notts County, where he had partnered England centre-forward Tommy Lawton. The fee, along with the value of precious metal at that time, had officially made him the first British player to be worth his weight in gold.

The clearing fog gave the crowd a clear view of an exciting end to the match. With two minutes remaining, Brown received the ball on the right, pulling it back from the by-line for Perry to head down. In one swift move, Taylor swivelled and volleyed in from close range. Blackpool's players and fans celebrated wildly but there was still time for a scare when Dooley went close.[8]

Blackpool were safely through, and Monday lunchtime's fourth-round draw gave them a home tie with Huddersfield, already well on course to regain their top-flight status at the first attempt. "I would rather meet a team playing the good football the Town are reported to be playing than one of these unknowns with everything to gain and nothing to lose," said Smith. "Success in the Second Division has given Town all the confidence, which makes such a difference, and I'm expecting no easy passage."

Bolton's course to the fourth round was yet to be charted after a week in which the weather had been the dominant feature in the town. Burnden Park groundsman Freddy Eckersley was spending most of his time, trousers rolled up over Wellington boots, sticking a fork into the playing surface in an effort to get rid of ice that lay half an inch thick in places. Even the goal areas, which had been covered in tarpaulin, were frozen. An appeal went out to Bolton Corporation to let the club have every brazier they could spare. An extra 50 tonnes of sand was ordered to add to the 50 already in stock, and was spread over the ice after the process of forking had been completed. Meanwhile, salt was scattered on the terraces to ensure that fans would be able to watch safely if the game went ahead.

The cold weather had Bolton's population as concerned about heating their homes as seeing their team's FA Cup tie against Second Division Fulham go ahead. JR Roscoe, the president and chairman of the Bolton and District Coal Traders' Association, was at pains to correct reports that

. . . .

8 Barely a month later, Dooley's football career was over. On 14th February he collided with Preston goalkeeper George Thompson in a game at Deepdale, causing a double fracture of his right leg. When it was discovered that a cut had become infected with gangrene, doctors were forced to amputate his leg.

there was an adequate amount of coal in the town. It was, he said, a result of comments by "certain dealers who are not authorised to make such statements", adding that there was less than two weeks' worth left. "Stocks and supplies have been nearly exhausted," he warned.

With the game only 24 hours away, optimism had grown that there would be no further overnight freeze, but now the concern was the fog, which had been lying low in the Manchester area for two days. Fulham set off regardless on their journey north, electing to stay in Manchester rather than Bolton because of the greater options it offered to take their players to a Friday evening show.

Fans of the London team followed, most of them travelling by road through the early hours of Saturday morning, although only 100 tickets of the club's allocation of 2,000 had been sold. It proved a wasted journey. At 1.30pm referee Bell, who had travelled from his home in Seaton Delaval, postponed the game. Visibility was down to a few yards and when the official walked from the touchline on to the pitch he disappeared from view inside less than 20 paces. Bolton manager Bill Ridding allowed the disappointed Fulham fans inside the ground to see the conditions for themselves.

None could argue that the game should have been played. Some announced their intention to salvage something from the day, including one female fan who said her group planned to attend a dance in Bolton before driving home later that night. "We will make the best of it," she said. "It is a trip for us and we will have it out in full."

Besides, for Londoners, this layer of Lancashire fog was nothing. Barely a month earlier, smog had engulfed the capital for four days, the consequence of a combination of weather conditions and airborne pollutants, caused mainly by coal being burned on open fires. Accepted initially as one of London's 'pea soupers' it quickly turned into the country's worst-ever air pollution event, accountable for anything up to 12,000 deaths, mostly elderly people who developed respiratory problems. One filmed news report labelled the smog "the greatest mass murderer of modern times".

Eager to make for the clear air of the coast, the Fulham players headed to Manchester to take in City's game against Swindon while arrangements were made for them to stay in Blackpool for four days rather than going home. No one posed the question of whether they had packed enough underwear.

The extra preparation time didn't affect Bolton's team selection. Inside-left Harold Hassall was still not fit to play, although the three others who had been named in Saturday's team after winning their fitness battles had time for further recuperation. Nat Lofthouse had been among that trio after fracturing his nose against Charlton on New Year's Day. While his team-mates had been beating Blackpool he had been in a nursing home having the injury attended to. When, three days before the originally scheduled game, the *Bolton Evening News* had spoken to Fulham manager Bill Dodgin, he had jumped in with the first question of the interview: "Do you know whether Nat Lofthouse will be fit?" Dodgin went on to admit that he had not seen Wanderers play all season, but had been using "spy reports".

Having completed their training on Tuesday and then jumped in a coach to attend Burnley's afternoon game against Portsmouth, Bolton named a line-up that included three men making their Cup debuts: full-back Roy Hartle, who had played only two senior matches and was still being called "Les" by the local paper at that point in his career; Ray Parry, who stood in for Hassall to become the club's youngest-ever Cup player at six days short of his 17th birthday; and left-half Eric Bell, whose role in this year's drama was to be a significant one.

The inquest into the identity of the Middlesbrough-based printing firm selling unofficial programmes outside the ground could wait because, with only seven minutes played, Bolton had more pressing matters to worry about. With players of several other teams watching in the crowd of 32,235, the home team found themselves trailing – even after Langton and Wheeler had forced Fulham keeper Ian Black into the first saves of the day. Bobby Robson, the future England manager, released Bobby Brennan on the right and his cross was converted by the former Manchester United winger Charlie Mitten.

Lofthouse spurned what seemed an easy chance when he chose not to get on the end of Willie Moir's header, wrongly assuming the ball to be goal-bound. Then, after 20 minutes, Parry took a ball from Langton and hit a powerful shot on the run that Black turned against the bar.

Robson and future England skipper Johnny Haynes always suggested they could threaten for the visitors, but Langton was by now settling into an outstanding performance and it was his prompting that led to a turnaround in the game's fortunes. He rounded off a neat dribble by cutting inside and passing to Lofthouse, who brushed aside the challenge of Jeff Taylor to equalise. Two minutes later, Langton began another move before Lofthouse charged left with the ball and his cross went via a defender to Doug Holden, who scored with an angled volley. Lofthouse almost added a third before half-time with a low shot after beating two defenders.

Langton's running and crossing was at the heart of heavy Bolton pressure early in the second half, during which time Lofthouse shot disappointingly wide. Fulham forward Bedford Jezzard reminded Bolton that the game was not won yet by twice forcing Stan Hanson to save bravely at his feet, before Lofthouse had two more efforts turned round the post. Bolton's wastefulness around the box looked worryingly as though it could cost them victory and they were relieved to see Robson balloon his shot after Jimmy Hill had hit the bar from a corner. It was not until three minutes from time that victory was secured when Langton advanced and sent a low ball into a dangerous area for Moir to push into the goal.

Former Bolton Mayor Jim Entwhistle, the club chairman, had told the *Bolton Evening News*: "Of course I most certainly hope that we enjoy a good Cup run with a Wembley appearance at the end." And, with the benefit of hindsight, Lofthouse would end up saying that this Wanderers team "had the right blend" and were "the ideal Cup combination". He explained: "Bobby Langton and Doug Holden, who was just coming through, were fast skilful wingers. The inside-forwards were Harold Hassall, with his strong loping run and a fine shot, and Willie Moir, the skipper and brains of the side." He felt that the half-backs combined the bluntness of Barrass with the more creative instincts of Wheeler and Bell. "A strong side with good team spirit," he concluded.

Yet at this early stage of the competition, *Evening News* reporter Haydn Berry was unconvinced. His verdict on the team's third-round success was that "the Wanderers won a well-played match without quite looking like a Wembley combination".

* * * * *

HAVING DEFIED Berry's reservations and gone all the way, Bolton so far bear little resemblance to potential Cup winners, despite their early lead against Blackpool. They contribute further to the early clumsiness of the final when Moir hits a crossfield pass that looks like it has been attempted by a man with his boots on the wrong feet. The ball slices behind him and lands at the feet of Matthews, who slips it forward to Mortensen. He nudges it into the box, but Perry can't bring it under control.

The next time the ball comes in Mortensen's direction, driven low by Shimwell, he turns it first time to Matthews on the right wing; something that has become an instinctive action during the previous six years. Matthews slides past Banks and crosses to the edge of the six-yard box, where Barrass heads out of play. The resulting corner is cut out and carried away to safety, but Matthews will recall: "The fact I was getting the ball into the danger area gave me confidence."

Ten minutes have been played when Mortensen links again with Matthews, whose one-two with Ernie Taylor takes him beyond two men and helps him win another corner, a quintessential piece of Blackpool build-up play. This time the corner is over-hit, as is a lofted ball into the box by Mudie a few moments later. Soon, Johnston is playing a thoughtful pass out of defence to the left wing, where Bolton have been quick into the tackle on Perry. On this occasion, Mudie's pass on the turn frees Perry beyond his marker, allowing him to cut inside and square the ball to Taylor. The move breaks down, but at least Blackpool are enjoying greater possession and showing a direction and purpose in their play.

Bolton respond with Hassall slipping away from a couple of challenges and sending a harmless cross-shot into the grasp of George Farm, although Kenneth Wolstenholme points out: "Farm must be a little nervy about shots like that after Lofthouse's goal."

As is usual for the era, there is little chanting or singing coming from the crowd. The practice of orchestrated vocal support will not find its way into English football until the early 1960s, prompted in part by television viewers hearing the rhythmic chants of the Brazil fans during the 1962 World Cup. Instead, the crowd noise at Wembley is a general buzz, rising to a roar at moments of higher excitement. On the DVD of the game you can clearly hear individual shouts of "Up the Pool!" and the like.

Matthews, however, needs no musical accompaniment, picking up possession in his own half. He plays the ball inside to Mortensen and brings the crowd noise to a crescendo as he takes a return pass and pushes the ball past Banks, hurdling a desperate attempt at a tackle. Barrass is quick to cover from his central position, forcing Matthews back inside, where the recovering Banks is able to smother the ball. That forces a bounce-up that leads to Barrass sliding the ball to the left wing for Langton, who lays it inside for Lofthouse to surge forward. Johnston refuses to succumb to Lofthouse's attempted dummy and dispossesses him with a well-timed tackle.

As Matthews says later: "The one Harry never relished playing was Nat Lofthouse. [He] was like a bull; strong, pacey and very difficult to knock off the ball. He was a barnstorming centre-forward with class and the desperate look of a haunted man who knew his job would be to run head first into a brick wall if called upon to do so. Nat in full flight was an awesome and frightening figure."

Already it is clear that those two are going to give each other a long afternoon.

3

A TALE OF TWO TOWNS

"The real England is not the England of the guide books. Blackpool is more typical than Ascot." – George Orwell (1943).

"It is a strange commentary on our modern way of life that a football club like the Wanderers may do more to foster the sense of community in Bolton than does a governing body like the Town Council." – Bolton Journal (1949).

FOREVER CONJOINED by the 1953 FA Cup Final, Blackpool and Bolton's historical connectivity in football continued when the clubs' match at Bloomfield Road in 1961 was selected as the first League game to be broadcast live as part of a short-lived experiment of televised Friday night matches. A more sombre association was forged when their 1974 game produced the first death attributed to football hooliganism; the fatal stabbing of a Blackpool fan.

The links between the two towns, however, date back further and extend beyond the sporting context.

In the first half of the 20th century, when the people of Lancashire escaped the dirty and stifling environment of the cotton mills for their summer breaks they mostly went to Blackpool. So intriguing was this considered that in 1937 and 1938 researchers from the Mass-Observation organisation went along to view the people of Bolton at play at the seaside, stating that they expected "to see copulation everywhere".

Somewhat regretfully, they ended up reporting that Blackpool offered no "special outlet for sex", certainly no more than they could find in Bolton on any Saturday night. The saucy postcards, jokes about lusty landladies and the 'What The Butler Saw' machines on the piers added up to no more than an orgy of innuendo. To experience the real thing required the finances to secure a hotel room away from the prying eyes and curfews of the average boarding house; something beyond the means of most Bolton workers.

Sex might not have been easily acquired, then, but what Blackpool prided itself on offering above any other commodity was fun, and had done so since it first began advertising itself as a holiday destination in mill-town newspapers in 1876. Having developed more slowly than southern resorts such as Margate and Brighton, Blackpool was determined to make up for lost time when a period of deflation helped to create more spending power and leisure time among the working classes. It was the first English resort to levy a local rate on its residents to fund tourism promotion and by the turn of the century a high-brow location previously known for genteel promenade walks and the quality of its bathing had taken a profitable turn down-market.

Over a period of two months in the summer the whole of the Lancashire cotton industry would, town by town, close down for a two-week period – known as wakes – and Blackpool subsequently became the host to phased holidays known as Bolton Wakes, Oldham Wakes and so forth. Even for those left at home, these periods of rest provided some kind of respite from the daily dourness of industrial urban life.

Recalling his post-war childhood on the *Bolton Revisited* website, town native Brian Farris recalled that "clothes hung out on the back street washing lines… often were dirtier from the chimney smuts than they were when they went out". He explained: "The June holidays when the town closed down were by repute the only time you could see across town. I know it as a fact from the 1950s looking out across Bolton from the lofty Scout Road at the top of Smithills. All those mill chimneys quiescent."

Meanwhile, excited families of all ages would pile onto trains taking almost entire towns to the coast. Passengers would hang precariously out of windows once they got past Preston, looking for their first glimpse of Blackpool Tower – the symbol of the town, opened in 1894 and modelled, as any attentive schoolchild knew, on Paris's Eiffel Tower.

They came from across the Pennines, too. Yorkshire-born Jimmy Greenhoff, who would be involved in FA Cup semi-finals with Leeds and Stoke and win the trophy at Manchester United, was a regular visitor in the post-war years. "A fleet of coaches would leave Barnsley at the same time – it was known as Barnsley week in Blackpool. Everyone I knew went, including the three children in our family. We thought Blackpool was the bright lights, a really special place."

As architectural writer Sir Nikolaus Pevsner would comment: "English social history of the second half of the 19th century and the first half of the 20th century could not be written without Blackpool."

The town's famous Golden Mile evolved after opportunistic traders were banned by the town council from selling their wares – everything from foot ointment to

novelty hats – on the packed beaches. They headed instead
to the forecourts of the cottage owners along the sea front,
paying them rent for use of their land and creating the name
by which this bustling stretch of Blackpool would forever
be identified. Even in winter, the town discovered ways to
maximise revenues, with the theatres that kept the thrill-
seekers entertained on summer evenings being used to stage
conferences.

Blackpool in the middle of the 20th century was a popular
venue for the newsreel cameras. Many such clips still exist,
specialising in somewhat patronising pieces where the
message was: "Look at the common people at play." It was
a similar tone to that projected annually when Lancashire
towns sent their fans down to London for the FA Cup Final.
The working classes, especially those from the north, still
clearly had a quaintness in the eyes of those controlling the
media.

Looking past such superficiality, the BBC's 1954
programme, *The Blackpool Story*, scripted by future *Z-Cars*
writer Allan Prior, suggested: "Blackpool is built on an idea:
people like people. If you don't like people at close quarters
then you could never like this. Blackpool is built on an idea:
give people what they want. For that you need imagination.
You need to guess what they want, before they want it."

While the town was making its name by welcoming the
outside world within its boundaries, it was taking much
longer for its football team to become known to the wider
public in the manner of the Pleasure Beach and the piers.

Blackpool Football Club was founded in a meeting at
the Stanley Arms Hotel on 26th July 1887, when members
of St John's FC decided to form a club that featured the
town's name. After becoming one of the founder members
of the Lancashire League, Blackpool played their first
Football League game in 1896, following a successful third
application for election. They slipped out of the League

in 1899, but were back to stay a year later, resisting the temptation to drop back into minor football during the decades of hardship that followed. At times it was only the benevolence of club directors that kept them afloat, dipping into their own pockets to ensure that players were paid.

By 1930, Blackpool had achieved greater financial security. Winning the Second Division title saw them begin a three-year run in the top flight, the first coastal club to feature in the First Division. But it was the arrival during the 1935/36 season of a new manager, ironically a man who had been a symbol of success at Bolton Wanderers, that heralded the start of a new chapter for the team from the seaside.

* * * * *

FOOTBALL IN Lancashire had developed in geographical concert with rugby league throughout the latter years of the 19th century. Rugby had become the preferred sport throughout the textile towns of the east, from Salford to Rochdale, and in the west, from St Helens to Warrington. The towns of Darwen, Blackburn and Bolton formed a triangle of football country in the middle, with all 28 founder members of the Lancashire Football Association in 1878 emanating from that small region.

The area was also in the vanguard of the spread of professionalism, with players – many of them brought down from Scotland – offered dubious testimonial matches or secret payments to work in local firms. Bolton were rumoured to be at the forefront of such practices.

In his history of Bolton Wanderers, Percy Young referred to the town in terms of its "strong traditions of community and independence; the religious fervour and cognate political loyalties that were there engendered from at least the time of the Reformation; the influential country gentlemen who, from their sturdy and often beautiful manor houses in the moors, dominated the surrounding peasantry; and the Industrial Revolution, which made Lancashire the centre of the commercial world in the nineteenth century, and also the focal point of world football".

Gentry and religion had, indeed, played a significant role in the formation of the club, which had its roots in the setting up of Turton Football Club by the Kay family, prominent figures in local agriculture for two centuries who had seen two of their number introduced to football while at Harrow School. Thomas Ogden, a local schoolmaster at Christ Church, studied the Turton club with a view to introducing the sport to his pupils. In 1874, he raised enough money from prospective players to buy a five shilling football and Christ Church FC was formed.

Conflict ensued when the Vicar of Christ Church, JF Wright, who was club president, refused to allow the team officers to make any decisions without him being present at meetings. In frustration the officers walked out of the Christ Church school, where they usually held meetings, and met instead at the Gladstone Hotel, near Pikes Lane. On 28th August 1877, they became Bolton Wanderers FC. After a few nomadic years, the club settled at Pikes Lane in 1881, but despite having their first permanent home, they resisted the efforts by town leaders to make them drop the Wanderers from the club name.

The identity of the town that the club represented had its foundations in the 15th century arrival of Flemish settlers, bringing their wool and cotton weaving traditions with them. It survived the Bolton Massacre of 1644, when 1,600 townspeople were killed by Royalist troops during the English Civil War, to become one of the most important mill towns in the world. Textile manufacturing – which was accelerated by the spinning machines created by local inventors Richard Arkwright and Samuel Crompton –

brought about the urbanisation of Bolton and, at its peak in 1929, boasted 216 cotton mills and 26 bleaching and dying works in the north-west of England.

Most children growing up in Bolton who escaped the prospect of a working life spent in the mills believed they had experienced a lucky escape. Brian Farris explained:

> We were taught the fundamentals of the town's main trade at school but I consider myself fortunate not to have been forced to follow my mother and her family into the mill... I remember taking a message to her in the mill at the bottom of the street. The atmosphere was hot, dry and dusty. I couldn't hear myself speak but my mother, having worked from 13 years old in that environment, had no problem and was amused to see me in her work place.
>
> She said later that I looked as if I had stumbled on to another planet. I had often been near the entrances when the buzzer had sounded for the end of the working day and the mill workers had poured out like ants from a disturbed nest. They were covered in fluff and dust from the cotton and there was the all pervading smell of the cotton and the hot oil of the machines.

Yet even as early as the 1930s, the British cotton industry had been seeing the first signs of decline, with theories on its cause ranging from the lack of building materials for more modern mills to the greed and bad management of the owners, who remained stubbornly blind to the prospect of foreign competition. The formation in 1929 of the Lancashire Cotton Corporation by the Bank of England was an attempt to rationalise the industry, merging many companies. By 1935, the LCC had closed almost half of the 140 mills it had taken over. In 1950, its portfolio of mills stretched to only 53. During the latter stages of Bolton's Cup run of 1953, cloth output in the Lancashire mills did at least reach its highest level for 11 months, while manpower stood at 275,000, up 13,000 from a year earlier. Still, it was no wonder that Bolton Mayor Jim Entwhistle had made his New Year appeal on behalf of an industry that was historically so integral to the fortunes of his town.

It had been some time after their formation that Wanderers could claim to be adding much to the prestige bestowed upon Bolton by its industrial prominence. They lost their first-ever FA Cup match against Blackburn during the 1881/82 season and, a year later, were threatened with expulsion from the Lancashire FA when referee Sam Ormerod was booed off the field and assaulted at the local railway station after a game at Pikes Lane. The club's first trophy did arrive, however, in 1886 when they beat Blackburn to win the Lancashire Cup; and in 1888/89 they lined up as one of the 12 founder members of the Football League.

Their first FA Cup Final was reached in 1894, a 4-1 loss to Notts County at Goodison Park, where their only goal was a late consolation. One year later, Wanderers moved to Burnden Park, their home for the next century, which had first been used for the local athletics festival and attracted 35,000 spectators. Approximately 20,000 fewer saw Bolton's first League game there against Everton.

Between 1899 and 1911, Bolton were relegated and promoted four times, the final of those campaigns seeing the establishment of a partnership between Joe Smith and Ted Vizard that was to grace the club for 16 years. Outside-left Vizard, a Welshman who had played rugby for Penarth and Barry before settling on a career in football, was well-served by the man immediately next to him in the forward line. Smith, who hailed from the West Midlands, had begun his playing career at Crewe Alexandra, but it was at Bolton that he made his name as a dynamic on-field force and prolific scorer, either from inside-forward or playing more centrally.

It is Smith who links the football histories of Bolton and Blackpool prior to the final of 1953. He won the first of five England caps in 1913, two years after Vizard played the first of his 22 games for Wales, and the pair were strongly rumoured to be on their way to Chelsea late in 1918 after turning out for the London club during the First World War. Yet both remained and Vizard was even placed in temporary charge of the team for the second half of the 1918/19 season, before Charles Foweraker took over and named Smith as his captain. Thriving on the responsibility, Smith equalled the league record of 38 goals in 1920/21, including three in five minutes during a four-goal performance at home to Sunderland on Christmas Day. After scoring his final goal with his head he had to be taken off the field in a state of near unconsciousness, so heavy had the ball become on a wet surface.

By the beginning of the 1922/23 season, Bolton had proved themselves effective cup competitors by winning both the Lancashire and Manchester Senior Cups – then prestigious and sought-after prizes – in the previous campaign. They transferred that form to the national stage by qualifying for the first FA Cup Final to be played at the newly-built Empire Stadium, Wembley, beating holders Huddersfield along the way. Smith became the first Cup-winning captain at the new home of English football when his team defeated Second Division West Ham 2-0.

Anything between 125,000 and 150,000 were estimated to have forced their way inside "incontestably the finest sports ground in the world", as the match programme described it, and a white police horse called Billy went down in football folklore for his role in controlling the crowds. During the first half, after several stoppages to force the spectators back behind the touchlines, Smith reportedly declined the offer of West Ham captain George Kay, a former Bolton player, to abandon the game, insisting that he was happy to play until it was dark if necessary.

Three years later, Smith's goal in a second replay against Nottingham Forest put Bolton one game from Wembley again; then he scored two in a 3-0 win against Swansea in the semi-final. In the final, David Jack – scorer of the first Wembley goal three years earlier – was on target again inside the final 15 minutes to secure a 1-0 win against Manchester City.

The following season was Smith's last at the club, his colleagues expressing their appreciation of his service by presenting him with a canteen of cutlery. Two decades later, Charles Buchan, the former Sunderland and Arsenal great, would write of his on-field contemporary: "Joe Smith, with his all-out methods and forceful language, was the driving force behind the Wanderers' success." Smith had ended his Bolton career with 277 goals and continued to score freely for Stockport. In 1929, though, he transferred the leadership qualities of which Buchan would speak to a new role, becoming player-manager of Lancashire Combination side Darwen. After two years in which his club carried all before them, Smith retired from playing to become manager of Third Division South team Reading. During four seasons at Elm Park, he achieved two runners-up placings, plus a third and fourth.

By the time Bolton were back at Wembley in 1929, coming from behind to beat Huddersfield in the semi-finals, Jack had also left Burnden Park, becoming the country's first £10,000 footballer when he transferred to Arsenal earlier in the season. Having prepared for the final by staying just outside Blackpool, in Cleveleys, Bolton beat Portsmouth with two late goals. They had now won three finals in a seven-season span without conceding a single Wembley goal, keeper Richard Pym, a former fisherman from Exeter, having preserved an empty net on each occasion.

By the summer of 1935, Bolton had been relegated and promoted once more – reaching the FA Cup semi-finals and finishing as runners-up in the Second Division in the same season – while Blackpool were looking for a new manager following the departure of Sandy MacFarlane. The former Scottish international had set about rebuilding the team after their relegation from the First Division in 1933 and had signed the young Northern Ireland inside-forward Peter Doherty,[9] but missed out on promotion when finishing fourth in 1934/35.

Blackpool's approach to Smith succeeded mainly on the back of his professed enjoyment of the seaside. In fact, he loved it so much he remained as the club's boss for 23 years. "It was a very healthy place, Blackpool," he would tell local author Robin Daniels. "I fancied coming here. I never fancied one or two of the southern crowds, somehow. They would saunter about, even if it was two or three minutes before the start of the match. They would walk along as if next week would do. Whereas in the north they'd run to the ground, frightened of missing the match."

After his second season in charge, Blackpool were back in the top flight as runners-up in the Second Division. By the time they were next relegated, in 1966/67, they would rank behind only Arsenal as the First Division's longest-serving club.

The success that Blackpool went on to enjoy throughout and beyond the war years was an accurate reflection of the fortunes of the town itself. When war broke out in 1939, Blackpool was benefiting through its innovation, introducing entertainment centres, modern cinemas and new public houses – although John K Walton's history of the town also points out: "Not far behind the facade,

. . . .

9 Doherty was sold to Manchester City in 1936 for £10,000 because Blackpool needed the money.

however, could be found the crumbling slums of the earliest uncontrolled development," and adds that there was "no shortage of poverty."

The war years were prosperous ones for Blackpool – as they had been between 1914 and 1918 – with local aircraft production and the heavy military presence bringing important revenue into the area. Landladies crammed as many RAF personnel as they could behind the lace curtains of the town's 5,000 guest houses. By 1940, 1,700 civil servants had arrived from London, with the town's population up from 128,000 before the outbreak of hostilities to 143,000 in 1945. On the last Saturday of July in that year, it was estimated that 103,000 visitors arrived at Blackpool's train stations. Around 1,200 coaches turned up in an average week, carrying about 25 passengers each – most of them day-trippers.

Many wartime visitors returned for holidays and honeymoons, others to work or retire. Around the country, seaside resorts and sports events attracted huge crowds, and Blackpool was in a position to benefit from both. Even as some of the middle classes drifted away in favour of package holidays overseas, the slack was taken up by more working-class people being given paid holidays and being able to afford weeks at the coast.[10]

The parents of long-time Blackpool fan Mel McCarthy owned the Ribblesdale Hotel in Hesketh Avenue, by the north shore. "Christ, it was doing well," he recalled. "We came here in 1945 and Blackpool was booming. The hotel

. . . .

10 It was not until the 1960s that English resorts began to find foreign holidays biting into their revenues, along with the effects of lack of post-war investment. Towns would stagnate and become taken for granted; in the manner that the post-war football boom would lead the sport's authorities down a parallel path of complacency. Meanwhile, easier transportation encouraged the northern visitors who had formed Blackpool's captive audience to go further afield, particularly to the warmer resorts on the south coast.

was always busy. Britain's holidays resorts were booming because nobody went abroad. There were deckchairs on every inch of sand."

Future England captain Jimmy Armfield, who forced his way into the Blackpool team in the season after their FA Cup triumph, helped his mother run a boarding house in the town and recalled: "Blackpool during the war and immediately afterwards attracted a lot of people of all types and it was tough at times... the years from 1945 to 1950 were a boom time for Blackpool's boarding houses."

Ken Britton, a schoolboy Tangerines fan at that time, added: "If you went on the beach on a sunny day you simply wouldn't be able to move. You would be threading your way through all the people and there was no space to play. I can remember people coming to Blackpool on their holidays from as close as Preston."

More people were settling permanently in the town, a shift in population that by early 1953 was causing concern within the Town Hall about the slow pace of house building. The council's 1952 target of 800 new homes had been missed by more than 400. Councillor H Henson, the chairman of the housing committee, said: "If the builders build as they should, we should get 1,000 houses this year."

Many of those, it was hoped, would accommodate employees arriving to build jet planes for Hawker Aircraft Ltd, itself a new arrival in the town. Alderman Rhodes W Marshall warned: "Without key workers the factory cannot build up. They are already five months behind with their own building-up programme. In the national interests it is absolutely essential that new aircraft should come from the factory as soon as possible." Meanwhile, work opportunities continued to be plentiful, with Blackpool's unemployment figures for January 1953 standing at 4,229, despite a small monthly rise.

The resumption of Blackpool's famous seafront illuminations in 1949 had been a symbol of recovery from wartime hardship. Ceremonially switched on by Stanley Matthews in 1951 – and George Formby and Hollywood star Jayne Mansfield in later years – they extended the summer season by a further six weeks into the autumn, bringing in an estimated additional three million visitors. Their reappearance marked the beginning of a successful decade for the town's entertainment industry. Even deckchair rental revenue was 20 per cent higher in 1955 than in 1950 as visitors headed for the Fylde Coast from points as distant as Dundee and Devon.

Walton explains: "The town and its amusements brought people together from a variety of provincial cultures in a way that nowhere else could." There were endless shops selling nothing but items intended for fun, the store fronts providing the backdrop for joyful flirting as men and women walked along the promenade.[11]

Blackpool considered itself the centre of the entertainment world, with attractions such as Reginald Dixon and his Mighty Wurlitzer at the Tower Ballroom and clown prince Charlie Caroli in the Tower Circus. Of course, much of what it offered was parochial, earthy Lancashire humour as performed by the crude, belching character of Frank Randle, who regularly filled the town's theatres. The brand of escapism he offered to local audiences never translated outside the area in the way that the exploits of the football club developed an appeal stretching well beyond the county boundaries. "In sport, as in entertainment, the 1950s had given Blackpool a primacy it was never to reclaim," Walton writes.

. . . .

11 A decade later, the innocent air had dissipated, according to actor
David Thewlis, who grew up in the town. "I was brought up constantly
surrounded by drunk people," he said. "All the tourists, my image of all the
people who visited, was that they were always drunk."

In the early spring of 1953, towns such as Bolton were warned that there was a danger of paying through the nose for the attractions of Blackpool because of the established schedule of 'wakes' weeks. A survey of 100 north-west textile towns found that all were taking their annual holidays between 20th June and 22nd August. Vain attempts had been made to get them to extend that vacation period and the message reaching them from the landladies was summarised as: "Don't blame us if your holiday is a crowded one and costs more."

Harry Cunningham, general secretary of the British Federation of Hotel and Boarding House Associations, explained: "There appears to have been no careful study in the choosing of holiday dates. If prices for holiday are not to be put out of the reach of the average working man and his family – which would be disastrous to the hotel and boarding house trade – there must be a wider spread-over. Since all the cotton workers cannot agree to these proposals it is hoped that the hotel industry will not be blamed for taking advantage of the present situation when the holidaymakers find that the terms quoted for accommodation have been increased for the 1953 season."

Meanwhile, professional footballers, as well as tourists, had long since felt the allure of Blackpool as a town. Scot Hugh Kelly, who signed for the club in 1943 as a 19-year-old, remembered that "everybody I knew had been there on holiday". He told Mike Prestage, author of *Blackpool: The Glory Years Remembered*: "Everything about the place pleased me so much. As I took my first tram ride along the front I thought it was the loveliest town I had ever been in. Playing for Blackpool and living in the town fulfilled my ambition."

Winger Bill Perry arrived from South Africa in 1949 to find: "Blackpool was packed during the summer season. The town was buzzing." And being local celebrities meant that Blackpool players had easy access to the biggest shows at a time when venues such as the Winter Gardens could attract international stars as big as Bob Hope, as well as the best of British.

Stan Mortensen explained that there was "plenty to entertain us in the evenings" and even admitted: "From the point of view of club officials there may be too many distractions in Blackpool. Luckily I found the right companions at once and I had no temptation to go off the rails. Twice a week a bunch of the younger professionals would take a long walk, and there were plenty of cinemas – if we could afford them."

In the early years of the 1950s, four out of ten adults went to the cinema at least once every week, while the second largest entertainment sector was dancing, with 200 million admissions to the country's dance halls annually. In the days before rock and roll and the burgeoning youth culture, that still meant predominantly ballroom dancing, mostly polite teetotal occasions.

Among the rules that Blackpool's footballers were obliged to follow was that they were not allowed to dance from Wednesday onwards. Additionally, they were expected home each night by 11.30pm (or 10.30pm on the night before a match) and they were not allowed to ride motorcycles. "Once a week or so we might go to a dance," said Mortensen. "One could dance on Saturday after the match, and on Monday. For the rest of the week the dance floor was out of bounds." Yet Wednesday remained a popular night out among the team and, according to Mortensen, "Around nine o'clock it was no uncommon sight for anything up to a dozen Blackpool players to be footing the light fantastic to the strains of a famous band!"

If the party wasn't broken up by the arrival of one of the club trainers sending the players scurrying for the doors, then landladies could be relied upon to pass on tidbits of information. "Everything we did was known, sooner or later, to the officials at Bloomfield Road," said Mortensen, who stopped short of accusing the landladies of being paid spies but said these "good-hearted women" might think they were "doing the right thing" for the players' welfare by keeping the club informed.

Cyril Robinson came from Bulwell, just outside Nottingham, but was one of many Seasiders players of the era who ended up settling in the town. "Blackpool wasn't a place you went to on your holidays if you were from Nottingham," he said, "but I liked it very quickly. We used to go to the pictures quite a lot, which a lot of people did, and we spent a long time along the prom. I was away for about eight weeks in the summer but I liked coming back and I wouldn't want to live anywhere else."

Robinson's explanation of his living arrangements when he first arrived in Blackpool was a common one for young footballers, right up until the more modern phenomenon of academies stocked by overseas signings. "To leave home was very unusual in those days and I was in digs. That could be a very different experience, depending on what digs you are getting. I thought they should have had a hostel thing so the lads were together. The first digs I had was run by an old couple and at four o'clock the radio used to come on for *Mrs Dale's Diary* and as soon as that had finished they turned it off. I turned it on one night and there was music on. The landlady came in and said: 'What are you doing with this noise on?' She switched it off. I thought: 'Bloody hell.'

"Saturdays we used to go to the Winter Gardens, which was where I met Kath, my wife. If we were coming back from a reserve game we knew the driver so we would say 'put your foot down' because they used to finish at 11. We went dancing, walked home, got back about 11 and I would get 'where have you been until this time?' I just left in the end. A lad I knew had recommended somewhere else. It is amazing how many young boys finished with football through being homesick. But I don't think the club took an interest particularly. That was because of Joe Smith. You could have had a flat on your own and he wouldn't have known, although he wouldn't have liked that. He didn't take a lot of notice of the young lads."

As Smith led his team to the 1948 and 1951 FA Cup Finals and watched Stanley Matthews filling the terraces at Bloomfield Road, it was clear that the success of Blackpool FC both reflected and added to the town's growing profile and lustre. The club fell neatly into the category of "artificial attractions" that, Walton notes, held the key to the town's fortune at that time.

Bolton Wanderers, of course, had less ability to sell the attractions of their town when looking to attract new players. John Higgins, a Derbyshire-born defender who arrived at the club in 1952, recalled being singularly unimpressed by his new environment. "I trained the first Tuesday night I came here and there were a lot of little lads with dark eyes and they had been in the pit all day and the muck was that bad that night I couldn't believe it. The bath was that thick with scum. When I got home I said: 'I'm not going back any more, Dad.' Anyway, I went back the following week and they were the best set of lads I've ever known in my life."

The close bond among the Wanderers players had been emphasised at the outbreak of war in 1939. Several months earlier, 15 players had enlisted with the army and 13 were called up immediately hostilities began, the other two still being too young to fight. Those off to join the 53rd Regiment Royal Artillery included Stan Hanson, goalkeeper in the 1953 final, and club captain Harry Goslin, who was to be killed late in 1943 while seeing action with the 8th Army Mediterranean Forces. Another player, Walter Sidebottom, died when his ship was torpedoed.

Having won the War Cup North in 1945, thanks to two goals by Malcolm Barrass in the second leg against Manchester United, Bolton then came from behind to beat Chelsea in the national final. But there were only a few highlights in the first years of official post-war football. These included Willie Moir's feat of leading the First Division with 25 goals in 1948/49; the club-record signing of winger Bobby Langton for £20,000 from Preston; and the representative honours and international accolades earned by centre-forward Nat Lofthouse.

* * * * *

NOW BOLTON have another Wembley final to add to their club history. Still 1-0 up after 17 minutes, they threaten briefly through a good interchange between Moir and Bell but Robinson intervenes to guide the ball back to Farm. Then, a further two minutes on, comes one of the pivotal moments of the game. When Robinson is halted from taking a throw, Kenneth Wolstenholme brings viewers' attention to the fact that someone is injured, identifying him as Bolton left-half Eric Bell. For the second year running, the course of the Cup Final will be partly determined by injury, Arsenal having lost full-back Walley Barnes to a damaged knee inside half an hour of their defeat to Newcastle a season earlier. Bolton trainer Bert Sproston can do no more than escort Bell to the touchline, strap his left thigh and send him back out to hobble along the wing. Outside-left Langton moves inside and Harold Hassall drops back from inside-left to left-half.

Interestingly, Barrass will venture decades later: "It was an advantage because Ding-Dong [Bell] got out of the way and we had to convert other positions. Harold was a good wing-half."

But Barrass's view remains a minority one, and Bolton manager Bill Ridding seems to be guilty of failing to consider the implications of weakening that side of his team in the face of the greatest right-winger in the game. Although it will take until the later stages of the game for Matthews to completely hit his stride, there is no doubt that left-back Ralph Banks is eventually left exposed without a more experienced defensive-minded player close by to offer assistance. According to Doug Holden: "There was no help for Ralph Banks. We had Bell hobbling on the wing and Harold Hassall had to fill in at left-half, but that's the way it was in those days."

Even before the game, Lofthouse stressed the importance of Bell's role by saying: "We all hope Bell will be able to lend the support necessary to help Ralph Banks at left-back to keep the great Stanley in check."

Additionally, without a left-winger able to tackle or cover, it means that Bolton will find it harder to prevent the ball being fed to Matthews in the first place. Stan Mortensen will describe the Bolton reshuffle as "the biggest blunder of all time". Talking to Matthews's biographer, David Miller, he explains: "If there was one thing Matthews hated it was the opposing winger on his flank tackling back. I've even heard him tell wingers to go away and get on with their own job."

Banks will become a vocal critic of Bolton's failure to properly compensate for Bell's injury, feeling that a makeshift left-half and the support offered to Matthews by Taylor effectively left him outnumbered two to one on far too many occasions. But perhaps Ridding should not be held too culpable for acting on auto-pilot and adhering to the formational rigidity of English football. In these days before substitutes, outside-left is traditionally the position to which crocked players are posted. And this is hardly a period in the game known for managers going against the grain and introducing innovative tactical thinking.

4

SAME OLD BALL GAME

"England was stuck in the Thirties until the Sixties." – Jonathan Miller.

A S THE end of January 1953 approached, most of Britain was gripped by the efforts of Derek Bentley's father, William, to have his 19-year-old son spared from execution after he and a 16-year-old companion, Christopher Craig, had been found guilty of murdering a policeman during a burglary attempt three months earlier. No one disputed the truth that Craig had pulled the trigger but Bentley's alleged shout of "let him have it, Chris" to Craig was judged to have been an incitement to open fire rather than a plea to surrender his firearm. On Wednesday 28th January, with demonstrators clamouring outside Wandsworth Prison, Bentley was hanged.[12]

Even in the days before footballers became as closeted from real life as they are in modern times, such human tragedy struggled to fully penetrate the insulated world of

. . . .

12 Bentley and Craig claimed that the "let him have it" comment was never even spoken and in 1998, following a long campaign led by his sister, Iris, Bentley had his conviction posthumously overturned when the Court of Appeal ruled that he had been denied a fair trial.

preparations for an important FA Cup tie. It is doubtful that too many Blackpool players spent much time at their habitual retreat in Buxton discussing the moral dilemma of capital punishment. Likewise, the Huddersfield players, passing the week at Blackpool's Norbreck Hydro Hotel before their fourth-round contest, would have quickly turned away from the serious headlines on the front page of the *Evening Gazette* to seek out information on their opponents in the sports pages.

Instead, they found it was they who were being talked about. "Why this hush, hush?" the paper asked when Huddersfield manager Andy Beattie took the entirely reasonable step of declining to name his team a full three days in advance. Combining suspicion, naivety and a desperation to fill its columns while its own players were out of town, the *Gazette* conjectured: "Could it be he has a secret plan?" Exhibit A was the memory of Beattie – who the following year would become Scotland's first manager – bringing his Stockport team to Bloomfield Road a couple of years previously and double-teaming Stanley Matthews by posting the left-half close to the left-back in what the *Gazette* referred to as a "freak formation".

With such attitudes prevailing, it was little wonder that the Hungarians would be looked upon as men from another planet when they allowed their number nine, Nándor Hidegkuti, to drop into midfield to orchestrate the infamous humiliation of England at Wembley later in 1953. British football still considered it downright underhand to allow someone to roam more than temporarily from the position on the field to which his jersey number supposedly tethered him. Manchester City would discover the same thing when they began using their own centre-forward, Don Revie, in a similar role – with great success. "Centre-halves were conditioned to going with the centre-forward, just as wingers had a battle with full-backs," Revie's team-mate Johnny Williamson told *Backpass* magazine. "If they followed Don, another forward slipped into the gap they had left."

Bolton centre-half Malcolm Barrass, an England international, said: "I covered the opposing centre-forward and that was basically it. Where he went, I went."

Football's tactical rigidity, it could be argued, did nothing more than reflect the strict moral and social boundaries that existed in post-war England. Anything as outrageous as tactical thinking was generally considered as desirable as communism or pre-marital pregnancy.

In his 1952 book, *40 Years in Football*, journalist and former amateur international Ivan Sharpe reported a conversation with Vittorio Pozzo, the mastermind of Italy's two World Cup wins during the 1930s. Pozzo suggested that the pressure to win in English football was greater than in other countries, thereby stifling any sense of adventure and innovation. He noted that English teams all had the "same styles, same moves, same tactics, same tendencies" and added: "New tactics to upset the opposition are now the feature of football on the Continent. [In Italy] you seldom come across two teams playing the same way."

While Pozzo was guiding his country to their triumphs of 1934 and 1938 the idea of tactics and coaching was still anathema to all but the most enlightened thinkers in English football. Nothing much changed when the Football League resumed after the war, although Arthur Rowe's Tottenham side did demonstrate their manager's original thinking in winning the 1950/51 championship one year after promotion. They did so with a style of play known as "push and run" due to the players' clever – and at that time, revolutionary – use of space off the ball.

Yet it should be remembered that the role of football manager as we know it in modern times was still in its relative infancy in the early 1950s. It had not existed at all in the early days of the Football League, little more than half a century earlier. Clubs were run at that time by the directors; professional businessmen who added the selection of players to their administrative responsibilities. The club secretary, a paid employee, was the man who liaised between the board and players.

As the growth of the sport made the task of running the club too big for part-time directors, the secretary's role expanded into team affairs. The secretary-manager was still a shadowy background figure – until the directors required a scapegoat for poor results, at which point the unfortunate employee was usually thrust forward to announce his 'resignation'. Yet as fans become more passionate about their team, the demand increased for someone to be the club's focal point on a daily basis. The directors, acknowledging the dangers posed to their companies and products through association with an unsuccessful club, happily fostered this heightening of the manager's profile.

Finally, more managers began to realise that if the board were going to make them the fall guys they might as well do whatever they could to influence events on the field. Pioneers such as Herbert Chapman, the great Huddersfield and Arsenal manager of the 1920s and 1930s, showed their profession the way forward. He was one of the earliest to introduce previously alien concepts like mental and physical preparation for games. Rightly acknowledged as one of football's visionaries, he commented in 1934: "Football today is too big a job to be a director's hobby. In my opinion the club manager ought to pick the team" – a radical statement for the time, when the secretary-manager rarely had the opportunity to choose which players would be entrusted with the fate of his own employment. "Team picking is a complicated and scientific matter requiring expert knowledge and, in my experience, comparatively few directors are qualified to undertake it," he wrote in the *Sunday Express*.

Chapman was one of the first to take tactics seriously, developing the custom of pre-game team talks. He spurred players to study the game, to discuss it with team-mates, to contribute ideas in meetings and to think about their own contribution to the collective effort. He complained that players were "keen and ready enough to hold an inquest on the playing of a hand of solo, but they did not bother to inquire why they had lost a match or how the play of the side might be improved".

Tactically, his most notable contribution came to be acknowledged as the introduction of the stopper centre-half, a practical solution to the problem posed by a new offside law, which stated that only two, not three, defenders had to be between the attacker and the goal for him to remain onside. Recognising the advantage that the forwards now had against the traditional formation of two defensive full-backs and three midfield-dwelling half-backs, Chapman pulled back the centre-half to become a third defender.

The employment in British football of brains such as Chapman was, however, still a rarity. As late as September 1954, in his season preview in *Football Monthly*, Charles Buchan was highlighting the captain as the "most valuable man in the modern League team" and as good as urging the manager to keep his nose out of it. "How often have I seen during a League game a manager issuing orders during the game or even at half-time! A real old-time skipper would never have allowed this." Buchan's view was that the captain "is in a better position, in closer touch with events, than the man sitting in the grandstand" and argued "[Managers] set up as dictators and fall down on the job, especially as far as it concerns the playing side".

It was little wonder that, more often than not, anyone showing a desire to think about the game and a flair for implementing their thoughts via on-field strategy had been forced by England's narrow minds to seek employment overseas. Most famously, Jimmy Hogan, an unspectacular player with Burnley and Bolton, spent two decades earning a reputation as a coaching pioneer in the Netherlands, Switzerland, Germany, France, Hungary and Austria, whose team he led to the 1936 Olympic Final.

And there were others. Fred Pentland, a former England centre-forward, was a successful coach in Spain; Jack Reynolds, a well-travelled Football League professional, spent a quarter of a century as coach of Ajax in three spells and is credited with laying the foundations for the 'Total Football' style of play that became their trademark. George Raynor, from Barnsley, led Sweden to Olympic medals and a World Cup Final and helped them earn a 2-2 draw against Hungary six months before that famous team destroyed England 6-3. Raynor combated the threat of Hidegkuti by man-marking him in his deeper position – something beyond the wit of England at Wembley. In 1959, he advised Sweden on a 3-2 win at the home of English football, but commented sadly: "I would much rather have been doing the same thing for the country of my birth."

In his book *The Anatomy of England*, Jonathan Wilson comments: "This of course was the shameful irony of England's conservatism: it wasn't that forward thinkers didn't exist; it was that coaching was so scorned that they were forced abroad. Not only did they not help English football they ended up helping England's rivals."

At home, those few who craved a more cerebral approach to the game were at least able in the 1950s to sign up for coaching courses at the FA's training centre in Lilleshall, where the likes of future coaches Malcolm Allison, Don Howe and Alan Brown studied at the feet of England manager Walter Winterbottom. Allison, indulged by his West Ham manager Ted Fenton, would go as far as taking over organisation of his club's training sessions and introducing specific skills training along with the use of weights.

Stanley Matthews was among those scratching their heads to work out why the general approach of English football was to be suspicious of anyone who sought to do things differently. Even though England had lost to a continental team for the first time as long ago as 1929, when they were beaten in Spain, the feeling persisted that traditional virtues such as muscle and power would, on most occasions, beat overseas trickery and tactics. Matthews couldn't understand why clubs stuck rigidly to fitness training on most days. "Although Stoke and Blackpool used a ball in training more than most clubs, it was still nowhere near enough as far as I was concerned," he commented.

He also failed to see why the admiration he and Tom Finney shared for the Brazilians in the 1950 World Cup finals was not reflected by a hierarchy who saw the event as a gimmick. It was back to the old days of blaming England's early overseas defeats on hard grounds or hot weather, as if home-grown mud on a wet day in February were the only relevant conditions in which to judge a team. The FA's technical committee met only once to review the tournament and quickly concluded that Brazilian methods were not suited to the English game.

England had boasted a strong team in the immediate post-war years, able to field perhaps its most illustrious forward line ever: Matthews, Mortensen, Lawton, Mannion and Finney. They also had their first team manager, Winterbottom, an inventive choice for which the FA should be applauded as it went against the grain of club football. Winterbottom had studied as a coach and trainer while at Manchester United and entered the profession full-time when spinal problems curtailed his playing career. Yet he was constantly hampered by prejudice and short-sightedness within the game, including his employers and even some of his players, the most senior of whom –

uncoached for much of their careers – could not see what he could teach them. Even Matthews, a more enlightened thinker than many, ascribed England's failures in Brazil to too much tactical emphasis by Winterbottom, commenting: "You cannot tell star players how they must play."

A 10-0 win against Portugal in Stan Mortensen's debut game and a 4-0 win against Italy in May 1948 had contributed towards England's best run since the First World War. But this was followed by the disorganised entry into the 1950 World Cup, where Winterbottom's team was effectively chosen for him by the one FA official on the trip, Grimsby fishmonger Arthur Drewery.

The typical view was that football was a game played by 11 individuals in matching shirts; and that a team approach had no value. Wilson calls it "symptomatic of the anti-intellectualism that has habitually undermined English football", while David Goldblatt says in *The Ball is Round*: "Like the wider culture, British football was suspicious of intellectuals, distrustful of theory, disdainful of certified expertise." When a combined Britain team beat a Europe XI 6-1 at Hampden Park in 1949, it was heralded as a triumph of robust British character over continental technique and coaching.

Neither of the two Cup Final leaders of 1953 could be said to have ploughed a deep strategic furrow through football management. *Football Monthly* might have said of Joe Smith that "his forthright character has moulded the side into the best that has worn the tangerine jerseys", yet, in keeping with most of his profession, the Blackpool manager – scorer of more than 250 goals in his playing career – was no great tactician. "But he knew a good player when he saw one," said Harry Johnston, his captain and on-field brains. "He got a good team together and he more or less let it take care of itself. He wasn't the type of man to interfere when things were going well."

Bill Perry said: "Joe's strength as a manager was that he brought players into the team to suit certain positions. We were not coached as such… Joe never talked about tactics." According to Mortensen: "We did not see a lot of Joe Smith but I have not the slightest doubt that he saw and heard more than we imagined."

Matthews recalled: "Joe was a wily old bird but he was my type of manager. He had assembled good players and he believed that you don't have to tell good players what to do." Even Matthews, however, looked back on Blackpool's defeat to Manchester United in the 1948 Cup Final and wondered whether Smith could have done more to prepare his team for the threat posed by the opposition; an approach he knew that Matt Busby would have taken on United's training ground. Interestingly, United winger Charlie Mitten suggested Busby got it wrong by making him track back to cover Matthews in the first half, which saw United trailing 2-1. In the second half, Busby changed tactics, freeing his winger to attack and instructing his team to press against Blackpool half-backs Johnston and Hugh Kelly in order to cut off Matthews's supply at source. Matthews confessed that his team was "completely flummoxed".

Smith ignored such lessons, insisting that time in preparation for games was better spent working on practicalities on the field rather than theorising on a blackboard. Without prior knowledge of what the other team would do, he argued, plans were "a load of old tripe". Opposition was discussed in an open forum, with attributes of key players given an airing, but formalised systems rarely, if ever, emerged as a result of those talks.

In the dressing room, Smith, short and stocky with dark hair that he parted high on the right side of his head, believed more in lightening the mood than striving for enlightenment. According to Johnston: "He always had a joke. Relieving tension is part of a manager's job."

Full-back Eddie Shimwell recalled that Smith "fostered a good spirit among us", encouraging the players to bolster team-mates who were out of form and relying on the dressing room veterans to look after the interests of younger colleagues.

One of Smith's favourite recurring team talks was: "Get two goals up before half-time, lads, so I can enjoy my cigar in the second half." If things were going well he was happy to stay quiet, Johnston recalled. "He wasn't the man to say to himself 'well I am the manager and I must say something, just for the sake of saying something'."

Although he would leave players in no doubt about his dissatisfaction over any perceived lack of effort, Smith felt that being continually harsh on a team could damage morale. He was happy to apply his own brand of psychology, rather than bombast, after a bad performance. One often-repeated story had him warning his team after one poor display that he had something important to tell them. The players spent all week dreading the announcement and fretting over their places. But, Smith was happy to observe, they also elevated their performance and trained with a purpose that had been missing. By quarter to three the following Saturday he appeared before them in the dressing room at Cardiff's Ninian Park and declared: "Right. That important thing I have been meaning to tell you: the train leaves at five so get changed as quickly as you can."

That, at least, was Johnston's version. Cyril Robinson recalled it being a game at Fratton Park. "Joe had no tactics at all," he said. "We played down at Portsmouth and ten minutes before kick-off it was 'OK lads, everybody get together'. We all looked at each other. 'Is he drunk?' He said: 'Don't mess around after the game, lads. We want to catch the 5.15pm train to London.'"

Hugh Kelly told the same story about a game at Chelsea, while Allan Brown was another who remembered it as

Cardiff. The probability is that it was a line Smith used on more than one occasion.

Matthews described Smith to author Robin Daniels as "a comedian" who "had a personality about him" and added: "He could tell the same joke 20 times in a day and you would laugh every time." Smith's easy relationship with his senior players helped maintain a healthy team spirit, while the familiarity within the squad ensured that tactics and teamwork evolved naturally for the most part.

Among younger players such as Robinson, however, there existed a craving for a more serious, technical approach and a greater appreciation for the talents of the fringe players. "My first game for the first team, we played Middlesbrough at home," Robinson recalled. "I am a left-half and I kick with my left foot but Joe has me playing right-half. Their inside-left was Wilf Mannion and Joe knew I liked to go in and tackle pretty hard so he said: 'Mark Mannion.' At half time I came in and said: 'Is he playing? I haven't seen him.' You couldn't mark Wilf Mannion; he was one of the best players I have ever played against. Anyway, we drew 2-2 and that was me over as right-half."

Smith told Daniels many years after his retirement that he treated all his players equally, whether they were internationals or journeymen. But it didn't always seem that way to Robinson, who admittedly had some kind of axe to grind after several years on the fringes of the team. "You didn't get in and have ten games, even if you played well and the injured man played badly. Joe always relied on experienced players. He wouldn't look at youngsters. That was one of his worst faults. He would ignore you. In general, you rarely saw him around the club to speak to him. He didn't take training; he used to stop in his office. I wouldn't call him a bad manager, but he wasn't in my eyes a good manager. The players never had much to do with him. Some of them liked him, but you couldn't talk to him and have a joke with him – he was a bloody joke. You would definitely get on better with him if you were in the first team."

Bolton's Bill Ridding had entered management earlier than he might have planned, having seen his career ended by a knee injury at the age of 24. Known as "Nibbler" as a player, he bounced around Tranmere (twice), both Manchester teams – top scoring with 11 goals for United in the Second Division in 1932/33 – Northampton and Oldham before resigning himself to medical reality.

The beginning of his managerial career was also curtailed, this time by war after he had taken charge of 20 Tranmere games following his appointment at the age of 28. His impact after taking over at Bolton during the 1950/51 season was immediate and, mirroring Smith's longevity at Blackpool, he was to remain in his position until 1968.

Ridding, a balding figure who was rarely seen without a couple of pens clipped into the breast pocket of his suit, was described by Wanderers historian Percy Young as "a man of Cheshire and a countryman at heart, [who] has never sought nor achieved the more strident headlines".

Having trained during and after the war as a physiotherapist and looked after Lancashire's cricketers, as well as the England football team, he remained a physio at heart, according to more than one Bolton player. "He was a good rubber-downer," said defender Bryan Edwards, who signed for Bolton in 1947 and missed the 1953 FA Cup run because of National Service before picking up a winner's medal five years later.

"Bill Ridding? He was a good physiotherapist," was how a dismissive Doug Holden recalled his former manager. "I remember him standing on the cinder track watching us run round, smoking a cigar and with his fingers in the pockets of his waistcoat."

Barrass, who joined Bolton from amateur football in 1944, remembered being thankful for Ridding's long memory. "I took advantage of Bill because he had been at Manchester City when my dad played there. He had seen me play in my knickerbockers and had already assessed me by the time he got to Bolton. I wouldn't necessarily say he thought I was a good player – it was a question of familiarity. Bill wasn't a good manager. George Taylor did most of the training. Most of the teams had similar tactics most of the time and we just did what we were told and got on with the game. The players all made good decisions on the field."

Holden continued: "George used to do most of the coaching and anything tactical but I don't know how the team got picked. We just waited for the team sheet to go up. I don't know who had the input into the team selection. There were no tactics, no team talk. We would have a talk in midweek about the opponents but that was more about individual players we had to be aware of rather than their style of play. We played our way and would stick to that, getting the ball forward quickly. Against Wolves, who had good wingers, I might be asked to come back a bit more and help stop the supply to them."

Barrass's wife, Joyce, recalled that – contrary to Joe Smith's tendency to favour the older players – Ridding was more comfortable with the less experienced team members. "He was a great fellow, but he changed once he became manager. He liked the young ones who said 'yes, Mr Ridding; of course, Mr Ridding', rather than the lads who had known him coming up from a trainer. Malcolm was a bit uncomfortable with that and didn't want any bother."

Edwards did have a memory of some strategic discussion. "When we had our talks on Fridays, Bill used to come over with the salt cellar and pepper and move them on the table to show us tactics. He had a good coach, a very good defensive coach, in George Taylor."

The importance in the Bolton managerial set-up of Taylor, whose playing career at Bolton straddled the war, was also acknowledged by Nat Lofthouse, who called him "a source of inspiration to the young players on the field". And he could be a hard-arse. After Lofthouse had scored two goals against Yugoslavia in his England debut at Highbury, he returned to Bolton to play poorly in a League game against Chelsea.

"Right, Lofty. I'll see you in my office on Monday morning. 8.30 sharp," Taylor barked at Lofthouse as he left the field. Having turned up for the meeting in the naive expectation of being praised for his international performance, Lofthouse recalled: "Instead he gave me the biggest rollicking I have ever had." Taylor had identified an over-confidence in his player that had made him attempt too much elaboration. "There are only three things you can do in this game," Taylor told him. "Run, shoot and head. Leave the fancy stuff to those more capable." Lofthouse remembered it as "the best piece of advice I ever received" and would insist that the appointment of Taylor as coach was one of the club's shrewdest moves. "He had the gift of making people play for him," he said.

Taylor's methods were no more sophisticated than was common for the time, with sprints up and down the Burnden Park terracing and five-a-side matches on the area outside the stadium featuring highly. Defender Tommy Banks said: "Basically, everything we did was kicking lumps out of each other. We would hammer each other."

Holden recalled: "When we played five- or six-a-sides, it used to be the hard guys like the defenders against the ball players. At the back of the Bolton playing pitch they had a little area of gravel and we used to call these guys the 'Gravel Hangers' because they used to play together. Even in training there was no quarter given and you could end up on the gravel. We were a physical side. We played with our shoulders."

According to Lofthouse, handing responsibility for preparation to Taylor was one of Ridding's most important contributions to the team. "Bill left George to get on with what he was good at – coaching and handling people. [George] preached that the club was always bigger than the individual. We were playing for the club, the town, the people of Bolton."

And it was the view of those people – in towns all around the country – that the football they were watching was captivating and thrilling; in most cases, the highlight of their week. They cared little for the technical niceties. Nor, in these early days of England's venture into international competition, did the failures of the national team disturb their Saturday afternoons on the terraces or cause banner headlines to be thrust in front of them.

The goals they saw being scored in club football – whether through exciting, technical forward play or defensive clumsiness – were more important than any advances on the international stage. It was the First Division and the FA Cup that defined the nation's football identity, not the new-fangled World Cup and certainly not the notion of European club competition that was beginning to surface. The 1951/52 *FA Yearbook* spoke out against such an idea, claiming it would devalue the Home Internationals, a view Matthews summarised by claiming: "The FA still believed our domestic game to be superior to anyone else's and they were reluctant to allow English clubs to enter any competition where it might be proved otherwise."

While it is easy, and often justifiable, to look back and highlight the deficiencies and backward thinking in the game, those who witnessed English football in vast numbers between 1945 and 1953 had few complaints. The working man wanted an easy escape at the end of the week; a piece of romance and intrigue when he switched on the radio or picked up his newspaper. Football didn't need to be too cerebral.

By 1952/53, crowds had dropped somewhat from the immediate post-war boom, when more than 40 million per season had gone through the turnstiles, but the sport was still attracting massive crowds. Charles Buchan suggested that any decline was down to that season's increase in admission from one shilling and sixpence (seven and a half pence) to one and nine, rather than any dissatisfaction with the technical ability of the players they watched. And if the fans had been asked to swap the high-scoring, sometimes shambolic, crash-bang-wallop excitement of English club football for a more thoughtful, measured approach that might have brought greater success to the national team, they would almost certainly have declined.

Buchan probably accurately reflected the majority view when he wrote of the season: "There was often a mediocrity about some of the matches I saw… It is no wonder that some of the public stayed away. They were not getting value for their money. In my view the over-stressing of teamwork is largely to blame for the lack of sparkle in the majority of games… many young players are scared to express their own individuality in style on the field."

So here is evidence, then, that while greater coaching and continuity might help the national team it wasn't necessarily what the people wanted to see. In the 21st century, with the Premier League hailed as the most exciting in the world and the England team floundering at major finals, it appears that the discussion has not changed all that much.

* * * * *

FROM HIS position in the BBC's commentary box at Wembley, Kenneth Wolstenholme is getting all the innovation he can handle by watching Matthews wandering the pitch. Bolton keep him at a safe distance for most of the first half, preventing him from making his way to his favourite attacking position at the by-line and forcing him into a nomadic role. When, after quarter of an hour, Matthews receives the ball on the left wing, Wolstenholme chuckles: "I should imagine he'll turn up with these cameras any minute now."

Later in the game, when Matthews drops deep into his own half in the middle of the field, the commentator gasps: "I think he must get underneath the ground and bob up through a hole somewhere." It is easy to hear in Wolstenholme's commentary a desire to make Matthews the hero of the game even though, in the early stages, inside-right Ernie Taylor is the focus for most Blackpool attacks, linking with Perry and Mudie to his left.

Throughout the game Wolstenholme appears to waver between the journalist's desire to see the Matthews fairytale materialise and his own affection for Bolton. The latter is almost betrayed after 19 minutes by one of those breathless passages of play that English fans love and which owes little to continental subtlety. Lofthouse heads down a lofted clearance and Moir prods the loose ball through for his centre-forward, running unchallenged into the right of the box. As Farm comes out, Lofthouse slides to send a low shot against the base of the keeper's right-hand post. Hassall follows up with another skidding effort that is blocked by Shimwell. Matthews will claim that amid the din of 100,000 people he had "heard him grunt and strain as he stretched every sinew". Matthews also describes Shimwell as "racing back" but in fact he is already in the six-yard box and in position to block. Fenton is then at the centre of the ensuing scramble, which ends with the ball going out for a corner and Wolstenholme yelling: "It must be a penalty there surely. I am sure someone got their hand to that one!"

Blackpool's next attack sees them win a free-kick in what should be a dangerous position on the right, level with the edge of the box. Nowadays you would wait for a ball curled wickedly into the six-yard box just in front of the keeper, but Shimwell simply wellies it all along the ground and out for a goal kick. "Well, he can take them like that all day," comments Wolstenholme, echoing Bolton sentiments. Following a minor delay to replace a broken corner flag after Lofthouse has run into it, Hassall breaks forward from his new, deeper position, resists the challenge of Shimwell and sends over a deep cross that Garrett heads to safety at the far post. With 25 minutes played, Bolton still lead 1-0.

* * * * *

ANDY BEATTIE'S Huddersfield team had company in the Norbreck Hydro when Blackpool's players checked in to the same hotel after returning from Buxton on the Friday afternoon before their fourth-round tie. Whether by design or not, the two sets of players were kept apart in the evening, Huddersfield's squad watching the professional boxing at Blackpool Tower and the home team going to the cinema.

The following morning found the coastline being buffeted by gale-force winds. The four trainloads of sup-porters arriving from Huddersfield were sledge-hammered by gusts of up to 70mph, but still the majority battled their way to the seafront. There they gazed upon a raging tide that had almost drowned a Lytham lifeboat man earlier in the day and whose often violent incursion onto the promenade had halted the running of some trams. Meanwhile, fans who queued for tickets outside Bloomfield Road from 11am resembled those New Yorkers in disaster movies who huddle for their lives in grimy alleyways as the aliens send their death rays down Seventh Avenue. Dustbins and A-frame shop signs clattered past them as they tried to discuss the day's team news over the stormy blasts.

Farm was able to play in Blackpool's goal, despite disloc-ating a finger at Sunderland a week earlier, while Allan

Brown was another whose injury had cleared up. Full-back Jackie Wright was still missing, but would have been unlikely to dislodge Shimwell and Garrett in any case. Stan Mortensen, therefore, was the only major absentee.

The wind was to be a major contributor to a game played in front of a crowd of 29,239. Visiting captain Len Quested won the toss and chose to have the elements in his favour in the first half. Blown back towards their own goal, Blackpool even needed Matthews to carry out defensive duties. "It was so windy, it was impossible," he explained. "Every time we kicked the ball it was coming back. You've never seen anything like it."

Blackpool did enjoy their own brief period of pressure, during which Bill Perry tested keeper Jack Wheeler with a low cross-shot, but then Jimmy Glazzard, who in two years' time would be the First Division's leading scorer, should have made more of a clear opening for the Second Division side. It was against the run of play when Perry set up Brown after 38 minutes, but his shot deflected to safety off the heels of a defender.

It all changed when the home team had the wind at their backs after half-time. Matthews's shot was cleared for a corner and Mudie was denied by an unwitting defender on the line, although Huddersfield broke out to claim a penalty when they felt John Crosland had fouled Glazzard. The only goal arrived in the 84th minute, two minutes after Garrett's long free-kick had sailed on the wind over the head of everyone in the penalty area and into the Spion Kop. When the left-back received the ball just inside his own half, he again banged it downfield.

Ironically, Garrett was not renowned as a hit-and-hope defender, a description that could more comfortably be applied to his full-back partner Shimwell, a racing pigeon breeder who could easily boot the ball from deep in his own area into the opponents' half in an era when such feats were admired. Garrett had a calmness and style about him in possession and, when confronted by an opposing winger, a deliberate method of attempting to keep him pinned to the touchline. A native of the north-east, he had signed for Blackpool in 1942 after being spotted playing for Hordern Colliery. He was there as a "Bevin Boy", the group of young men conscripted to work in the mines rather than in the armed services in a scheme introduced by Ernest Bevin, the Minister of Labour and National Service. Having made his senior debut in 1947, he succeeded Ron Suart to become Blackpool's regular left-back, although he had been an inside-forward in junior football and even played a few games for his club in the number nine shirt. In April 1952, he won the first of three England caps.

Garrett's long ball forward again caught the wind, but this time just enough to make it drift over the head of Wheeler and drop underneath the crossbar. "I decided to loft the ball high into the goalmouth," he explained. "No, I'll be fair; it wasn't a shot, but as soon as I saw the wind take it away I knew it was going to finish in the net."

Skipper Johnston confessed: "This was an example of the luck you've got to have in order to achieve anything," with Perry reflecting: "It was a fluke and their keeper got the blame for it. It was a lucky break and everyone says you need luck to win the FA Cup, and we had our share that day."

5

LOFTY AMBITIONS

"Give me a decent cross to go for and it was never less than 50-50 between me and the centre-half."
– Nat Lofthouse.

OR ONCE, Nat Lofthouse finds enough unoccupied Wembley turf to make a clean turn with the ball. Receiving it after the hobbling Eric Bell has played it forward, he appears so taken aback by the lack of close attention from his Blackpool marker, Harry Johnston, that he clumsily misdirects his intended return pass. Now he has to watch as Blackpool mount an attack. He admires the well-timed tackle with which Johnny Ball prevents Bill Perry getting on the end of a ball clipped into the box by Jackie Mudie. Then he sees Stan Hanson, the team-mate with whom he shared the darkest day of his professional career, punch away a Stanley Matthews cross after the winger has been fed the ball close to the by-line.

Lofthouse is soon off on another forward run, only for Bobby Langton to over-hit a through ball. Just as his colleagues continue to look to their centre-forward with their passes and crosses, it is to their most famous player that Wanderers fans most eagerly entrust their hopes of victory.

It is Lofthouse, after all, who has come to symbolise his team and town – and will continue to do so right up until his death almost six decades later. Perhaps only the case of Tom Finney and Preston is comparable to the tale of Lofthouse and Bolton.

* * * * *

THE SON of a coal-bagger and one of four brothers, Lofthouse was like many of his townsfolk: obsessed with Wanderers. He would watch them whenever he could, paying 3d (one pence) to go in as a schoolboy and stand on the Burnden Park embankment – on the days when he didn't get in for nothing by climbing up a drainpipe. Ray Westwood, the England inside-left, was his hero; a man so popular in Bolton that if he was doubtful for a game because of injury the town's cinemas would flash the news on their screens when he was declared fit.

Typical of football-mad boys of his time, the young Lofthouse played endless games in the street, using makeshift balls and throwing down articles of clothing as goalposts. His earliest on-field memory was standing in for a missing goalkeeper, conceding seven goals and ruining a new pair of shoes. And one of his first football lessons was delivered by Tommy Lawton after young Nat met the future England centre-forward at a bus stop. Lawton, on his way to playing a game for Burnley, asked for the name of his young fan and told him: "I have heard about you in the town team." Then he advised: "No matter how you play, always try to score. That's the important thing."[13]

. . . .

13 It was reported for a long time that Lawton had preceded Lofthouse at their school, but Lofthouse corrected this in a Sky Sports interview with Dickie Davies in 1998. "There has been a little bit of a mistake about this," he said. "Tommy went to Falls Road and I went to Castle Hill – some people thought I went to school with Tommy."

Lofthouse took the advice to heart, netting seven goals in one game for Bolton Schools against Bury. Established as a centre-forward – "I didn't have the brain to be an inside-forward or wing-half" – he spent hours practising his heading and shooting. He was weighing in at more than 12 stones by his early teenage years and admitted: "I always felt more confident if I could jump up at the ball than if I had it at my feet."

Despite the attention he was devoting to football, he had not considered a professional career until Bolton's Mayor, Jim Entwhistle, visited his school for prize-giving day. A board member at Wanderers, Entwhistle asked Lofthouse if he would like to play for them. "I went home and told my dad," he said. "I thought it must be a joke or something. But Bolton contacted us soon afterwards."

Only just 14 years old, he signed for the club on 4th September 1939, the day after the Second World War had begun. "As I walked through the gates of Burnden Park all the players were lining up in rows on the field," he said. "They were disbanding."

For three and a half years he worked at Peter Caffery and Sons, making reeds for the mills, before going down the mines at Mossley Colliery as one of the "Bevin Boys". "That was one of the best things that ever happened to me. I was still playing all the football I could. I was still pretty fit. But working down there took off a lot of puppy fat, hardened me up. They were good days and they made me all the more determined to be a footballer rather than go back down the pit and work for a living. I never thought being a footballer was working. It was a privilege."

Wartime football might have been somewhat disorganised at times, but it was an important enough distraction from the realities of life to merit continued serious coverage in the regional newspapers. With the Wanderers team having gone off to battle *en masse*, Haydn Berry was left to reflect in the *Bolton Evening News* in April 1941: "Of the groundstaff there is none and the club is pulling through with spare-time players... It is a big opportunity for local talent and the club are eager to find players who will be ready for serious duty when normal football resumes."

The dark-haired, 15-year-old Lofthouse had already displayed the first signs of such readiness with two goals on his debut against Bury a month earlier and would go on to score more than 100 times for his club in wartime competition. Like Blackpool before them, his team would win the biggest prize on offer at the time by beating Chelsea in the last wartime cup final and he remembered: "Men like Ralph Banks, Matt Barrass and Willie Moir were making their way into the side with me. Men with whom I would share some of my happiest days. I wouldn't dispute for a minute how lucky I was. If I'd signed for Wanderers under normal circumstances in peacetime, there's no way I would have played over 100 games between 1941 and 1946. I learned my trade in the senior side."

The transient nature of football during the years of conflict also gave him the opportunity to play alongside men such as Tom Finney and Bill Shankly. "They were very patient. I was very limited," he confessed.

The generosity of the man who lost his centre-forward position to Lofthouse, former club top scorer George Hunt, played an important part in the development of a player who still felt, by age 19, that he was failing to make the necessary progress to succeed as a professional and was considering his future in the sport. Hunt would take his young replacement aside for individual coaching, proving as skilled at imparting his knowledge as he had been in front of goal at the peak of his own career. "I learned more from George in an hour than I could from most people in a year," Lofthouse admitted.

It was the FA Cup that marked football's return to something approaching normality after the cessation of hostilities in Europe. Peace came too late for the Football League to organise a schedule for the 1945/46 season but the FA Cup was quickly reinstated, albeit with ties to be played over two legs rather than the traditional dramatic one-off.

It was during that first post-war Cup campaign that the competition, which would provide Nat Lofthouse and Stanley Matthews with their crowning moments, also produced the most tragic episode of their careers.

Bolton and Stoke had advanced to meet in the quarter-finals, where two goals by Ray Westwood earned Matthews's team a 2-0 victory in the first leg of the tie at Victoria Road in front of more than 50,000. More than half as many again were estimated to have attempted to attend the return match on 9th March, not least for the opportunity to see the great Matthews in action. Burnden Park was filling up steadily from 1pm, with the railway embankment area of terracing apparently full 25 minutes before kick-off. Fans, however, were still being allowed in, while even more waited their turn impatiently outside. Once inside the ground, the latecomers found that there was nowhere for them to go and at last police ordered the gates to be closed. Meanwhile, many people were deciding to leave, frustrated by their failure to find a vantage point.

At around 2.40pm, police began helping fans on to the perimeter track at the north-west corner of the ground to ease the congestion. Even after the order to close the turnstiles had belatedly been carried out, the fans still came. Some simply barged through the barricades; others, on the Burnden side of the ground, began clambering over the railway line fence. Forced to guard the food rations that were stored below the stand, police were powerless to redeploy to that area.

At 2.50pm a father, eager to protect his son, picked a lock on the gate next to the boys' entrance in order to create an exit. Inevitably, according to the Home Office report issued later, those outside took the opportunity to rush in. Under further police instructions, a section of wooden perimeter fencing was pulled down to ease the overcrowding. But when other gates were ordered open to allow people to leave, no one could be found to implement that command.

When Lofthouse and Matthews took the field with their respective teams they were taken aback to see how many people were on the railway lines. "I have never seen Burnden Park so full," Lofthouse recalled. "If you'd thrown a golf ball into the air it would have come down on someone's head. There was no space at all."

A surge of the crowd from the top of the terrace forced more people towards the bottom corner. Two barriers collapsed. People were now piling on top of each other, while hundreds ended up on the field. As the game kicked off, Lofthouse could see fans being lifted out of the melee by police and ambulance men, while bodies lay outside the touchline. "I thought they had fainted," he said.

Matthews recalled that "a sound like muffled thunder followed by a terrific roar ripped through the ground". Turning to look at the terracing, he saw the crowd behind the goal tumbling forward. "People were screaming and clambering over the perimeter wall," he said, aware that this was more than a mere case of big-game overcrowding.

Only 12 minutes of play were possible before the referee took the players back to the dressing rooms. One young local resident, Brian Farris, explained: "I seem to remember the dreadful day when, after early cheers, the ground was unusually quiet. As older boys and men returned quietly along the street we heard of the dreadful disaster that had happened."

While they waited to be recalled to the field, the players watched injured people being carried on stretchers to receive medical aid. A total of 33 dead bodies were pulled from the terraces, initially being laid out on the pitch in view of the returning players and photographers. It was only then that the extent of the catastrophe began to suggest itself to the game's participants. Even then, according to Lofthouse, they had to wait until the following day's newspapers for confirmation of what they had witnessed.

A further 500 spectators received treatment for injuries, although play was delayed for only 13 minutes and some parts of the ground remained unaware of the full nature of what had happened. Matthews would describe feeling physically sick and running around with tears in his eyes as the teams distractedly played out a goalless draw. The result put Bolton into the semi-finals – where they would lose to Charlton – but there was no celebration in the town that weekend. Families who had spent six years fearing the visitation of death found it invading their lives as the result of the kind of sporting event that was meant to create greater distance from the hardships of wartime.

It was easy to blame events on the unpreparedness of the ground in the rush to bring big-time football back to places such as Burnden Park in those first post-war months. Yet even as early as March 1929, the *Bolton Evening News* had commented on a 65,000 crowd by warning: "One means of entrance to the huge railway embankment is tragically inadequate." Eleven years later, the paper had pursued the same complaints about a ground whose facilities had remained pretty well unchanged for decades. In that regard, however, it was hardly unique in English football.

Lofthouse, who remembered the town being in a "state of shock", visited Burnden Park on the Sunday morning after the quarter-final. "It was a pitiful sight. There were shoes, ties, gloves, hats and other bits of clothing on the running track around the ground. We all felt so helpless."

There was no training for several days and, at that point, no player involved in the game could imagine ever being excited about football again. The townspeople apparently felt the same. When the stadium hosted Bolton's Football League North game against Bradford four days later, a little over five thousand showed up.

While a relief fund that would raise £40,000 was established, evidence for an official inquiry was gathered. The hearing was told that 85,000 had attempted to get into the ground, which was equipped for 50,000 (the official attendance was announced as 65,419). Far from highlighting any inadequacies in the stadium, however, the inquiry effectively ruled that the spectators had caused the tragedy through their own actions on the day, although £5,500 of improvements would be made to the embankment area and improved safety regulations were imposed upon all grounds.

Yet little was done to use the events at Burnden Park as a catalyst for more wide-ranging change and, as had happened in the past and would happen again, the sport returned to normality as the memories of the day were softened by time. Only two years later, Notts County – with crowds flocking to see new signing Tommy Lawton – were urging fans to: "Please pack together as closely as possible." Calling for "utmost cooperation in this matter", the club warned that "without it we cannot possibly accommodate the numbers who wish to see our matches".

In Bolton, a plaque was put up "in remembrance *(sic)* of the 33 supporters who lost their lives". The lack of attention given to the spelling seemed a somehow appropriate reflection of the events of 9th March 1946.

As a Bolton native and Wanderers fan, Lofthouse felt the grief as deeply as any of the players. It was another factor in the deep mutual affection that existed between the home fans and the man who marked the immediate post-war years by establishing himself as the nation's leading centre-forward. "I learned very early on that you won't find better fans anywhere," he said. "They never criticise a trier."

It was always qualities such as effort and strength that characterised Lofthouse's game, assets that Italian club Fiorentina would attempt to purchase in 1952. Putting aside the severe restrictions on players' abilities to move from club to club at that time, Lofthouse considered the "kind-hearted, good-natured" people of Bolton his second family and was in no hurry to exile himself from them, even for the £60 per week that was on offer. "I was happy to play for Bolton. My £14 a week was a reasonable amount at the time." He added that "I could never dream of living anywhere else" and even stated: "There's nothing to match those two lions outside Bolton Town Hall."

By the time of Fiorentina's approach, Lofthouse was an established England international, having heard on the radio of his initial call-up to face Yugoslavia at Highbury in November 1950, by which time he had been married for three years to Alma and had a son, Jeff. With a £900 mortgage and repayments of £6 per month, he had, according to his father, "put a rope round your neck for life", which meant that the £30 fee for the England game was as welcome as the honour and recognition it carried. Lofthouse's selection sparked debate about whether England should just pick the best player in each position or look more at the team dynamic and structure. Lofthouse's individual qualities were apparent but, despite scoring two goals on his debut, there was clearly some doubt about his value to the collective and it was another 11 months before he was chosen again. In the meantime, the number nine shirt was given to Blackpool's Stan Mortensen. This was also a time when the England selection panel tended to reward club form between internationals more readily than performances in previous England games.

When he finally regained his place against Wales a year later, he produced a performance that was praised highly in *Charles Buchan's Football Monthly*. "His speed off the mark, his ability to shoot on the turn, his agile heading and excellent anticipation of where a rival defence would least expect to see him were dominating features of the English revival," wrote John Thompson.

A run of 18 goals in 18 games ensured that the England jersey stayed in his possession, although he remained down-to-earth about the qualities he brought to the team compared to some of his illustrious team-mates. Remembering his first game alongside Matthews, he said: "I just realised there was one thing [to do]. Just get to the box because he will get down to the by-line, he'll get to the corner flag and he'll get the ball over, lace away so it won't hurt."

He described Matthews and Finney as "fantastic players to play with" and added: "You always knew that if you gave them the ball they'd either beat a man and get a cross over to you or they'd manage somehow to give you the ball back. They'd always do something. They wouldn't just lose the thing."

Even more impressive to Lofthouse was the level of close skill that they brought to bear on the game in an era when playing surfaces were far from conducive to such activities. "Especially late November to the end of February, the grounds were not all that brilliant. We liked playing Blackpool and Preston when the ground was that deep in mud."

Despite his self-deprecation, there was one match, played in Vienna in May 1952, that would secure Lofthouse his place alongside Matthews and Finney in football legend. In the second game of their summer tour, England faced an Austrian team anchored by a technically gifted centre-back in Ernst Ocwirk. They were, said Lofthouse, "a yardstick; our chance to see how we measured up against the continentals".

Lofthouse knew he had not played well in the 1-1 draw with Italy in the previous game and was forced to endure the newspapers' calls for Newcastle's Jackie Milburn to play in Vienna. A healthy percentage of the 30,000 British soldiers based along the Rhein at that time found their way into the ground for a match billed – by those unaware of the Hungarians, at least – as the unofficial championship of Europe.

Lofthouse converted a pass from Jackie Sewell to give England the lead, but the game was tied at 2-2 going into the final stages when Austria piled forward for a corner. England keeper Gil Merrick caught the ball and released it quickly to Finney, who set off towards the Austrian half and delivered a perfect ball beyond the last defender into the path of Lofthouse, the only player England had left up front. Lofthouse found himself bearing down on Austrian keeper Musil.

"These chances are in many ways more difficult than the instinctive ones where you put the ball in the net without thinking about it," he said later. Musil hesitated; so did Lofthouse, not wanting to hit the ball too early. The inevitable happened. Musil slammed into Lofthouse just as he shot, clattering him to the ground. The reaction of the crowd told the prone England man that the ball had gone in to earn England a victory. Taken away on a stretcher, he dragged himself back to the field and even hit the post before being carried off once again at the final whistle; this time by jubilant British soldiers.

During the post-match celebrations, one reporter who had been particularly critical of Lofthouse before the game sent him a bottle of wine. The following morning's headlines told of the brave display by "The Lion of

Vienna", the title he would carry proudly for the rest of his career.

"He could always win a game for you," said Doug Holden. "There was always a feeling that he could pull it out for you. He was a good header of the ball and after he left we tried to find a direct replacement but nobody was as good a header. We had to try a new style of play."

Centre-half Malcolm Barrass added: "I played against him in training more often than not. As a footballer he was a trier. He just kept going and was very adept at scoring goals. He always managed to thump the ball into the back of the net."

That straightforward approach to his game was reflected in his down-to-earth relationship with his team-mates. While the star status of Matthews could often create complication and tension within the teams for which he played, there was no such ambiguity surrounding Lofthouse. "Nat was one of the fellows," said Holden.

"He was one of the lads," echoed Barrass – who invited his team-mate to be godfather to his daughter Lynne. It was a description far less frequently attributed to Matthews.

By 1953, Lofthouse scarcely needed to do anything to increase his popularity in the Bolton dressing room, but he ended up earning even more pats on the back after making a decisive contribution in the FA Cup fourth-round contest against Notts County, a tie that proved more troublesome than expected. Drawn at home against another Second Division opponent, it took three matches and a controversial goal of the type that would soon be outlawed to send them through to the final 16.

Bolton's initial concern, before the first game, was responding to recent criticism of their crowd management. After many fans complained about the amount of time it took to get inside Burnden Park, the club announced that turnstiles would be open from 1pm – for a 2.45pm kick-off – and spectators were asked to spread their arrival over the full period of available time. "Come in good time and have your money ready, the exact amount if possible, and there will be no hold-ups," the club urged. The only advance tickets still available as matchday approached were restricted view seats in the Manchester Road stand. In a better example of customer service than effectively telling spectators that the turnstile hold-ups were their own fault, visitors to the ground were allowed inside to observe the seats in question before committing to purchase.

Those turning up to buy those tickets were confronted by Wanderers players using any available piece of land to practise on after the weather had made the pitch unavailable for training. Some played head tennis behind the stands, while one woman who had arrived for an unsuccessful attempt to buy tickets almost took the ball in the face as Stan Hanson, Roy Hartle and Harold Hassall staged a kickabout outside the main entrance.

The elements, however, were no hindrance to what was becoming an important part of Bolton's ritual for the tournament. The ceremony of 'The Cup Drink', carried out after Friday training before every round, involved mixing two dozen eggs with two bottles of sherry and passing the sickly result around among the players. With all football superstitions, no one was going to suggest changing something once it had worked so the players' gag reflexes were on trial all the way to Wembley.

The Saturday of the fourth round saw five trainloads of Notts County supporters disembarking at Trinity Station between midday and 1.30pm, part of a fleet of 30 spectator trains that were estimated to be arriving in the north-west around the same time, with Sunderland playing at Burnley; Tottenham at Preston; Huddersfield at Blackpool; and Luton and non-league Walthamstow Avenue at Manchester's City and United respectively.

The same wind that was creating havoc in Blackpool was swirling around Bolton's home ground, although not with as much force as that morning's rumour that Lofthouse had been injured in a car accident and would miss the game. The early entrants to the ground filled up those corners that offered the greatest shelter from the elements and all were relieved to see Lofthouse run out unharmed. The gales, however, proved more stubborn than the gossip.

Bolton played into the wind in the first half, but their opponents – supposedly with the conditions to their advantage – found that the ball kept running away from them. Just when it appeared that the home team were quicker in coming to grips with their surroundings, County grabbed a seventh-minute lead. There seemed to be no danger when forward Ken McPherson took possession 35 yards out, but he shot quickly and saw the wind aid the ball's path towards goal, with a shocked Hanson able merely to get a slight touch as it flew past him.

Doug Holden and Bobby Langton switched wings for variety as Bolton, for the second round running, sought to cancel out an early deficit. But Lofthouse, who thought he should have had a penalty instead of an indirect free-kick in the box, was lost for several minutes after falling heavily under another challenge from three County defenders.

The selection of Ralph Banks at left-back had been a talking point, brought in for ever-present but out-of-form George Higgins. Yet he and Eric Bell provided a consistent barrier down the left of Bolton's defence and the visitors, despite their enthusiasm in the tackle, were only an intermittent danger. Of course, a good deal of damage had already been done and Tommy Deans, the visitors' balding left-back, typified their determination to maintain their lead with the enthusiastic way he continually belted the ball out of play rather than attempt anything risky. Meanwhile, according to *Evening News* man Haydn Berry, the Bolton forwards "fiddled away too much as individuals and rarely found a way to serve Lofthouse up the middle".

The equaliser eventually arrived in the second half, a well-executed finish by Lofthouse, who once said of his goal-scoring craft: "The moment I hit it I always knew when it was going in. I think most players do." There could even have been a late winner when Langton's drive hit the bar. But the game as a spectacle had largely fallen foul of the difficult conditions.

Perhaps it had been a gust of wind between the ears that had led to the extraordinary performance of referee Bob Smith after he awarded a second-half free-kick at County's end. While he became embroiled in an argument with players from both teams, another group carried on playing and nearly contrived a goal at the other end, with Smith oblivious. At the end of the passage he never bothered to enforce the original free-kick. It was not the last time that Smith's decisions would be the cause of dispute.

Details of how Bolton fans could obtain one of the 1,000 tickets available to them for the Thursday night replay in Nottingham took secondary importance in Monday's newspapers to news that the townspeople were facing a likely rise in rates of two shillings and sixpence in the pound, taking the rates to a record 26 shillings in the pound.[14] The cost of running Bolton in the 1953/54 financial year was forecast to be £2.5m. Education accounted for £1.39m, an increase of £120,000, with the government contributing £876,000 and the rest to come from the ratepayers. A further £322,000 would be spent on the police force and fire brigade, with highways costing £244,000 and health services £233,000.

. . . .

14 In the days before council tax, a household paid for local services according to an amount per pound of the 'rateable value' ascribed to the home.

By Wednesday, however, the *Evening News* was confident that Bolton fans would have their priorities re-ordered. "The public is asked NOT to ring the Evening News tomorrow afternoon to find out the score in the Wanderers Cup tie at Nottingham," it wrote in prominent bold type. "The telephone lines are needed for urgent messages connected with the production of the paper and unnecessary calls cause inconvenience and delay." Local anxiety would not have eased the following afternoon, however, when the game went into extra-time, denying *News* readers the chance of seeing the final score in their evening paper.

The refusal of many Nottingham works to allow their staff to take time off meant that only 33,669 were inside a stadium capable of holding 50,000 to watch a contest to determine who would earn a fifth-round tie at Luton, who had overwhelmed Manchester City 5-1 in a replay. Bell had the first shot of the game – too high – and Hanson had to wait until ten minutes had been played to touch the ball for the first time via a back-pass.

Lofthouse scooped the ball over the bar with a first-time effort and as the quality of play on both sides improved Hanson did well to keep out a low drive by McPherson after 20 minutes. Lofthouse then headed wide from a Holden cross and Hanson had to make a timely interception, a sign that neither defence looked entirely at ease. County's defensive discomfort was at its most extreme after Scottish keeper Jimmy Linton pushed away a corner and saw Johnny Wheeler's header loop back towards an unguarded net – only for it to drop just over the bar. Then Linton stretched to save from Lofthouse after he chased a long ball down the middle. He saved well again from Langton, one of the more constructive players on view.

One minute before half-time, the first goal arrived amid controversy after County inside-forward Bob Crookes received a pass from McPherson with the linesman flagging

127

for offside. Yet referee Smith waved play on and the ball was pulled back for Jimmy Jackson to send a bouncing header into the net.

The goal precipitated a frantic opening five minutes to the second half. Bolton were level within half a minute after defender Leon Leuty made a rare mistake with his clearance, allowing Hassall to free Langton. His shot was charged down by Linton and Moir followed up to score. At the other end, McPherson headed over the bar, but was quickly given another opportunity. This time he beat Hanson to Crookes's corner to force the ball over the line for a 2-1 lead.

Lofthouse came close with a header from Holden's cross and Wheeler thought he should have had a penalty, before Moir hit a fierce shot narrowly wide. At times Bolton were becoming over-anxious in their attempts to draw level, their lack of composure allowing County to keep them at bay. Moir came close again with a flicked header and, with 15 minutes to play, Bolton got their equaliser. Banks hit the ball long, Hassall squared a pass to Moir and the skipper shot inside the post from 20 yards for his second goal.

Moir's goalscoring ability had been a feature of his play since signing for Bolton after being spotted playing for the RAF by the club's chief scout, Bob Jackson. Born in the Bucksburn area of Aberdeen, he had converted successfully from the wing to form a profitable partnership with Lofthouse from the inside-forward position. He had even outscored his team-mate in 1948/49, his first season in his new position, when his 25 goals included four in one match against Aston Villa. The Scotland selectors, however, seemed reluctant to cast their gaze so far south, picking him for a solitary international, against England in 1950.

Wanderers fans appreciated exactly what his native country was missing and as Bolton went looking to win this game without the help of extra-time it was he and Lofthouse who created the first opportunities for a winner. Then

Linton saved from Hassall, and Langton missed by inches before setting up a near-miss for Wheeler.

Seven minutes into the additional half-hour, the referee was back at the centre of the action when he ruled out a Lofthouse effort for offside. Bolton's players argued that Moir's pass had come off the leg of a defender, which should have made it a legitimate goal. In fact, how Wanderers didn't settle the tie before the final whistle was something of a mystery after forcing Linton into several top-class saves and seeing Moir and Lofthouse hit the woodwork.

So it was off to Hillsborough the following Monday, Wanderers fans having queued up on the Saturday morning at Burnden Park to secure their tickets. Snowfall on the day before the match threw the game into doubt for a while, but it was a greater weather event a few days earlier that had been occupying the minds of many of Bolton's citizens.

Massive storms on the east coast had sunk a car ferry heading out of Stranraer, killing 133 people, while a further 307 perished along the coastline and 37,000 were evacuated from their homes. Author David Kynaston notes the disappearance of this tragedy from the history of the period by suggesting that "it did not chime in with the much-desired early to mid-1950s narrative of material progress and increasing optimism, perhaps also because most of its victims were poor people living on low-lying marginal land".

At the time, though, its impact was significant. With the Women's Volunteer Service at the centre of the effort, the people of Bolton were, like those in many other towns, donating clothes and bedding for those affected by the disaster. "We have been inundated with goods," said the organisers. The Bolton Dramatic Society donated funds from their run of *Open Verdict* at the Miners' Hall, while Bolton greyhound track arranged a fund-raising meeting.

When the FA Cup returned to centre stage, it was the match officials who, for the third time in the tie, wrote themselves a controversial role. The second replay ended, according to Haydn Berry, in "an atmosphere of argument and some acrimony". Surface water on top of a previously frozen ground made for difficult playing conditions, with players struggling to keep their footing when they attempted to change direction. With 11 minutes remaining, the crowd of 23,000 appeared destined to be watching an extra half-hour.

Langton had continued his good Cup form and was denied twice in the first ten minutes by Linton, firstly as he cut inside to shoot and then by an outstanding tip-over after he burst through the middle. Lofthouse saw a good-looking goal disallowed for offside, while County's nearest misses came via a Wheeler clearance that sliced against his own crossbar and a goal-bound effort by McPherson that was blocked by Hartle.

With Barrass standing firm at the back, Bolton created the greater openings. It was only in the final few minutes that the lower division side could be said to be on top – by which time they were aided by injuries to Bell and Hassall, forcing the latter out to the left wing and Langton to inside-right. County were also driven through the closing moments of the game by indignation at their opponents' goal.

With 79 minutes played, Moir had received the ball from a throw and lobbed it into the penalty area. As it dropped underneath the bar, Lofthouse charged at Linton, knocking goalkeeper and ball over the line in a similar manner to the controversial Wembley goal he would score against Manchester United's Harry Gregg in 1958. Both referee and linesman gave a clear and immediate signal for a goal and the linesman was even reported later to have said that the ball was already over the line when Lofthouse struck, although the record books recorded the centre-forward as the scorer.

"They say I gave goalies some stick," argued Lofthouse many years later, "but I used to get stick as well. You could get an elbow in the back of the head, which wasn't too helpful. There were no holds barred but no malice about it."

* * * * *

FOLLOWING THE Notts County contest Harold Hassall was one of the Bolton players criticised by the *Evening News* for his early-round Cup performances. Now, as a makeshift left-half at Wembley, he earns general praise with some well-executed covering as Bill Perry tries to release Mortensen into the penalty area. But then he is unable to prevent Ernie Taylor gliding past him as he cuts in from the right. The elusive schemer also beats Langton before laying off to Mortensen. This time it is Barrass who alertly smothers the shot before it has barely left the forward's boot.

Langton is immediately dispossessed by Blackpool's half-backs near the centre line and stays down under the weight of the challenges as Taylor advances unopposed on Bolton's area. He is eventually closed down by Hassall, who, having done his bit in clearing, simply stands on the arc of his penalty area with his hands on his hips, watching the play continue no more than 20 yards away. Such notions as defenders pushing up to condense space were well in the future. Referee Mervyn Griffith blows play dead and Langton receives treatment in the centre circle. "Good gracious," remarks the easily-astonished Kenneth Wolstenholme. "They can't carry two passengers."

With a shake of the head and a grimace, Langton dismisses the trainer and carries on.

Johnston picks up a knock-down in his own half and fires the ball low to the right for Matthews, who passes inside to Taylor. Recovering from a near loss of possession, he passes in the direction of his winger, but Hassall is quick to cover and win his team a throw. As Bolton prepare to take it, Blackpool right-half Fenton can be seen in the foreground of the television picture kicking at thin air in apparent disappointment at the disintegration of another move.

There is no doubt that Blackpool are in control at this stage, however, with Bolton unable to keep the ball away from their own territory for any length of time. After 32 minutes, it arrives once more with Matthews, who, faced with two opponents, cuts in from the touchline and plays the ball forward with his left foot to Fenton. It is a smooth, effortless action. He might not be dominating the game at this stage, but that easy ability to exert his will is in stark contrast to most other players, who appear very deliberate in their attempts to control the heavy ball, especially when it is bouncing. Receiving Matthews's pass, Fenton plays in Taylor, whose path is blocked. The ball ricochets back to Fenton on the edge of the box, from where his left-foot shot goes harmlessly beyond the far post.

It has been a promising passage of play, throughout which Wolstenholme has sat in total silence. The next few minutes will bring the commentator – and Blackpool's hopes of victory – back to life.

6

MORTY AND THE MONEY MEN

"There was nothing from the FA. You couldn't go on any type of course. You just got what job you could. If you knew somebody, or if you were higher up in a football sense and had been a good player, then you probably got into some kind of firm." – Cyril Robinson on life after football.

BLACKPOOL ARE attacking with intent now. Jackie Mudie bursts through on a loose ball just inside his half and rides the challenge of Johnny Wheeler to knock it into the path of Stan Mortensen, who plays it wide to Stanley Matthews as he is challenged by Malcolm Barrass. A high cross into the six-yard box sees Mortensen beaten by the punch of Stan Hanson, but the ball falls invitingly to Taylor, who badly miscues a shot from the edge of the box. Another move begins unpromisingly, an ugly hack by Tommy Garrett followed by Cyril Robinson's untidy header. But the ball lands fortuitously with Bill

Perry on halfway and it needs a wall of white shirts to bar his path.

Bolton respond by spreading the ball from right to left through Doug Holden, Bobby Langton and Wheeler, only for the move to break down when it reaches the hobbling Eric Bell on the left edge of the box. When Eddie Shimwell clears to the halfway line, Mortensen links with Ernie Taylor and he finds Perry, who has moved into a central position. Ralph Banks's clearance offers only brief respite as Blackpool resume their attack down the left, Taylor's pass into the box being met by Perry's first-time shot, which slides narrowly outside the far post.

What by now seems like an inevitable equaliser materialises after 35 minutes, although it has an ungainly conception as Garrett gathers up a goal kick by Hanson and bangs it back downfield with little apparent intent. The ball travels, via a flick by Taylor, to Mortensen, approximately 35 yards from goal. He appears to attempt a first-time pass to a team-mate, but as he turns towards goal he finds the ball still at his feet. Perry now plays an important role by moving inside to the centre-forward position, leaving Mortensen with more open space in front of him as he charges into the left side of the box. Going outside full-back Johnny Ball, he shoots left-footed across goal towards the far post and Harold Hassall, racing back to cover, diverts the ball inside the near, leaving Hanson helpless.

At this stage Kenneth Wolstenholme is not only pointing out that it was the first goal conceded by Bolton in a Wembley final, but crediting it to Hassall as an own goal. The keeper seems likely to have saved Mortensen's scuffed shot had it not been deflected and, in modern times, the Premier League's dubious goals panel would most certainly have ruled against the Blackpool striker. But, somewhere in the game's aftermath, Mortensen's Cup Final hat-trick will become established as historical fact.

* * * * *

FEW BEGRUDGED the achievement of one of the most popular men in the game. Charles Buchan, who watched Mortensen's career from the press box, summarised his universal popularity when he called him "a wonderful character" and "one of the finest inside-forwards in the game". In his autobiography, Buchan commented: "His electric dashes through opposing defences have brought many goals and a name comparable with that of Steve Bloomer, one of the old immortals. He had the same sallow complexion, the same slight build and the same happy knack of scoring vital goals."

Mortensen's reputation for sportsmanship would even manifest itself at half-time at Wembley, where he approached Nat Lofthouse as they left the pitch with a cheery: "Congratulations, Lofty."

"What for?" asked his confused adversary. "We haven't won yet."

"I know you haven't, but you've scored in every round," came the reply – a feat Mortensen had achieved five seasons earlier. Lofthouse recalled the moment as "a great gesture from a great player".

Well known, too, was the adversity Mortensen had overcome to be on the Wembley pitch in May 1953 as one of England's most successful post-war footballers. The grandson of a South Shields-based Norwegian sailor, he had suffered the death of his father, a timber yard worker, when only five years old.

During the Second World War, serving as a wireless operator and gunner in the RAF, Mortensen had two lucky escapes; first when a practice parachute jump almost went tragically wrong and, more seriously, when his Wellington bomber crashed near Lossiemouth, killing two of the crew and causing another to lose a leg. Mortensen survived, although the accident left him fighting to recover from a head injury and insomnia.

What was true for much of Mortensen's generation, therefore, was even more so of him; the realisation that sport, however seriously taken, had no connection to life and death, which he had witnessed so painfully from close range. Anything that happened on a football field, such as losing the 1948 and 1951 FA Cup Finals, could be met with philosophical acceptance.

It was why he was able to leave the Wembley arena with "tears of real happiness" in his eyes after the loss to Manchester United in the first of those games, thanks to the rousing, moving reception he had been given by the disappointed Blackpool fans close to the tunnel.

The war had interrupted his professional career a year after he had signed for the Seasiders. The club had been so impressed by his performance for South Shields Ex-Schoolboys in an Easter Monday challenge match against a team from Leeds at Bloomfield Road that secretary William Parkinson sent for him and, having checked that he was indeed the inside-right he had summoned, posed the question: "Would you like to become a Blackpool player?" before composing an offer letter to his mother. As well as seeing him represent the RAF and making guest appearances for numerous clubs, wartime football also gave Mortensen a first taste of international competition when he played for Wales, stepping in at the last minute for injured half-back Ivor Powell because their team had no replacement players.

Indebted to the patience, criticism and technical input of former Blackpool and Preston defender Billy Tremelling on the club's coaching staff, Mortensen quickly became established in the post-war Blackpool team, for whom he would end up scoring 197 league goals. He made his England debut in 1947, scoring four times in the 10-0 win over Portugal. Effective at the apex of the forward line or at inside-forward, Mortensen told author Robin Daniels: "I was quite happy to play anywhere as long as I was playing in the team. My preference was centre-forward, although as an inside-forward I was still an attacking player."

Nicknamed "The Mighty Atom" or the "Blackpool Bombshell" by reporters and fans, Mortensen had quickly earned a reputation as a strong and resilient player. "I can't recall him ever being knocked off the ball," said Matthews, who described him as having "cornflake box shoulders and legs like bags of concrete".

Lofthouse called him "one of the bravest players I have ever seen" and added: "I've known Morty put his head where you wouldn't put an iron bar. He would go for anything, in the air or on the ground."

Mortensen was quick in his changes of direction and brave and skilled in the air, the result of hours of lonely practice against a school wall. And he was capable of scoring goals through close-range poaching or powerful shooting from distance – "a monstrous and explosive shot with either foot", according to Matthews.

Mortensen explained: "A player has got to have the confidence to hit balls from outside the penalty area. It was instilled into me that if I missed a couple of chances, well, I'd got to make up for it; and the only way to do that is to have the confidence to try more shots at goal."

His positional awareness and accuracy with the ball was an asset to Matthews, who recalled never having to look back or break stride when running on to a pass from his colleague. In return, he remembered: "Wherever I was on the wing I knew where Morty would be in the middle."

Mortensen built on his feats against Portugal with a hat-trick against Sweden, going on to score 23 times in 25 appearances for England over a six-year span. His most famous international goal came in a 4-0 win against Italy in Turin. Having beaten two defenders, he was running out of room but stunned the stadium with a dazzling shot from the narrowest of angles as his body tumbled over the by-line. England boss Walter Winterbottom commented: "I've never known a stadium fall so silent."

Dressing rooms were rarely quiet with Mortensen around. "Morty was a great comedian," said Cyril Robinson. "You couldn't have wished for anybody any better. He was a Geordie and I think they are that way."

On England duty, he became renowned for his double act with Manchester City goalkeeper Frank Swift. Whenever shoes went missing from outside hotel rooms in the middle of the night, you could bet that that those two were responsible; if moods needed lifting they would roll out their ventriloquist act, in which Mortensen wrapped himself in a sheet and climbed into his colleague's arms to play baby to Swift's 'mummy'. International team-mate Tom Finney stated: "If you couldn't hit it off with Stan then it was your fault because he made friendship easy."

Highly superstitious, Mortensen would insist on being the last out of the dressing room, as well as frequently being the last one in. Robinson continued: "On a match day, I remember at ten to three Joe Smith would often be saying: 'Where's Morty?' He'd be outside talking to somebody and Joe would say: 'Go and bloody well fetch him in.' Morty was ready in two minutes. He was very untidy. When he became a manager he had good results and people liked him. They could speak to him. If you said something to him you shouldn't have done he would probably laugh at you."

Mortensen would depart Blackpool as a player in 1955 but was back at Bloomfield Road as manager between 1967 and 1969. Both in reality and emotionally, he never left the town, having married a local girl called Jean, opened his own shops there and gone on to become a town councillor. His presence remains even into the 21st century, with the erection of a bronze statue outside the club's home ground in 2005. "Any opportunities I have had in life were created in the first place by coming to Blackpool Football Club as a young lad," he once said. "I married a Blackpool girl and fell very much in love with the town."

Blackpool fan and resident Mel McCarthy said: "Morty was fantastic. He had a shop and, unknown to me, my parents had ordered a football for me for Christmas. I will never forget it because Morty was my idol and on Christmas Day I was downstairs messing around and playing a few games when the door to our hotel goes. I have gone to the door and who is there? Stan Mortensen. With a leather ball with the old T-panels. He had signed it and everything. On Christmas Day! I couldn't believe it."

Mortensen was one of several Blackpool players who strengthened their links with the community and looked to safeguard their financial future by establishing themselves as businessmen within the town. While Stanley Matthews purchased a private hotel, *Stanley Mortensen – Fancy Goods and Postcards* became a well-known destination for seaside visitors, especially those who knew their football and hoped to run into the owner serving behind the counter. Full-back Eddie Shimwell's transfer from Sheffield United in 1946 had come about following a transfer request prompted by the Yorkshire club's refusal to allow him to run a pub in the Derbyshire Dales.

Such ventures were more than mere vehicles to which players could attach their name to make a bit extra to supplement their earnings. In the days of the maximum wage, which by the start of the 1952/53 season stood at only £14 per week, these were serious undertakings, to be supervised personally, and designed to see players through the remaining three decades of working life after retirement from football. When he collapsed unconscious during half-time of a home game against Wolves during 1947/48 –

before coming round and belatedly joining the second half – Mortensen put it down to a combination of a physical first half and the lack of sleep caused by living above his shop in a busy street.

Mortensen's store was among the enterprises featured in an August 1949 Pathé News film highlighting the plight of footballers who, while the money was rolling into the sport via the turnstiles, were left scratching around for ways to make a living beyond their playing days. It had only been the threat of strike action in 1945 that had forced a rise in the maximum wage to £9 per week, before the National Arbitration Tribunal increased it to £12 two years later. Of course, only a small proportion of professionals, estimated at 30 per cent, earned the top salary, while many lower division players and reserves at the leading clubs had to make do with less than the average British weekly wage.

Certainly, some clubs made use of illegal payments and tactics such as presents to players' wives, along with use of club cars and houses and the provision of household goods. But while such seedy activities might have eased financial burdens, they did nothing to increase the footballer's professional pride, while newspapers had a field day when they unearthed a new scam.[15]

The Pathé piece, somewhat misleadingly titled *Soccer Stars Kick Off with New Deal*, showed Arsenal players benignly studying fabric at the College of Distributive Trades in Charing Cross before featuring some of the personal enterprises of the stars of the day. As well as Mortensen and Matthews, these included Tom Finney at work in his plumbing business in Preston, Tottenham

. . . .

15 Things came to a head in 1957 when a long-running illegal payment racket at Sunderland led to a £5,000 club fine; a life ban for the chairman, chief financial officer and three other directors; while various players were temporarily suspended after refusing to give evidence to the FA's investigation.

goalkeeper Ted Ditchburn selling theatre tickets and Willie Hall, the former Notts County, Spurs and England man who'd had the lower parts of both legs amputated because of illness four years earlier, serving a customer with golf balls in his sports shop.

The film could easily have included Blackpool skipper Harry Johnston, who in 1948 bought a newsagent, hairdresser and general store in Central Drive. "I might get injured and, with the best will in the world, the football crowds would soon forget Harry Johnston. You can't live on past glories," he explained, noting that too many players were forced to attempt to remain in the game, "living almost on the charity of old friends who remember them from better days".

Johnston seemed happy enough with his lot, even though it meant getting up shortly after 6am to organise paper rounds before dealing with wholesalers and helping in the shop prior to training at Bloomfield Road and returning to the store to prepare for the evening papers. "I no longer have to rely on what I make from football to save up for the years ahead," he commented.

The Pathé film, however, signed off with the kind of challenge that must have sounded like revolution to any club chairmen who heard it in their local cinema. "Unlike the turnstiles and the pools promoters, the men who make the game seldom make fortunes," the clipped voiceover concluded. "As the new season opens may soccer see an end to the tragedy of its good sportsmen unsportingly treated. Soccer must learn to play the game."

Football in the late 1940s had exploded like never before, with the source of the boom emanating from the war years, when the sport – for all its haphazard organisation – had become even more integral to the British way of life. The headlong dash into mainstream public consciousness that football had undertaken during the 1930s accelerated further when people's lives were in dire need of some kind of anchor of familiarity in a time of fear, grief and uncertainty. Those in power had seen the importance of keeping the morale of the country high at a time when many were suffering bereavement and had recognised the need to maintain the population's confidence in authority. Much like a beleaguered Roman emperor putting on 150 days of games in the Coliseum to win the hearts of his people, the government decided that football had to continue, even with the constraints on transport and the inherent issues of public safety.

Once peace had been restored, the fretting over important trivialities such as the results of one's favourite team became a symbol of the restoration of normality. Servicemen returning with back pay in their pockets and workers who had saved their money during the years when there had been little opportunity to splash out meant that there was cash to be spent, but few luxuries or goods on which to spend it. A balance of payments deficit forced the Labour government to review its economic policy in 1947, with a resulting reduction on imported goods and the imposition of further rationing. The football match remained an available and, for more and more people, affordable option.

On one Saturday in October 1948, a record 1,171,173 people attended Football League games. Despite the mediocrity of their team, Chelsea drew 78,000 to Stamford Bridge for the visit of Blackpool, with an estimated 25,000 locked out. Some of those inside the ground began demanding their money back when they discovered that they had no way of getting on to the terraces to see the action and were eventually allowed to sit on the dog track.

The 1948/49 season saw a record total Football League attendance of 41.3 million and the single-day high was beaten twice more over Christmas 1949. It fell again on the opening day of the 1950/51 season, when Blackpool's trip to Tottenham was the largest individual crowd, almost 65,000 seeing Johnston score twice in a 4-1 win against the eventual First Division champions.

Meanwhile, the football pools, introduced in the 1920s, both fed off and helped to fuel interest in the sport, with an estimated ten million people every week filling in their Littlewoods or Vernons coupons by the early 1950s. The Saturday evening ritual in many homes was for dad to sit intently checking his predictions against the results in the sports *Pink 'Un*. Half the population was reckoned to have done the pools at one time and, with betting still illegal away from the racecourse, it was most of the population's one regular flirtation with gambling, whatever their background and level of interest in football.

The renowned diarist of the time, the housewife Nella Last, was certainly no sports fan, but even she noted in January 1951: "My one extravagance… is one shilling a week for a football coupon." She spoke of listening to the 6pm news bulletin and checking the scores against the fixture list in the *Daily Express*. "I certainly get a lot of entertainment from the one shilling," she wrote, adding: "I pick towns I've visited; places where I'd like to go."

As author Peter Lewis observed in his book about the decade, "'When I come up on the pools' became the Fifties' equivalent of breaking the bank of Monte Carlo for the Edwardians."

Yet the impact all of this football-generated income[16] had on the wage packets of the players was minimal. Unlike the modern era, where a gifted teenager knows that a few good

. . . .

16 It should be noted that football gained no direct income from the estimated £60m generated annually by the pools companies. In 1950, the FA lamented this state of affairs in its annual yearbook by stating: "If there must be betting on football, there are at least grounds for arguing that the game, instead of being a passive instrument of betting, should make more positive gain therefrom."

years with a top club can set him up for life, young post-war professionals were encouraged to take up an apprenticeship, both to safeguard them against the early curtailment of their sporting ambitions and to give them a trade after the cheering stopped. For those dissenters such as Mortensen – who, despite his mother's urgings, quickly gave up his evening classes in joinery – investing their football salaries in a business became vital if they were to avoid spending their later years in constant search of the next pay packet.

According to Robinson: "People said we were on a good wage. I would say: 'Yes, but we could be finished at 26. Then what do we do?' We did whatever we could. I didn't have a trade; I had done two years in the RAF. From stopping playing I have had a newsagent's, flats and a boarding house; I worked for an insurance company, in building management and I have sold ice cream. I have done all of them."

As a squad player, Robinson had to fight for every penny and he painted a frustrating picture of the ongoing battle to receive the wage he felt he was due. "One Saturday, Spurs came up from London and one of their players took sick," he recalled. "They didn't bring reserve players, so they had to panic and get one up. We were playing at Arsenal the Saturday after, so Joe took two reserves to be safe; a forward and me. They might normally have taken one. Everyone was fit to play but when we came back I thought: 'Right, we're on top money this week.' At the end of the week I got the pay packet and it was the usual eight quid. Me and Alan Withers, an outside-left, went into see Joe in his little office at the back of the stand. I said: 'I thought we would be on top money; you took us down with the first team.' He just said: 'We took you down for the ride.' That was the type of man he was. He wouldn't give us it. I had to go to the bloody captain, Harry Johnston, and he got us the money.

"After the Cup Final in 1953, we got a yearly contract for the same terms. At the time it was about £8 in the reserves, with £6 in the summer. I saw Joe again and he humbled and bumbled and I got nothing from him. The chairman at the time, Harry Evans, was a plumber and had an office in town so I went to see him and told him what I wanted. He had a big board on the wall, with names, wages and everything. He got a ruler and went across and said: 'You are on top money already, Cyril.' I pointed out that the bloody ruler was sloping, so he said: 'We'll see what we can do.' I got an extra couple of quid. There was another instance. If you were there four years you could get a benefit payment. It was about £250 or £500. I went up to Joe and said: 'What about my benefit?' He said: 'You'll get the benefit of the doubt.' That was it."

Clubs were able to rely on the special nature of the employment they offered to prevent their players from becoming militant. In *The Life of a Journeyman 1950s Footballer*, former Aldershot, Tottenham and Southampton goalkeeper Ron Reynolds said: "It wasn't a particularly well paid job, it didn't put you on a different financial footing to most other people." And he confessed: "I suppose we were more innocent or naive in general in those days and becoming involved with a football club seemed such an unlikely or remarkable thing to do."

Matthews, admittedly cushioned financially by his off-field earning opportunities, told Robin Daniels: "I didn't feel I was very much underpaid. I love the game. Somehow, when I was playing on the field, money didn't mean a thing."

While the players – whether through naivety or impotence – remained undervalued in the context of the money they helped their clubs generate, the notion of an egalitarian pay scale was supported by many. Discussing the potential for "animosity" bred by the modern superstar system, Bill Perry expressed a view that was not untypical of his era. "If I was playing and I was the best on the field, I would still not like to think that a team-mate was earning less than me.

Knowing Stan [Matthews], he wouldn't begrudge anyone earning the same as him. Certainly I never remember hearing about him arguing for more for himself."

According to Bolton's Doug Holden, wages were rarely a topic of dressing room conversation. "I got a £10 signing-on fee and everyone got the same. It helped make everyone part of a close-knit team. It never entered my mind about what anyone else was making. When the time came for signing a new contract, they would say: 'There you are. It's the same as last time,' and I signed. There may have been some others who looked for a few extra quid but I wasn't interest in money, just kicking a ball. I was young and single and it was a good wage compared to the normal man. It wasn't until later when I was married that money started to become an issue.

"When you were getting to the end of your career, you always had that thought in the back of your mind: 'What am I going to do?' Especially if you weren't talented or skilled in any other way. It is why I ended up going to Australia because a lot of players were going there at the end of their careers. I never did consciously make plans but I started to think more when I got into my 30s. You can still play at that age but you start wondering what you'll do when you stop."

Arsenal and Wales full-back Walley Barnes wrote in 1953: "Bearing in mind the amount of money brought into the game by the efforts of the players at the top of the profession, I consider they are grossly underpaid." He, too, agreed with the imposition of a ceiling on salaries, but added: "I would like to see a higher basic wage for the skilled tradesman and, in addition, a more imaginative system of payment by results." He supported an idea proposed by Arsenal manager Tom Whittaker whereby players should be made shareholders in the club for the duration of their contracts and therefore entitled to a slice of the profits. Barnes felt that such a scheme would offer greater reward to undervalued players and even suggested that "unfashionable teams would have to play winning football – the kind that would draw the crowds and create a profit margin".

Blackpool's Eddie Shimwell argued that "they didn't over-pay you, they didn't under-pay you; you all got what you were entitled to". But football's approach to its players' entitlement during the days of booming revenues was born of the same head-in-the-sand attitude that pervaded much of the national game. It was the same mindset that forced spectators to be squeezed into stadia that offered little shelter against the elements, poor toilet facilities and minimal catering.

This was all, according to *The Ball is Round* author David Goldblatt, a reflection of authority in general at that time:

> The general tenor of the governance of English football in the 1950s and early 1960s bore a remarkable resemblance to the antiquated, complacent, self-importance of the Macmillan and Home administrations that governed the country. Both the Football League and FA remained suspicious of many of the key innovations of the era. The pools industry was resisted until the late 1950s; floodlit league football was opposed until 1956; television coverage was sharply restricted.

In the summer of 1950, the League Management Committee had at least brought in a scheme where players, upon retirement, earned a pay-off of ten per cent of their earnings during their career. This was intended to replace the system of awarding a player a benefit after five years of service, which might amount to a little over £500 once the taxman had his cut. Manchester United winger Charlie Mitten's comment that "you couldn't even buy a house" by the time a player retired was a typical one. The new arrangements offered greater security, but this still only amounted to the approximate financial equivalent of an extra year on the field and did nothing to counter the culture of fear that existed in many dressing rooms.[17]

Clubs wielded total power over the players' current and future salaries and their transfer prospects, thanks to the maximum wage and the retain-and-transfer system. Even when players reached the end of their contracts they remained tied to their clubs. Until England inside-forward George Eastham successfully challenged the system in court following his 1960 move from Newcastle to Arsenal, the frequent fate of any player who attempted to force a transfer would be to find himself an outcast. Alternative income streams would have to be found while bloody-minded directors adopted the approach that "if you don't play here, you don't play anywhere". Such a fate befell Eastham, who spent several months working as a cork salesman, before at last being allowed to escape St James' Park.

It meant that players were, for the most part, content not to rock the boat when it came to money. Nor would they voice concerns they might have about on-field matters. A player who earned a reputation for challenging the manager or even, God forbid, being a union activist ran the risk of becoming alienated within his club, shunned by directors, coaches and sometimes even team-mates.

Bill Albury, a wing-half at Portsmouth and Gillingham throughout the 1950s, commented: "Come Christmas, if you weren't in the first team or established in the reserves you were worried you would be on your bike and not signed on for the next season. I remember once thinking I had done quite well during the season so I went to see if I could get a £1 rise. I was offered the same terms – but you took it and cleared off. You were made to feel it was a privilege to be

. . . .

17 By 1956, the percentage had decreased, first to nine per cent and then to seven and a half, as clubs faced up to lower income at the gate.

able to play football as a living instead of being a welder or bricklayer."

The plight of the English player was highlighted by the 'Bogota Affair' in the early summer of 1950, when Neil Franklin, the Stoke City and England centre-half, along with George Mountford, Charlie Mitten and Billy Higgins, went to play in Colombia – at the time not a member of FIFA. All were subsequently suspended. Franklin explained that he went to Santa Fe for a reported £3,000 signing-on fee and £300 per month, plus win bonuses ranging up to £150. He lasted only two months, admitting: "I made a mistake, but at the time I thought I was doing the right thing, not only for myself but also my wife and family."

Mitten, who said his signing fee had been £5,000, stayed for an entire season before returning to find himself banned by English football for six months, a longer period than his fellow exiles. "Any player in the land would have gone if offered such an opportunity," he told author Richard Adamson many years later. "Even Stan Matthews was interested in playing out there."

He also explained his own motivation for the move, noting that, at 29 years of age, he was only expecting another five years in the First Division. "Then I'd find myself back where I started as a 17 year old – with no money in the bank, a wife and children to support and looking for another living… all I had to show for my career to date was an old second-hand car."

Most of his peers found themselves in the same situation, which was why Mitten reckoned he knew 60 players interested in following his path to Colombia. The grievances of the professional footballer were articulated later in the decade by players' union chairman Jimmy Hill in an article in *FA News*. Pointing out that the average weekly wage of a professional footballer was only £1 higher than the average wage in industry, he argued: "Although he may be on a pedestal, the footballer's purchasing power is no greater than his neighbour's." He added: "Unlike the man next door, he must perform in public in front of perhaps a million people in a season, as well as having to contend with 11 opponents who do their utmost to ensure he makes a mess of his job."

Hill continued: "Sometimes, publicly, he is a hero. In the nature of things he must at times look a blundering fool." Stressing that such failure could lead to a drop in wages or a confidence-sapping banishment to a lower level of the game, he concluded: "What a shameful advertisement it is to attract young men of higher intellectual ability into a great sport."

* * * * *

THERE IS nothing particularly intellectual in the play at Wembley immediately following Mortensen's equaliser, which seems to have robbed both teams of their composure. In fact, it appears to have become a contest between Shimwell and Barrass to see who can lump the ball furthest downfield, until Matthews adds some temporary composure with a neat pass inside to Mudie. He promptly launches a long ball for Perry to chase, but he is beaten by Ball, who celebrates by leathering a clearance beyond the halfway line.

Mortensen, with his back to goal, is allowed the space to control a Taylor pass and slip it to Matthews. He turns inside to play the ball left-footed into the box and Hanson has to dive to gather after seeing another deflection off the ill-fated Hassall. A few moments later Matthews, almost apologetically, robs the injured Bell and hits an adventurous pass across field. Again, he looks like he is playing a different game to many others, although this time Ball makes a timely intervention to deny Perry.

Twice in the space of a few minutes, a possible, unexpected benefit to Bolton of Bell's injury becomes apparent. With no outside-left to speak of, Lofthouse begins to drift further to that side of the field, meaning that when the ball is aimed at him he is up against right-back Shimwell instead of centre-half Johnston. When Hassall delivers a long clearance, Shimwell misjudges his attempted header and Lofthouse is able to run into the space behind him. He strides into the box and fires just over with his left foot – a similar effort to that with which Geoff Hurst will famously score from a nearby patch of grass 13 years later.

Before long Hanson is booting the ball deep and, once again, Shimwell, having a horrible first half, errs in his positioning. The ball skims off his head into the path of Lofthouse, enjoying his freedom to roam, and Johnston has to cover quickly to drive him wide, forcing his cross to go harmlessly behind the goal. At this stage, Bolton are coping well with their depleted forces and will soon be ahead once more.

7

ON A WING AND A PRAYER

"We mostly just used to stay up by the halfway line. The game was tactically more fixed then and it was just you against the full-back. Work-rate, tackling back and closing down came into fashion later on." – Bolton outside-right Doug Holden.

"RIGHT, LADS. Pack your bags now and meet in the lobby. Quick as you can." Within minutes of Joe Smith's orders, Blackpool's players were on their way to Buxton station in the hope of catching the one train leaving the snow-bound town. Reports of the rushed exit from their hotel conjured up images of hastily-packed clothes flapping from barely-fastened suitcases in the manner of businessmen caught cheating with their secretaries.

The weather had become the dominant feature of the week preceding the fifth round of the FA Cup, to be played on 14th February, Valentine's Day. Displaying a reckless abandon in keeping with their attack-orientated style of play, Blackpool – in readiness to play at home against Second Division strugglers Southampton – set off for their traditional Derbyshire retreat in spite of the heavy snow that was falling over the country. Having travelled by coach on the Tuesday, navigating through the white mounds to arrive only an hour behind schedule, they found themselves effectively trapped in their hotel the following day as blizzards piled snow upon snow.

While the RAC spoke of "some of the worst road conditions experienced in northern and central England for many years", motorists were warned to stay out of the triangle formed by Manchester, Stoke-on-Trent and Sheffield. A group of 29 elderly women returning from a pantomime in Sheffield were marooned on the Derbyshire moors for six hours, finally rescued by police and ambulance services at midnight. In Bolton, snow ploughs worked non-stop to keep buses running. Back in Blackpool, the cricket club's newly-arrived Northern League professional, Australian Bill Alley – the future Test match umpire – sent his car skidding off the North Promenade into a road sign. Although he escaped injury, his wife, Betty, suffered a cut nose and concussion.

This was all happening while the Queen and Duke of Edinburgh were engaged in visits to the east coast areas hit by the recent floods. And, ironically, the BBC had only this week announced that, by arrangement with the Automobile Association, it would be including news of adverse road conditions in its weather reports from 22nd February onwards.

Blackpool had ventured to Buxton with all but one of the team that had beaten Huddersfield in the fourth round – Jackie Mudie again absent on RAF duty – plus half-backs Eric Hayward and Hugh Kelly and reserve forward David Durie. Asked why the team was returning to the countryside, Smith had explained: "Because [the players] have asked to go and because, away from the town, they escape all these ticket hunters who always plague them at this time of year. It's good psychology too. They have gone to Buxton twice this year and won each time. There's something in this sort of approach to Cup football."

Now, as every major road in the surrounding area of Buxton became impassable, it appeared there was no way of getting those players home again. They might still be there come kick-off time on Saturday. The best they could manage was a morning visit to the local ice rink for a few stretches and exercises.

Hope arrived in the form of news that snow ploughs had cleared one railway line and that a solitary train would shortly be setting off for Manchester. Only Blackpool's bus driver and his vehicle were left behind to wait for the thaw as Smith and his men fought their way home. "We had to get out while we could," the manager explained later, from the warm sanctuary of the Norbreck Hydro Hotel, where another bus had carefully taken them after their train ride. "There was not a field within a radius of miles where the players could have trained."

Opponents Southampton, who had won only twice away from The Dell all season, had seen their own plans for relaxed preparation upset. Manager George Roughton had intended to treat his players to a round of golf in the New Forest on the Wednesday, but gales and sleet put paid to that. They did. manage one final training session the following day before setting off north on a sleeper train, arriving at the Clifton Hotel mid-morning on Friday. They were greeted by cagey local weather reports saying that "it is possible that snow will fall on Saturday" and "we may have some hard frost".

Roughton, a former Huddersfield and Manchester United full-back, warned that the game might be no more predictable than the weather. Having seen his team reach the fifth round by beating Second Division Lincoln after a replay and lowly Third Division side Shrewsbury, Roughton announced: "I am not pretending we are favourites. But in the Cup you've always a chance and we've one tomorrow. Everything to win, not a lot to lose; that's how we go into this match." In the end, after no more snowfall and only a hint of an overnight freeze, he proved more prescient than the Squires Gate Meteorological Office.

No one could ever accuse the owners of Blackpool's eateries of being slow to recognise a business opportunity. When, at 7.30am on Saturday, 1,200 Southampton supporters stepped noisily off the overnight trains that had transported them north to Central Station, they found rows of seaside cafes welcoming them in with promises of "Cup-tie breakfasts". And just as Premier League fans would see Blackpool's promotion half a century later as an excuse for a weekend at the seaside, the Saints followers were determined that their day out would encompass much more than a mere football match.

Fully replete, they spilled out of the restaurants with their bells and bugles heralding their noisy path to Blackpool's tourists attractions and shops. The local paper caught up with the Gladwyn family, on their first trip to Blackpool, who explained: "Our train doesn't leave until 11 o'clock tonight and, before then, we want to visit the Winter Gardens and some of the other entertainment centres."

They made sure they were at Bloomfield Road in plenty of time to take their positions among a crowd of 25,743, although what they saw in the first 15 minutes resembled an end-of-the-pier boxing booth as much as a football match as referee JB Flanagan was obliged to award 23 free-kicks for fouls.

Smith had been unimpressed with the Southampton performance he had witnessed a week earlier against Bury, although he had the good sense to warn that "a team one week can be an entirely different team a week later". And it was Saints forward Charles Purves who squandered the first chance of the match before Blackpool began to threaten via Stanley Matthews's mastery of opposing full-back Peter Sillett. Having beaten his man and had his cross blocked, Matthews repeated the trick and fed Mudie, scorer of a brace for the RAF against Oxford University two days earlier, but the resulting shot was blocked.

Sillett wasn't the only full-back on the field having problems, with Eddie Shimwell, recovering from a groin injury, given a going-over by John Hoskins. Growing anxiety among the home fans escalated into outright panic when they saw the ball sitting in the back of their team's net after Frank Dudley had converted a pass down the middle. Relief followed, however, when the referee was seen indicating a free-kick to Blackpool. And it was the Southampton contingent's turn to exhale deeply when Ernie Taylor's shot emerged from a crowd of players to skip teasingly wide.

The second half began with play switching from end to end without any clear chances. Good defensive work by Johnston and Tommy Garrett ensured Blackpool's goal was unthreatened, as did wayward shooting from Johnny Walker. The home team's appeals for a penalty were correctly ignored after Bill Perry went down in chasing a pass from Mudie, before Saints keeper John Christie executed a comfortable save to his left when Johnston attempted an ambitious shot on the run from 30 yards.

With 63 minutes played, Blackpool took the lead in somewhat fortuitous circumstances, although the sheer effort of winger Perry was worthy of reward as he gamely chased, apparently in vain, after an aimless long ball down the middle. Perry, Christie and a defender all converged on the ball simultaneously, but as the trio collided Perry managed to make contact with the ball and watched it trundle across the line.

Blackpool could hardly be said to be playing well, however. Their forwards were frequently outmuscled by quick-tackling Southampton defenders and their passes went astray too often for them to seal the game. With six minutes remaining, the away team earned a replay after Taylor was penalised for a foul and Henry Horton greeted Sillett's free-kick from the left with a powerful header into the net from the edge of the six-yard box. Johnston confessed: "Southampton played very well and were unlucky to draw."

Bolton, too, had been facing Second Division opposition, although *Evening News* man Haydn Berry had warned that Wanderers might be considered underdogs at Luton Town. This was, he suggested, because of the tiring nature of the recent tie against Notts County and the "peculiarities" of the narrow, sloping pitch at Kenilworth Road, with its tightly-packed stands. He balanced his thoughts with this assessment of the Bolton team: "They are an unpredictable collection of individual players with, in some cases, the talent for any company. Thus no task is beyond them on the right day in the right mood."

Berry was also forced to apologise to *Evening News* readers for giving the impression that more tickets were available to Bolton fans than was the case. In fact, all 750 – out of a stadium capacity of 28,000 – had already been sold. With only one day to go before the game, the pitch that was waiting for them was still covered in two inches of snow, although lines had been cleared in readiness. More snow had arrived by Saturday morning, but volunteers, including 30 early-arriving Bolton fans, helped clear the excess to ensure that the match went ahead.

Wanderers, having spent the night before the game in London, had George Higgins in at left-back in place of Ralph Banks, who had pulled a muscle in the second replay against Notts County. Luton, meanwhile, were pleased to have captain and centre-half Syd Owen back to combat the threat of Lofthouse after missing three games with fibrositis.

The home side's forwards had been the stars of their Cup run so far, scoring six against Blackburn and five in a replay against Manchester City. And after the game kicked off in welcome sunshine, they forced Stan Hanson into the first save, charging down a shot from stalwart Bob Morton after Jesse Pye and Bernie Moore combined. There was still an opportunity for winger Bert Mitchell from the rebound but he fired over the bar.

When Bolton, in scarlet change shirts, attacked they were too often guilty of misplacing their final pass, with Doug Holden and Nat Lofthouse consequently denied shooting chances. A cross by Holden caused a goalmouth scramble but it was not until 20 minutes had been played that Wanderers had a clear shot, Moir's first-time effort going wide.

The only goal of the game owed something to the conditions; Moir opting to lift the ball forward in the direction of Lofthouse rather than attempting to thread it through on the snowy surface. It was a well-judged delivery, allowing Lofthouse to run between two defenders and head past goalkeeper Ron Baynham. "It was odd to watch that lob," said Moir. "After lifting the ball into the air the ball appeared to flatten out in its flight and carry, or drift, exactly the distance Nat needed to time his header for when Baynham would be advancing."

Moir's assist was an example of the way in which the Bolton players were in the end able to make their higher skill level combat the conditions more effectively than their opponents, rather than allowing the surface to nullify their advantage. Their half-backs grew in command as the game progressed and a couple of second-half goals would not have flattered the visitors. Luton had no alternative plan to fall back on when the Bolton defence, marshalled by Barrass, frustrated their efforts to direct their approach play through Pye, while Hanson looked composed on the occasions when his goal was threatened.

It was an accomplished performance and, far from succumbing to Berry's fears, they enabled him to report that there were "many more laughs and songs than miles in the journey home".

It was travelling to the game that provided one of the indelible memories of the Cup run for Joyce Barrass, wife of the Wanderers centre-half. "I had been quite poorly, I'd not long had [son] Robert and I didn't know whether I was going or not. But I did and I missed the bus. The other girls said later: 'We wouldn't have had any money in our pockets," but I got on a train and then I had no idea where I was. So I got in a taxi and I said: 'I want Luton's ground.' He dropped me off any old where because he wasn't allowed to go any further; there was only so long to go on his shift, so he had to stop. I was nearly in tears. I got in a phone box and found the number of the ground and I could hear someone talking. I said: "Excuse me, could I just speak to that person," because it was one of the coaches' wives. She said: 'It is no use coming now it is near the end. They have won by the way.' I remember I ended up sitting on a little seat waiting for them to pick me up."

Blackpool's failure to dispose of Southampton was greeted as one of the surprises of the fifth round, along with the 1-0 victory of Third Division Gateshead at Second Division promotion contenders Plymouth. Seasiders fans would rather not have seen their team make such unwanted headlines, however, and the immediate reaction of those who gathered outside the ground to vent their dissatisfaction was that they would not be making the long trip to the south coast for the replay. But as the red mist cleared, 500 bought tickets for the contest at The Dell and, as well as a special train leaving Central Station at midnight on Tuesday, six aeroplanes were chartered from the Lancashire Aircraft Corporation. Taking off at 11am, the eight-guineas per head deal would include a packed lunch.

Against expectations, Mudie was able to make the trip to Southampton. He was called off a train at Preston after setting off for an RAF game at Uxbridge to be given the news that he and Saints full-back Sillett had been released from service obligations to play in the replay. Instead, he travelled with his club to London, where the team stayed on Tuesday night before journeying by train and taxi to The Dell on matchday. Shimwell's successful fitness test meant that the return of Hugh Kelly to the team for the first time since December – in place of Ewan Fenton – was the only change from the first game.

Replays had been The Dell's only experience of FA Cup action for the past five years and queues formed outside the ground from 9am, while the last of the snow was being cleared from the pitch. By 2.30pm, quarter of an hour before kick-off, the gates were locked on a crowd of 29,233, who had to wait only a few minutes for the first meaningful moments of the game. Johnny Crosland survived an appeal for handball in his own area and the belligerent Dudley, unmarked with only Farm to beat, shot over from near the penalty spot.

Perry fired at the keeper and Brown was wide from 25 yards, but most of the pressure was being applied by the home team. Sillett was making a better job of keeping Matthews in check this time and his colleagues were full of commitment and energy. It certainly was not against the run of play when Walker followed a one-two with Hoskins by shooting against Johnston and then curling his attempt from the rebound wide of Farm to give Southampton the lead.

Dudley shot within a yard of the post and Farm was kept busy by diving at Walker's feet, pushing Day's header

Blackpool keeper George Farm looks up in despair as an early shot from Nat Lofthouse (background) gives Bolton a 1-0 lead in the 1953 FA Cup Final.

Blackpool Tower and beach, pictured during the town's post-war boom years.

Training methods at Blackpool were basic, as they were at most clubs. Here Stanley Matthews and George Farm strive for all-important fitness by pounding the Bloomfield Road terracing.

Bolton's Harold Hassall (right) sees his attempted intervention send the ball past keeper Stan Hanson to give Blackpool an equaliser. Later, Stan Mortensen (grounded) would be credited with the goal, the first part of his hat-trick.

England star Raich Carter serves in his tobacco and confectionary store, the type of business opportunity that was the limit of the ambition of most 1950s footballers.

Electrical stores around England saw sales soaring throughout 1953 as the decision to televise the Coronation live prompted the purchase of millions of new television sets.

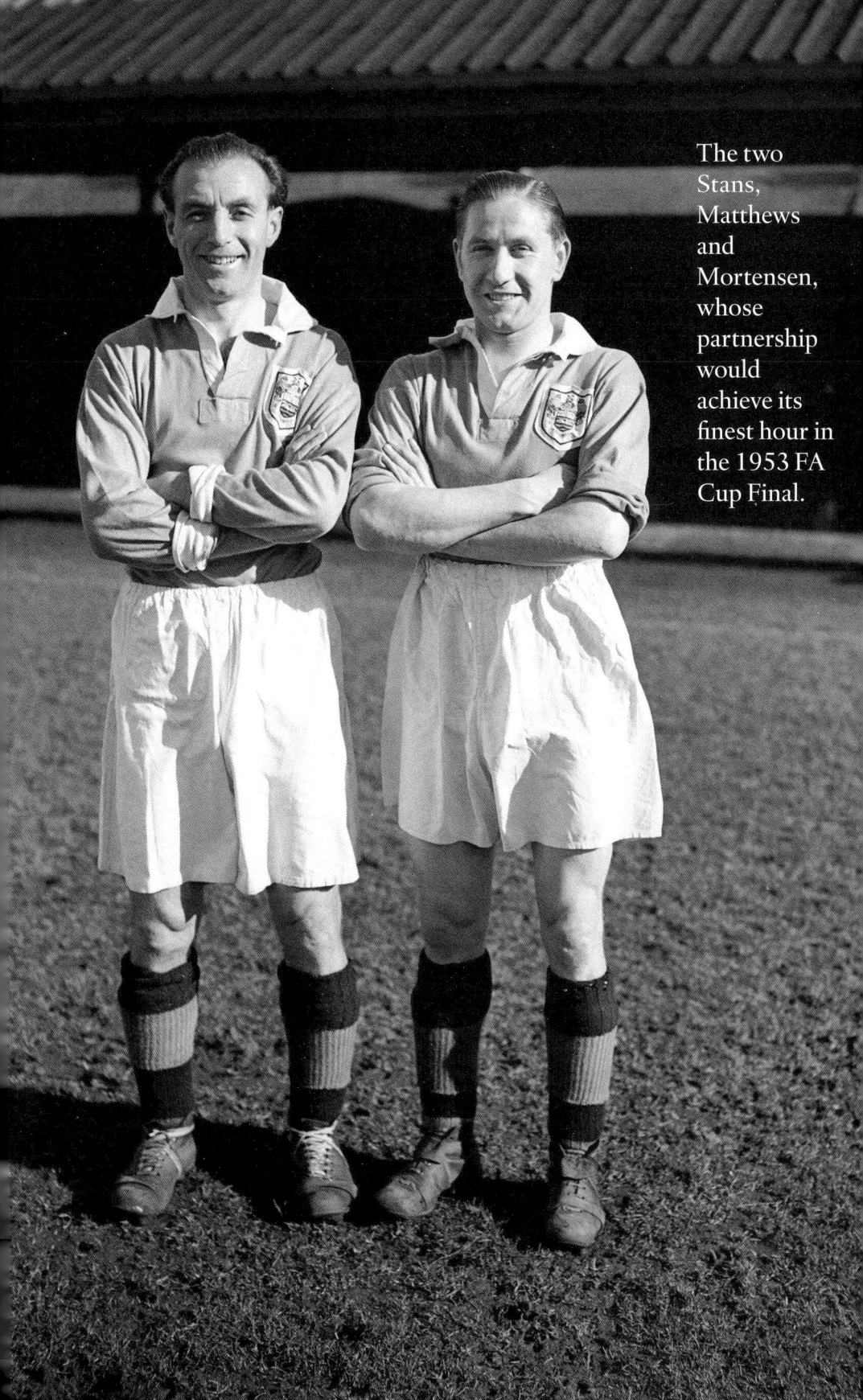

The two Stans, Matthews and Mortensen, whose partnership would achieve its finest hour in the 1953 FA Cup Final.

The BBC cameras were not always welcomed at Wembley for coverage of the FA Cup Final as clubs feared the damage live televised football could do to attendances.

Forward Allan Brown puts on a brave face as he is transported from hospital to the train station to return to Blackpool after breaking his leg in the quarter-final against Arsenal.

Blackpool's colourful fans, the Atomic Boys, march towards Downing Street on the morning of the FA Cup Final.

Stan Mortensen slides in Blackpool's second goal, beating the attention of Stan Hanson, Malcolm Barrass and Johnny Ball.

Stanley Matthews torments Bolton centre-half Malcolm Barrass at Wembley.

A first-time shot by Bill Perry (left) beats goalkeeper Stan Hanson and defender Johnny Ball to give Blackpool their dramatic injury-time winner.

Bolton captain Willie Moir (8) is among the first to congratulate Stanley Matthews as the final whistle blows to signal the achievement of his greatest ambition.

Stanley Matthews receives his coveted winner's medal from Queen Elizabeth II as the Duke of Edinburgh and FA secretary Stanley Rous look on approvingly.

Blackpool captain Harry Johnston, with manager Joe Smith to his left, leads the Wembley crowd in three cheers for the new Queen.

Skipper Harry
Johnston and
national hero
Matthews are carried
aloft by team-mates
as Blackpool begin
their lap of honour.

A month after
the final, crowds
cheer the newly-
crowned Queen
Elizabeth II back to
Buckingham Palace
after the Coronation
ceremony in
Westminster Abbey.
*(All pictures: Press
Association)*

over the bar and holding a drive by Purves. Garrett then scrambled away an effort by Hoskins. Incidents such as Taylor forcing a save at the other end were rare moments of first-half relief. "Blackpool were indescribably bad in the first half," was the verdict of Don Creedy in the *Evening Gazette* and skipper Johnston admitted: "[Southampton] almost ran off the field in the first half. They should have been at least three up."

Back in the dressing room, Johnston wasted no time in telling his team how badly they were playing. As usual, manager Smith was happy to let his captain have his say before adding a few terse comments of his own. "If you've got to lose, go out there and lose like fighters," he spat out. "At the moment you are playing like a lot of old washerwomen." The results were immediate. Within three minutes of the restart, Blackpool were ahead.

According to Perry: "We composed ourselves and took control of the game." In the first minute it was he who broke on the left and got in a shot just as two defenders closed in. Christie appeared to have the danger covered until Horton stretched out a leg and deflected the ball towards the goal. As Mudie moved in to force it over the line and a defender tried to clear, the linesman flagged to indicate a goal. "I could have touched it," Mudie said later, "but I saw that it was going over the line so I just followed it. It was Horton's goal."

Creedy was still too busy scribbling his notes about the equaliser to provide his readers with any details of the "four-man flowing move" that ended with Allan Brown hammering Blackpool's second goal with 48 minutes played. He was quick, however, to return to familiar terrain in attempting to analyse the action in front of him. That Blackpool were taking control was due to "forwards using the long pass to great effect". It was a common complaint of reporters of the era to blame any malfunction in forward play on attempts at a short passing game; just as an effective long-ball game was usually highlighted when things went well.

In fact, with Southampton running out of steam as the game went into its final quarter, a little more care and precision over their passing close to goal could have seen Blackpool creating more opportunities to extend their lead. Creedy would later also ascribe the fightback to the "inspiration of Farm, crisp tackling of Kelly and the whole-hearted efforts of Shimwell". Eventually Johnston was able to say: "At the finish we were playing like a First Division side."

* * * * *

WITH 39 minutes played at Wembley, disarray in the Blackpool defence allows Bolton to regain the lead – only four minutes after relinquishing it. Holden knocks the ball forward to the left edge of the Blackpool box, only for Fenton to arrive first. Yet the Blackpool right-half hesitates, apparently afraid to desert his designated zone and move out as far as the left touchline to claim the loose ball. Instead, he allows Holden to regain possession and run towards the box before laying it back and inside for Bobby Langton, who clips left-footed towards the far post. Arriving late, Willie Moir runs across George Farm's line of sight. As both men stretch for the ball – Moir with head and Farm with fist – it continues unimpeded on its path and nestles in the far bottom corner of the goal. Blackpool's players exchange disbelieving looks. They have been dominant for a long period, have come back to level the game and are up against only ten fit men. Yet they are behind again.

According to Kenneth Wolstenholme, it had been "a nasty, swervy, swinging ball" but it is still another disaster for Farm, now culpable for both Bolton goals. Even when

England goalkeeper Gil Merrick attempts to convince him after the game that he has been unlucky, Farm insists: "Nothing of the kind. I just made a mess of them." He admits later: "I would not have known what to do with myself if we had lost. I made some stupid mistakes. I don't know what went wrong with me. I suppose it was just that it was the Cup Final."

The injured Allan Brown both sympathises with his team-mate's plight and fears for further mishaps. "If George was as jittery as I was on the touchline, then it's a wonder he didn't let a few more through," he comments later.

* * * * *

SIGNED IN September 1948 for £2,700 from Hibernian, where he was third-team goalkeeper, Farm had already played in one Wembley final and represented Scotland, but this occasion certainly appeared to undermine his performance. "I'd seen George Farm collect such balls effortlessly on many occasions," Stanley Matthews observed of the second Bolton goal. "They were meat and drink to him."

Possessing the strong build required of a goalkeeper in the days of robust centre-forwards and little protection from officialdom, Farm did, however, have a far from classical method of catching. Instead of placing one hand on either side of the ball he would position his arms horizontally to put one hand on top and the other on the lower part of the ball. Criticism of his technique followed him around, but he was never afraid to spend additional time on the training ground perfecting it, urging colleagues to delay their games of snooker or golf to fire shots at him from all angles. "If ever I begin to suspect that something is going a little wrong with my game, I begin those afternoon practices again," he once explained.

Matthews described Farm as one of the greatest competitors he encountered in football; someone who treated an FA Cup tie or a five-a-side training game with the same intensity. A defeat in either would find him hurling his cap and gloves at his dressing-room peg and lighting up the air with his curses. Agile, brave and unconcerned about which part of his body he used to pull off a save, it is unfortunate for his legacy that the game in his 12-year Blackpool career that is remembered most is the one where he had a stinker.

Jimmy Armfield, who would play in front of Farm at right-back for several years, explained: "George went on after that final to be a really great goalkeeper. He was the most meticulous player I ever met. He took real pride in his appearance. He manicured his nails, hands and toenails and so important was it for him to look smart that he was the last to be ready in the dressing room."

Farm, who played seven times for his country and once scored against Preston from centre-forward after injuring his elbow, was also described by Armfield as "an enormously popular team player". Yet his inherent shyness meant that he was never entirely comfortable with any kind of attention from the fans.

"If we had lost the final they would have said it was his fault," said Cyril Robinson. "But he was all right, George. He was a funny character. He was very reluctant to sign autographs. He would just walk past. He was a man unto himself somehow; he would brush kids away and wouldn't sign. There weren't many players who would do that. He didn't want to be bothered."

Future FA chief executive Graham Kelly was one of those youngsters who experienced Farm's moodiness first hand. "He spent hours on his pedicure after training and was a terrible grouch when he eventually appeared at the players' entrance, glowering at the two or three kids still there while their lunch was going cold on mum's kitchen table."

After making a comment along the lines of "didn't I give it to you yesterday?" Farm would, on a good day, sign his name "Geo Farm" with his own fountain pen, although Kelly added: "You had to be particularly careful about which photograph to select for his autograph. It would have been a very reckless child who asked Farm to sign anything from the 1953 Cup Final, when he let in a couple of soft goals."

* * * * *

IF THE second Bolton goal has been aided in its set-up partly by the defensive inflexibility of the day – Fenton's refusal to pursue the ball too far to the left – then Blackpool are at least displaying more fluidity in their attacking positions. Matthews comes inside to combine with Taylor and Mudie but between them they are unable to find the final pass to set up Perry, who has turned up on the right.

Moments later Holden feeds the ball inside, receives a return pass from Langton and brings a collective gasp from the 100,000 crowd with a cross that, although mishit, drifts dangerously close to the crossbar of the nervous Farm. Wolstenholme puts it down to the way that "the wind swirling around can just lift these balls".

Perry runs strongly down the left, Taylor takes over and, as the ball runs loose, Mudie is fouled 25 yards out. Taylor plays the free-kick quickly to Matthews on the right and his cross is comfortably handled at full stretch by a leaping Hanson. "He's an old baseball player so he knows how to catch balls like that," explains Wolstenholme.

Then Lofthouse advances into the box on the right and hits a deep cross. The encumbered Bell is unable to attack the ball but recovers sufficiently to work it back to Langton, whose low drive – which looks as laboured as most other long shots in the game – is dealt with comfortably by the diving Farm. It is the last meaningful action of a first half in which Langton and Lofthouse have been dangerous for Bolton going forward and Ball and Barrass sound at the back. Matthews has been a marginal presence but still looks the class of the Blackpool team, with Taylor's energy and close skill making him a consistent threat.

In Blackpool's dressing room, manager Joe Smith is keen to convey a mood of calm. "You can beat this bloody lot; just keep playing your normal game," he reassures his team.

With Bolton effectively a man short, he does, however, suggest an increased tempo. "Quicken it up. The passing is too slow and too precise," he urges, before warning Matthews not to drop too deep and instructing Taylor to give him the ball as often as possible.

Typically, captain Johnston is more vocal in his instructions. "Tighten up," he tells his fellow defenders. "Ewan, get Stan more into the game. Morty, get into the box and make a nuisance of yourself. Eddie, Tommy, Cyril and me, we will deal with the rough and tumble and win the ball and I'll take care of Lofthouse. You lot who can play, do your bit. We've got the ball players to win this Cup, so let's get out and bloody well win it."

* * * * *

THE ACTION that the Wembley crowd were left to discuss while the players took their break was not vastly different to that which Bolton fans would have seen during any of their team's three Wembley appearances in the 1920s and pretty well identical in character to any match played in the 1930s.

Nor was there much difference in appearance and style among the participants. The shorts were still long and baggy, the jerseys heavy and the footwear cumbersome. It would not be until after the 1954 World Cup that button-up jerseys were regularly replaced by lighter slip-on tops and boots were cut away around the heel. Until then, the Hotshot football boot, officially endorsed by the FA, continued to reach a couple of inches above the ankle and offered reinforced toe-caps and protection. It had scarcely been altered in two decades. The balls had at least evolved a little and now featured dubbin to add a degree of water resistance, although it still took bravery and a tough skull to risk a header during the second half of a game played in the rain.

Courage and heading ability was a vital component of a game that continued to rely on a fundamental attacking basis of the WM formation; getting the ball forward as expediently as possible. Bolton defender Malcolm Barrass said: "That was our normal game; play it quickly and up the field. Long ball. Bang. The longer the better. You hoped you got on the end of it. The best way we could play it was kick and rush and we had players who could do it. Sides had to sacrifice the ball sometimes and lose the advantage. Blackpool did the same. Matthews held the ball up, but that might have been a disadvantage to them because we made sure we got back."

Once the ball had gone forward, it was transferred to the wingers, who were expected to get behind the defence to cross for an onrushing centre-forward. Herbert Chapman had long since described this as "a senseless policy" and even England captain Billy Wright would later deride his nation's football tactics of the time as: "Transfer the ball from the centre of the field to a winger, who makes as much ground as he can before crossing into the heart of an overcrowded penalty area."

Bolton outside-right Doug Holden added: "Wing play was the thing then. Football changed a bit later in 1953 when the Hungarians beat us because it set some people thinking, although others just carried on the same."

The WM, so-named because of the shapes formed by the front five and back five when looked at in formation on a team sheet, meant that wingers generally had space when they received the ball and were placed to beat their opponents with a well-timed burst of speed. This was especially true if the attacking team had quickly switched flanks, catching out the full-back as he moved infield to help protect the centre-half.

Even before Hungary reached Wembley in November 1953, observers had seen that more continental teams were turning to a back four, where the full-backs were able to play wider and deny space to the outside-forwards. English crowds had been given a glimpse of such tactics as early as the famous 1945 visit of Dynamo Moscow. Yet while wing play was beginning to fade from European fashion, it was more *à la mode* than ever in England. In fact, it had increased in popularity during wartime football, part of a general increase in attacking play. With players being part-timers, fitness and speed was less prevalent, meaning that one quick, sprightly wide man could wreak havoc.

The trend continued in the immediate years after the war and it was no coincidence that the game's two biggest draws, Matthews and Finney, were wingers. Author Jonathan Wilson points out in *The Anatomy Of England* that the prevalence of wing play also had a certain pragmatism attached to it, noting: "The concentration on the flanks was possibly an effect of conditions, that dribbling was only possible away from the centre, which had the tendency in the winter to become a mud bath; or it may be that it was simply that the hurly burly, blood-and-thunder of the English game meant creativity was possible only on the periphery."

The *FA Yearbook* for 1952/53 had at least picked up on some subtle changes creeping into the English game by virtue of wingers such as Matthews and Finney more frequently collecting the ball from deep positions. "Many club wingers have adopted this method, but it is open to the criticism that as a result they are seldom far enough forward to run for the diagonal pass behind the opposing full back." The article argued that it had led to a greater interchange of positions between forwards and prompted some defences to adopt a zonal system rather than more aggressive man-to-man marking.

No one would have realised it as the band's final half-time notes faded away, but the second 45 minutes of the 1953 FA Cup Final were to represent the pinnacle – and the death throes – of old-fashioned wing play. The match, underpinned by the romantic human tale of Matthews, served to reinforce the widely held view that England was the dominant football force; its style of play the ideal template for the world game. As Wilson notes: "At times the English obsession with wingers bordered on the pathological: England's greatest strength was also its greatest weakness."

Hungary would soon arrive and tear down the English game's misconceptions. By the time Sir Alf Ramsey restored the nation, temporarily, to the pinnacle in 1966, he did so with his team of "wingless wonders", where a three-man midfield sat in front of a holding player in Nobby Stiles and the width came from Alan Ball drifting out towards the wing or full-backs George Cohen and Ray Wilson being encouraged to advance into enemy territory.[18]

On this spring Saturday in May 1953, however, no one at Wembley or among the millions watching or listening around the country would have had a word said against the efficacy of wing play or the man who, over the previous 20 years, had become its greatest exponent.

· · · · · · · · · · · ·

18 Publishers appeared slower to catch on to what had been happening in the game over the previous decade. As late as 1966, a book called *Soccer Science*, most of it attributed to George Eastham, was running a chapter devoted to each position on the field, using the old WM as its basis, including wing-halves, inside-forwards and wing-forwards.

8

THE PEOPLE'S CHAMPION

"We remember him as a slightly humped, stiff-looking figure, rather like a Meccano man, darting suddenly towards and away from transfixed defenders, the ball not kicked by his feet but nudged between them, deftly and gently like butter being chopped up by a two-pat grocer." – Arthur Hopcraft, *The Football Man.*

IT WAS a simple rubber ball that helped turn Stanley Matthews into the great player he was universally acknowledged to be; the kind of sportsman to whom a nation was happy to give its wholehearted support as he strove to achieve his burning ambition. Whether banging that childhood toy against a wall for hours on end, or taking it down to the local waste ground with friends, Matthews never let it out of his sight.

In that respect, the man who would figuratively stand apart from most of his fellow professionals was just like the majority of his peers. "All we did was kick a ball around the street," said Doug Holden, who would wear the opposition's number seven jersey in the 1953 final. "We ran to school kicking a tennis ball, kicking it against the wall and trapping it. Everything is so coached and organised now from a young age, but we did our own thing."

By the age of nine, as a child growing up in the Staffordshire town of Hanley,[19] Matthews had advanced to dribbling his ball around strategically placed chairs in his back garden. "Any ball control I displayed later in life as a professional footballer can be traced back to those times," he acknowledged.

One of four brothers, he had initially been reluctant to admit to his father, Jack, that he had no intention of following the paternal sporting route into the boxing ring. But as Jack, a barber, watched his teenaged son's dedication to rising early to work on fitness and speed, he was driven to offer assistance, forging a close bond between father and son. No one was more proud than Jack when Stan was chosen to represent England Schoolboys and, at 14, was offered the chance to sign as an apprentice for Stoke City – an opportunity at which he jumped, despite being a fan of local rivals Port Vale.

It was a memorable first day at the Victoria Ground, where he was ordered to clean two changing rooms by trainer Jimmy Vallance, but also met Vallance's daughter, Betty, who was to become his first wife. His first season with the club, 1930/31, not only taught him the skills of a skivvy and an office boy, it also offered him the valuable realisation that he needed to adjust his style of wing play to achieve more consistent success. "In those days you waited until the defender was on top of you and then

. . . .

19 Hanley was one of six towns that joined together in 1910 to form Stoke-on-Trent.

tried to jink your way round him," he explained in his autobiography.

To remedy the occasions when such an approach didn't work, he developed a strategy to run straight at the full-back rather than waiting to invite the challenge. A successful experiment in a reserve game against Manchester City convinced him of this method. "Once on top of him, I'd put into operation the body swerve I'd been cultivating." This involved thrusting his body in one direction to make the opponent commit himself and then veering off in the other direction. "Sometimes all it needed was a drop of the shoulder."

Often followed by a cross that hovered around the penalty spot and left the goalkeeper uncertain of his best course of action, it was to become his trademark move, described thus by Arthur Hopcraft in *The Football Man*:

> When he moved with the ball, shuffling, leaning, edging ever closer to the defender, he was always the man teetering to the very brink of disaster, and we waited breathlessly to see whether this time he would fail or whether yet again he would come swaying back at the last possible moment to run on clear and free.

A playing career that would extend into a fourth decade began in earnest when Matthews signed as a full-time professional for Stoke on his 17th birthday in 1932, despite approaches from other teams. He became one of 40 full-time players at the club and, because of the salary restrictions of the time, found himself earning as much as many much more experienced men. Matthews was not about to let such relative riches go to his head. After training on most days he would spend another two hours working on his skills – roping in first-team defenders or youth players to help out – and undertaking short sprints to maximise his speed off the mark. Even before reporting to the training ground he would have been up at 7am to carry out stretching, sprints, longer runs and general exercises before breakfast. Such a routine, instilled by his father at an early age, had long since become habit.

By the 1937/38 season, he had scored 38 goals in four seasons in Stoke's first team, but found he was being marked more and more tightly. This prompted the second major tactical rethink of his career; the habit of dropping deeper in order to collect the ball in more space. As Holden said: "When you came back as winger, it gave the full-back the problem of what to do. Did he go with you?"

Maurice Reeday, a full-back with Leicester City, was one of the few opponents Matthews recalled making life difficult by shadowing him into those more withdrawn areas. "Haven't you got a home to go to?" a frustrated Matthews asked him during one encounter. "Yes, but it won't blow over before the game's over," came the quick reply.

Blackpool's Cyril Robinson, who played left-back against Matthews in practice games, explained: "The only way to get the better of him was to stand next to him. I stood by him when he was on the touchline and the ball was on the other side. He knew it was going to come across. He said: 'You shouldn't be here, Cyril. You should be in the middle because that ball is going to come across. You should cover the middle.' If he got the ball a yard or two away from you he would beat you. He would give you the body swerve, push the ball with the outside of his foot and he was gone. He might have done the same thing all the time but you still couldn't stop him. Some players you could weigh up, but not Stan. He was brilliant."

Arsenal's Walley Barnes, writing in his autobiography, gave this description of the task facing any full-back in opposition to Matthews:

Stan would reach out a foot to bring it under control and at once the ball appeared to become his personal property. He would not part with it until the opposition had been thoroughly undermined and confused, or until a colleague was in position to receive a gift opportunity from which to score.

Stanley's habit was to take the ball right up under the nose of his opponent, inviting – or rather demanding – a tackle. Sometimes he would stop dead in his tracks to force a defender to take the initiative. Meantime his fellow forwards raced into unmarked positions. Eventually the defender moved into the tackle, to one side or the other. Whichever way he chose, quick-witted Stan picked the right trick to hoodwink him. Once the defender moved a foot forwards towards the ball, Stan knew that his weight must be upon it, and during the instant while the defender was off balance he was ripe for beating.

Eddie Shimwell remembered the first time he faced Matthews. "He had such uncanny balance and speed off the mark," he said. "When I went in to tackle and thought the ball was mine, he whipped it away and was gone, and I was left high and dry."

The fact that Matthews would often drop back in search of the ball, as he did frequently in the 1953 final, could make him an even greater threat to the opposition. Often defenders would feel secure because of the distance away from their goal and believed that, even if beaten, they would have time for a further attempt at a tackle or for a team-mate to cover. Rarely did that second opportunity present itself as a burst of speed took Matthews clear and his cross or pass eluded any late-arriving reinforcements.

As well as attacking from deep, Matthews also made a conscious decision to cut inside for the penalty area less often and to concentrate instead on getting the ball to the by-line. These factors would combine to make him a more effective creator – eliminating the possibility of any offside decisions – but also resulted in a drastic reduction in his goals. He would score only 32 further goals in almost three more decades in League football.

Bolton defender Malcolm Barrass recalled Matthews as "a great fellow" and explained: "He didn't run back as quick as the others. If he got trapped by the corner flag he usually did a little victory roll and stopped there longer than some other players. But he was very capable of working his way inside from that kind of position, so it didn't happen very often."

The town that was to give Matthews the most successful years of his career had already begun to feature strongly in his life even before he found himself in the orange jersey of Blackpool Football Club. It was there he sought refuge during a difficult time at Stoke in the final season of football before the war. Ironically, he sold Betty on the idea by assuring her: "No one knows me there. We'll be able to get some peace and quiet."

His need for escape had arisen after he had heard stories of discontent among Stoke players resentful of his heightened profile. He suggested to the club that a transfer might be wise, but changed his mind after 3,000 fans attended a meeting intended to demonstrate the strength of feeling about such a move. One local firm had even announced: "Some of our employees are so upset at the prospect of losing him that they cannot do their work." Yet this would not be the final example during his career of rumblings of jealousy among team-mates.

The outbreak of war took Matthews back to the Fylde coast, his RAF posting finding him living just outside what he described as "this bright and breezy seaside town". As well as undertaking his basic training, he learned that the War Office wanted professional footballers to play as much as possible in order to provide entertainment and keep up public morale. Therefore he became an integral part of Blackpool's success in wartime football. According to another of the club's heroes at that time, Jock Dodds, speaking to author Michael Prestage in *Blackpool: The Glory Years Remembered*: "[Matthews] was at his peak when I played with him during the war and he was a magician... for the poor full-back, it was a case of now you see it now you don't when he had the ball."

Meanwhile, struck by the contrast between the bustling and busy Golden Mile and the tranquillity of the sand dunes on the edge of town, Matthews found living by the sea "a source of inspiration". Although initially worried that soft sand would put additional strain on his muscles, he soon began training regularly on the harder parts of the shoreline, including his daily four-mile run. Invigorated by his surroundings and with the proceeds of guest football appearances having supplemented his RAF wartime pay, Matthews invested in purchasing the Romford Private Hotel on the South Promenade.[20]

Back in Stoke's colours, Matthews resumed what he felt had never been a warm relationship with manager Bob McGrory. His boss, he believed, was reluctant to include his star player in any praise for a good team performance. "Although I'd describe our relationship for the most part as amiable, I never felt [he] batted for me at the club," was how Matthews described the situation. The fact that he was now living in Blackpool and training with the Seasiders rather than with his own club did nothing to bring the two men closer.

. . . .

20 These days the building is the Feng Shui House, one of the country's first hotels to be completely designed in line with the ancient Chinese practice of living in harmony with the environment. One suspects that Matthews, quick to embrace new and innovative ideas, would approve.

Having missed a series of games during the 1946/47 season with a knee injury, Matthews found that he was not restored to the team immediately he was fit again. Instead, he was given the option of playing in the reserves, an invitation he declined, believing there was no need for him to prove his physical health. Inevitably, the absence of Matthews prompted all kinds of speculation. Some suggested he had fallen out once more with McGrory; others that the Stoke first-team players had not wanted him back in their ranks. For a while, things appeared to have been patched up and Matthews was particularly pleased to have played well in a 4-1 victory over Blackpool in December in order to stifle gossip that he was suffering from mixed loyalties.

Back in the England team at the age of 32, he remained, he sensed, in McGrory's dog house and was left out of an Easter game against Huddersfield after he had already started getting changed. He believed it was a move deliberately designed to humiliate him. His mood deteriorated even more two weeks later when he discovered second-hand that he was only in the team to face Brentford because of an injury to a team-mate. He travelled home from the game convinced it was time to leave the Victoria Ground. "I felt a change of club would do me the world of good, rekindle the fire within and motivate me to even greater achievement."

Initially, his transfer request was denied, but then pragmatic club chairman Harry Booth asked Matthews if there was a particular club he would like contacted. With Stoke challenging for the title, there was an agreement to keep events under wraps to prevent any distractions, but once more the interest in Matthews made such secrecy impossible. The newspapers were full of discussion about his potential new employers. Worried about passing up possible bookings for his hotel, Matthews couldn't even ignore his telephone when it rang and spent hours trying to deflect questions about his future.

As it turned out, his new employer would come calling from just down the road. Blackpool manager Joe Smith had seen enough of Matthews at close quarters to have no fears about the effects of age on the England winger. After training, Smith approached Matthews. "I know you can give me at least two years," he said conspiratorially. "I'd be confident of putting you up against racing pigeons."

After helping Stoke to victory in his final game for them against Leeds, his transfer was concluded for a fee of £11,500; not the £20,000 originally demanded but still a considerable amount for a time when the record British fee was still the £14,500 Arsenal had paid Wolves for Bryn Jones before the war. Blackpool secretary William Parkinson, whom Matthews had discovered during the war to be "the most benevolent of men", handed over a cheque for the full amount to Booth. Stoke eventually missed the title on the final day when Liverpool beat Sheffield United to overhaul them. In a tight season, Stoke finished fourth, although only two points off the top. Even though Blackpool would come third four years later, this was – by points margin – the closest Matthews ever came to a championship medal.

The move of England's most famous player formed part of a post-war boom in transfer activity. Before the end of the year, a new record fee had been set on two occasions; first when inside-forward Billy Steel went from Morton to Derby for £15,500 and then when England centre-forward Tommy Lawton became the first £20,000 signing with his transfer from Chelsea to Notts County. The fact that a Third Division side had enough money to achieve this landmark is evidence of the money that was washing through the game.

Transfer activity at all levels was accelerating as teams completed evaluations of their squad strength after a six-year break from competitive play. In many cases clubs found they had to act quickly, a prime example being Charlton Athletic, who won the FA Cup in 1947 with only five of the men who had lost in the final 12 months earlier. Signing young talent became a less viable option because of National Service call-ups so demand grew for experienced players. Arsenal responded to a relegation battle in 1946/47 by signing old pros Joe Mercer and Ronnie Rooke, both in their mid-30s, and won the League a year later.

If Matthews had been suspicious of his relationship with his previous manager, then there was no disguising the near awe in which he was held by his new boss. "Play your own game, Stan," Smith told him before his Blackpool debut against Chelsea at the start of the new season. "There are no shackles here. You have freedom of mind and style to express yourself. Whatever you do out on the pitch, do it in the knowledge that you have my full support."

The view that Smith went too far in support of his older players in general, and Matthews in particular, would be borne out, according to the team's junior member, Cyril Robinson, by the manager's actions immediately after the final whistle at Wembley in 1953. "When we finished the Cup Final there was only one player he ran to. That was Matthews. He didn't shake hands with me and I don't think he did with many. Stan was brilliant but in a Cup Final when you have come from 3-1 behind you would think he would go round the team. I think it was too much trouble for him."

It had been defeat to Manchester United in the FA Cup Final at the end of his first season – after he had been named as the inaugural Footballer of the Year – that had provided Matthews's team-mates with further proof of the calm nature of his character. Harry Johnston had told his colleague "you have ice in your veins", yet Matthews viewed the cool head that helped him out of tight corners against opponents as part of the same personality that allowed him to accept Wembley defeat with "realism and unemotional acceptance".

He wrote: "By not allowing yourself to ride the emotional pendulum you temper disappointment, disillusionment, even depression and keep yourself on an even keel." It was an approach entirely out of sync with the passion and emotion he could instil in those watching him play, but was a reflection of the common sense approach that ensured he made the most of his fame and its attendant business opportunities.

Once hauled over the coals by the FA for claiming an extra sixpence for a tea and scone during a train journey to join up with the England party for a game at Hampden Park, Matthews was not shy of accepting earning opportunities when they came his way. In the summer of 1949, he even became part of the Blackpool entertainment scene when he and brother Ronnie played head tennis over an on-stage net as a variety bill support act.

His selection, albeit delayed, for the ill-fated England squad at the 1950 World Cup[21] impacted upon one deal that became a regular part of his matchday routine. Impressed by the lightweight, foot-hugging boots worn by the Brazilians – cut lower on the ankle and heel than the traditional English style and lacking the heavy toe-cap – he took a pair home and asked his own bootmaker to copy the style. His view was that losing the ankle protection offered by a heavier boot was a worthwhile trade for being quicker off the mark and made him less likely to be kicked in the first place.

Matthews found that he would wear out a pair in only three or four games, but when he signed a deal to promote Co-op boots he paid them to make the new boots for him

. . . .

21 He was summoned from an FA XI exhibition tour of Canada, but played only one match, missing the infamous 1-0 defeat to the United States at Belo Horizonte.

in their factory in Heckmondwike in Yorkshire. The deal earned him £15 a week – more than he earned at Blackpool – and required him to make personal appearances at sports stores around the country on the morning of away games, usually for a couple of hours between 9am and 11am. This was indulged by Joe Smith, who knew Matthews had been up at 6am to carry out his daily training routine. Future BBC commentator John Motson, raised in south-east London, was one of those who attended a department store appearance before a game at Charlton. "When I was growing up in Lewisham, [Matthews] was undoubtedly the most famous footballer in the country. He sat at a table in the store and we all queued up for his autograph. I remember being very shy and just said: 'Thank you very much.'"

Other commercial activities included advertising health foods and Smith's Watches, with pictures of him and son Stanley junior appearing next to the slogan: "A real man's watch and a good boy's watch." He even promoted Craven cigarettes – "The cigarettes for me" – in newspaper advertisements, despite admitting: "I've never smoked a cigarette in my life."

He was the first footballer to put his name to a newspaper column while still an active player, Ken Abram crafting Matthews's thoughts and opinions into articles for the *Sunday Express.* And there was money to be made from guest appearances in testimonial matches, the beneficiaries being more than happy to take care of Matthews in return for the boost he gave to the gate receipts. Journalist Mike Langley recalled Josh McCosh telling him of his successful benefit match for Dublin club Drumcondra. "I got in touch with Stan, offered to fly him from Blackpool and back in a day with £500 in notes for playing."

The fact that Matthews made many times more money from activities off the field than he ever did for simply playing kept him immune from some of his peers' grumbles about their lot as professionals. It was easier for him to say "I didn't feel I was very much underpaid" than some of his contemporaries, one of whom, Ernie Taylor, was recalled by Langley after Matthews's death as describing his famous team-mate as "the meanest man in football". Although the two men had enjoyed an almost telepathic understanding on the field, colleague Cyril Robinson added: "I think that Ernie always thought Matthews got a lot of publicity and opportunities and that he was missing out a little bit."

Nor did Matthews's elevated status in public consciousness and affection always hold sway with the England selectors. As well as being an afterthought for the 1950 World Cup, he was dropped by his country no fewer than 12 times throughout his career, sometimes in favour of Tom Finney, who on other occasions would play on the left so that both of England's great wingers could be accommodated. There is a story, probably apocryphal, of Finney replacing Matthews for one game and crossing for Stan Mortensen to head two goals, only for the Blackpool centre-forward to clutch his head and complain to Finney: "Stanley centres the ball so that the lace points away from me."

Bolton and England centre-forward Nat Lofthouse felt that Matthews "wasn't as easy to play with as Tom", suggesting that Finney would cross the ball to the number nine's favourite location whereas Matthews delivered the ball according to his own preference, meaning that it was "up to me to be there when it arrived". Lofthouse came to recognise that Matthews would habitually send the ball towards the penalty spot and it was down to him to anticipate how quickly he would reach the by-line and cross the ball. "The secret was to be thundering in just as that ball floated over the penalty spot. Nine times out of ten it would come."

While football amused itself with the ongoing Matthews–Finney debate, there was no doubt where support lay within their respective club dressing rooms. According to Bill Perry: "In Preston they always said they would rather have Finney in the team than Matthews, but I know that when Matthews was playing we always felt as if we had a goal start."

During the 23-year span of his England career, Matthews played only 54 times, frequently hearing accusations that he held on to the ball for too long. Others found England's reluctance to ink him into the team puzzling. Hungarian captain Ferenc Puskas called him "the very, very all-time greatest", while Finney argued: "There was nothing Stan liked more than playing on the big stages. He always seemed to bring his best football to the biggest games."

In particular, Charles Buchan always maintained that the presence of Matthews would have averted the disaster against the USA. "[His selection] would have had an important psychological effect on the American defenders and the inclusion of fresh new forwards would have added life and thrust to the most vital part of the team."

For his own part, Matthews was frequently perplexed by the haphazard nature of England's organisation, especially in the earlier stage of his career. Typically, the team would congregate the day before a game and receive a briefing on the morning of the match by whichever club trainer had been given the honour of looking after the team. The notion of continuity was as foreign as the idea of tactics. Matthews's recollection of a team talk before a pre-war game against Scotland was that "it wasn't worth the cost of hiring the private room".

According to former Irish international Johnny Giles, though, Matthews himself was not the deepest thinker about the game. Dickie Giles, a club manager in Ireland, told his son: "[Stan]'s a lovely man, but his knowledge of the game isn't great." Giles junior said he experienced that himself when he and a group of Leeds players chatted to Matthews in Dublin at a testimonial dinner for Liam Brady.

The 1950/51 season was memorable for the way in which Matthews led a Blackpool comeback for a dramatic 4-4 draw at Arsenal and the runaround he gave to Billy Wright when the Wolves and England captain was switched to left-back in an attempt to combat Blackpool's greatest threat. Matthews responded by setting up two goals for Mortensen.

It was the FA Cup Final that offered the greatest opportunity for indelible memories, though; opportunities that Newcastle were determined to grab for themselves. Preparing for the game at Buxton, where Blackpool would soon base their own out-of-town training, Newcastle decided to effectively double-team Matthews at Wembley, with either full-back Bobby Corbett or wing-half Charlie Crowe – whoever was closer – responsible for marking the winger. According to team-mate Jackie Mudie: "[Stan] was more nervous beforehand than anyone else in the team. He under-performed like the rest of us."

It added up to another Wembley setback – and another scene of dressing-room disappointment to be carved deep into his consciousness. He would recall the "almost trance-like state" that pervaded the team's inner sanctum; no words, no movement among the players sitting wearily underneath the street clothes hanging above their heads. Harry Johnston sat with a cup of tea in one hand and his second loser's medal in the other. For ten minutes he gazed distantly at the floor before silently slipping his medal into his jacket, picking up a towel and heading for the bath. The words of consolation offered by manager Smith bounced off each player's wall of introspection. Even the usually-lively Mortensen could do no more than absent-mindedly inspect a cut on his ankle before he, too, headed for the soothing water, leaving his medal on his bench. Players gazed without any trace of recognition at their colleagues.

The last player to remove his dirty kit was goalkeeper George Farm.

For a second time Matthews fought to be pragmatic and bury his disappointment, which he later admitted was probably the less healthy way of dealing with it. But those Wembley dressing room scenes were ones that he would replay in his mind when new FA Cup campaigns began – along with painful, immovable pictures of the day his father had died.

Lying in his hospital bed in 1945, Jack had struggled to lift himself up in order to whisper in his son's ear, making sure that none of the other family members present were able to hear. As well as making him promise to look after his mother he told him to fulfil the one remaining ambition he held for Stan's football career; to win the FA Cup. Within a few minutes he had died and Matthews never mentioned the conversation to anyone, not even close relatives. Even when he had delivered on his promise he decided to keep hidden the kind of human-interest story that even the less invasive media of the 1950s would have killed for, finally mentioning it only in the autobiography he published in 2000.

An ankle injury that dogged his 1951/52 season allowed Matthews more time than he would have desired to attend to affairs at his hotel. He helped with cleaning, restocking, reordering and even acted as a driver for his guests. Far from resenting the chores, he felt grateful that he had a business interest that was providing for him beyond football and preventing him from searching for summer jobs like many players he knew. It was at this time that he met an osteopath called Arthur Millward, a vegetarian, who introduced Matthews to the value of reducing his intake of red meat in favour of greater quantities of fish, fresh fruit and vegetables. He had already adopted the practice of cleansing his body by eating nothing at all on Mondays.

On the day of a game, Matthews's light breakfast would be followed, if playing at home, by a walk on the beach, a cold shower, some midday toast and another walk of one mile to Bloomfield Road. On arrival he would shower again and have a massage from trainer John Lynas. Matthews welcomed the pre-match nerves he often felt – "you've got to have butterflies" – and before big games he would usually be sick, claiming: "I felt it did me good, ridding my stomach of partially digested food that might lie heavy and impair my performance."

As eccentric as some of his practices might have seemed, they were, according to team-mate Hugh Kelly, what "kept him at the top long after his contemporaries had retired". Kelly explained: "Nobody took any notice that Stan didn't work out with us, but did his own thing. He had an agreement with the club and he was so respected. He also played a lot of tennis on his own court at home."

Robinson, however, felt that Smith "wrapped him in cotton wool", adding: "Stan was his favourite; he was a good signing. If Stan had been injured Joe would tell me to go and test him out. Not kick him, but just knock him a bit. Then he'd ask: 'You all right, Stan?' When you got to know Stan, he was laid back. You didn't discuss things with him; a bit of chatter, that was all. He went his own way. He was all right, but he was a bit different to the others and he kept to himself."

Jackie Mudie told Matthews biographer David Miller: "Undoubtedly there was a bit of envy and jealousy about him within the club," citing Taylor and even Mortensen as those who held such feelings. "Stan never went to the pubs, never went in and out of the players' entrance, but always through a side door. He didn't mix a lot, seldom went anywhere, always dashed off home." Mudie also suggested that Smith was guilty of favouritism and recalled: "In my time I complained about that."

Bill Perry described Matthews as "a loner", recalling him playing in five-a-sides and the Tuesday practice match against the reserve team but doing the rest of his training by himself. "He used to go into the gym with a ball. I'm still not sure what he did."

England colleague Lofthouse felt Matthews was "easy to get on with" and cited an example of him preventing American photographers taking a picture during an FA tour until his colleagues arrived. "Just a moment, gentlemen," Matthews instructed. "We have come here as a team and we shall have a team picture."

Lofthouse once said that there were only three things Matthews did not like: swearing, smoking and "the ball three yards either side of him". He explained: "Stanley knew exactly what he wanted. He was precise in everything… I've seen him come off the field in a Wembley international because his boots didn't feel quite right."

Joe Smith noted of Matthews that he was "an object lesson" but that "he didn't say a lot". Indeed, as willing as he might have been to share his theories with anyone who showed an interest, Matthews never tried to impose his methods on others and even admitted to being reticent of passing along his experience to junior colleagues. "I always felt that if I tried to help some of the younger players, it was going against the coach," he said.

Mudie admitted, however, that Matthews would bully him on the pitch and recalled going for six months without speaking to him after Matthews berated him for making a joke at his expense during a summer tour in which the England legend had been a reluctant participant.

On the field, though, there was no disguising the esteem in which Matthews was held by his colleagues. Mudie noted that "his speed of footwork bamboozled even the best defenders" and Allan Brown, speaking in 2000 for *Blackpool: The Glory Years Remembered*, said: "There isn't a player in football today who has his talent. Nobody can take on a player and beat him the way he did." Robinson continued: "His ball control was 100 per cent and his crosses were good, playing with the ball we did. Even new, it was heavy."

Interviewed by Brian Viner in *The Independent* in 2003, Perry insisted that Matthews could "cross the ball like Beckham" and gave a glowing account of his illustrious colleague. "When Stan got the ball anywhere near the halfway line, the rest of the forward line would just put their heads down and head for the goalmouth. I remember once playing against Aston Villa in the League. I have never seen a full-back so tormented. In the first half he jumped in as soon as Matthews got the ball, and Stan just beat him on either side. By the second half the manager had told this fellow to stand off him, but it didn't help. I remember Stan getting the ball on the halfway line and just walking with it towards the full-back, who was back-pedalling. He must have walked 15 yards. He would just demoralise them. Sometimes he'd beat them, then wait for them to come back and take them on again."

By the beginning of the 1952/53 season, recent injuries had raised questions about Matthews's effectiveness. There was even talk of Stoke being interested in re-signing him. Smith, conscious of his star player's determination to win at Wembley, was having none of it. "You think that we're destined never to win the FA Cup," he told him. "Well, I don't believe that to be the case. If I did, I wouldn't be sitting here now. I have every faith in you. I believe your best football is still to come."

Matthews himself was bothered even less by the rumblings that, with his 38th birthday being celebrated during the season, he should be considering retirement. Age to him was all in the mind. If he had a poor game, critics would put it down to age; Matthews preferred to believe it was merely the fluctuating fortunes that affect players of all ages. Once Blackpool had advanced as far as the quarter-finals of the Cup, so began the chatter about the possibility of him crowning his career with a winner's medal at Wembley. It was a prize that not one person in the country seemed to begrudge him.

In fact, it is impossible at the distance of six decades to appreciate the reverence in which Matthews was held by the British public. There is simply no parallel in the modern media age, when celebrities are built up and knocked down with bewildering speed and ruthlessness. There was no edge to the reports of his play or his life; no sense of people waiting for him to fall or tabloids attempting to catch him with his trousers down.

There was an innocence about the adulation surrounding him that was not merely the result of the gentler media of the time. That Blackpool were for many years the biggest draw in the game was down mostly to the public's love of Matthews. "Blackpool put 10,000 on the gate wherever they played, especially if Matthews was in the team," recalled fan Mel McCarthy. "They always used to keep it quiet if Stan had an injury because it would spoil the gate. He was the number one footballer in Europe at that time."

Even in the latter years of his career, when he was playing through his late 40s with Stoke, fans felt robbed if he was not in the line-up. Alexei Sayle recalled the disappointment of visiting Anfield with his father, Joe, only to find that Matthews was not playing. "It was only after I had asked Joe if every member of the Stoke team, then every member of the Liverpool team, then the referee and the two linesmen and the newspaper photographers behind each goal were Stanley Matthews, that I realised with a sinking feeling that he wasn't going to show."

There was a general feeling that Matthews should be treated as a protected species. Charles Buchan spoke out during the 1952/53 season against the sliding tackle; not merely from a safety point of view but because, it appeared, that he and Finney had a divine right not to be impeded in their work, even by fair means. "Let us do away with this chancy method that handicaps the artist and makes the habitual slider look much better than he really is," he wrote. "It is artists like Tom Finney and Stanley Matthews who suffer most from this type of tackle. How many of their efforts, when they have brilliantly worked the ball down to the goal line in order to put a pass across goal, have been brought to nothing because a defender has thrown himself bodily in their path?"

Fans would even show disapproval to their own players if they dished out rough treatment to Matthews. Remembering attending a match at Old Trafford, Ken Britton said: "They had a young full-back called Joe Carolan. He did a tackle when Matthews had his back to him and caught him up by the waist. The fans all turned on him for what he'd done to Stan."

Not only did opposition spectators wish to enjoy the spectacle of seeing Matthews in full flow – which in pre-television days was only possible on the one day a year he visited their ground – but he possessed a common touch, a simplicity if you like, that struck a chord with the populace. He didn't drink or smoke; he didn't argue with referees or kick opponents; he didn't make outrageous claims for himself; he was a family man and was careful with his money. Even at his age and with his history of achievement, he appeared shy, even vulnerable. There was no god-like air about him. Blackpool fan Tom Alder recounted for the *Stoke Sentinel*: "Stan was always a friendly man, always polite and ready to have a chat to anyone. He used to chat to all the children and my children had many a sixpence off him to go and buy a bag of sweets."

As blessed as he might be by talent, it was understood how hard Matthews worked at his craft; how he honoured and respected the game with his fullness of effort on the training ground and in every match. Bosses and factory workers alike admired him: the former because he reminded them what a good employee should be; the latter because he seemed to stand for the ordinary man. "He represented the kind of working-class man that the establishment liked to believe in," said authors Martin Johnes and Gavin Mellor. "He was respectful of his trade and social betters; he epitomised the image of the respectable working class." And as the country moved forward into an exciting, scary, unknown technological age, he reminded people of what they held most dear about traditional British values. In short, everyone loved Stan.

"He had a horse," Robinson recalled. "One day me and Len Stephenson were going to the races and one of Stan's friends said they were going racing at Liverpool and asked if we wanted to go with them. The first race is for two-year-olds and there are eight ruddy runners and I have had seven different tips. Everyone wanted to tip Stan Matthews. Of course, the one I wasn't tipped was the winner!"

9

SCREEN SHOTS

"The 1953 final should have been a testimony to television's potential to develop rather than undermine football's popularity." – Martin Johnes and Gavin Mellor, *The 1953 FA Cup Final: Modernity and Tradition in British Culture.*

JOHNNY BALL, in his first FA Cup game of the season, has been one of the outstanding defenders on display in the first half of the 1953 final and he begins the second by capitalising on a moment of hesitation by Bill Perry, intercepting and drilling an accurate ball forward to Nat Lofthouse deep in the Blackpool half. Lofthouse clips a pass to the feet of Eric Bell, who has done well to limp into the box, but he can manage only an ineffectual swing at the ball and sees it go harmlessly wide. Lofthouse makes a point of running over to him to give him an encouraging pat on the shoulder.

Casual in possession, Blackpool's Jackie Mudie is lucky to see his poor pass bounce straight back to him, enabling him to do better by pushing the ball forward to Ernie

Taylor. Malcolm Barrass and Stan Mortensen tumble to the ground as they contest Taylor's pass and the ball squirts left to Bill Perry. In one of his more nonsensical pieces of commentary – and there are a few to choose from – Kenneth Wolstenholme blurts: "It's a lovely chance for Perry." It is nothing of the sort and, more than 20 yards out, he is quickly closed down. "I do wish these Blackpool forwards wouldn't just push the ball a little too far forward," says the commentator, covering his tracks.

Wolstenholme has found his way into the BBC commentary box via a career as a newspaper journalist, interrupted by a wartime stint in the RAF. Born in Worsley, near Bolton, he grew up as a Wanderers fan and was working on a newspaper in Manchester before volunteering for pilot training. He had flown more than 100 missions over Germany as a bomber pilot by the age of 23 and earned the Distinguished Flying Cross, although in future years he would remain modest and reticent about his wartime exploits.

Returning to his former career, he worked as a freelance for BBC Radio before venturing into television in 1948. When he undertook his first commentary for the screen, a South versus North amateur international trial game at Romford, he said he had never seen a single television programme. A well-known voice on the radio, he began broadcasting more televised amateur football and was established in his BBC position by the time of this FA Cup Final.

Wolstenholme now watches Hassall give the ball away, but after pausing to berate a team-mate the Bolton player hurries back to offer a second line of defence when Matthews breezes past Banks. Then, as Taylor receives the ball on the edge of the box, Hassall makes a somewhat half-hearted attempt at a tackle and is relieved to see Hanson palm the ball away as the resulting shot heads towards the far post.

Banks draws cheers from the Bolton fans by pouncing on Matthews the moment he receives a crossfield pass by Taylor, forcing the ball out before the winger can work his magic. Lofthouse then commits one of the game's only 14 fouls and responds, not by haranguing the referee in the modern style, but by placing the ball for Eddie Shimwell to play a quick free-kick down the touchline. As Matthews approaches the box at no great pace, Banks this time backs further and further away as if scared to breathe the same air as the winger, preferring to let Hassall attempt vainly to get back to make a challenge. By the time Matthews delivers an unopposed cross into the penalty area, Banks is ten yards away from him, almost in his own six-yard box. Happily for Bolton, the ball drifts harmlessly over the bar, but Matthews says later: "The runs I had been making convinced me I had the beating of the Bolton defenders."

Lofthouse drifts right and sets up a half-break by Wheeler, broken up by Johnston, who plays the ball forward to Matthews in the inside-left channel. He lays it into the path of Perry, who checks and feeds inside to Mudie. His failure to control forces him out wide, from where another cross goes lamely out of play. Wolstenholme continues in his pedagogical tone: "See how Barrass was covering there. That's the sign of a good defence."

* * * * *

WHEN *MATCH of the Day* launched in 1964, it was Wolstenholme who greeted BBC 2 viewers from the Anfield touchline before Liverpool's game against Arsenal. And it was his voice that would be heard as the lead commentator on the programme – soon to move to BBC 1 – for the next eight seasons.

In general, Wolstenholme was a man of few words; some of them, it has to be stated, ridiculous or, often, plain wrong.

It was a style that characterised his two decades as the BBC's main football commentator. But who is to say that his minimalist style was any less palatable than many of the new breed of non-stop ramblers whose pre-prepared verbal contortions can anaesthetise the most vital of football occasions? At least Wolstenholme would find the perfect words when his country most needed them, as Geoff Hurst banged in England's fourth goal in the 1966 World Cup Final. For that alone he deserves his place in televised sport's Hall of Fame.

Wolstenholme's commentary of the 1953 final was estimated at the time to have been heard by a television audience of around ten million, approximately half of whom watched the game in the homes of others. That so many people were able to tune in was undoubtedly due largely to the excitement over the impending Coronation of Queen Elizabeth II.

The announcement that the ceremonies in Westminster Abbey would be televised live came as a result of the weight of public opinion after initial resistance led by the combined forces of Winston Churchill, the Coronation Commission – headed by the Duke of Norfolk – and the Queen herself, known to be nervous about the presence of cameras. After several approaches by the BBC were rebuffed, it was a poll in the *Daily Express*, which showed 78 per cent in favour of live coverage, that helped produce a change in policy.

That prompted a rush to electrical stores to pick up TV sets and a battle between retailers looking to capitalise on the surge of interest. Newspapers in 1953 were packed with advertisements like those in the *West Lancashire Gazette*, in which the Radio and Electrical Equipment Co was offering 16-inch Ferguson models for 105 guineas, with hire purchase terms available. Or that taken out by the Murphy dealer in Talbot Road, Blackpool, who reminded readers: "Now with the whole of this Happy and Glorious New Year to unfold, is the time for you too to have TELEVISION." And customers who went to Waring of Cleveleys in search of a Bush television ranging from 49 to 65 guineas were being told to "ask your Bush dealer to take the back off to show you an example of fine television engineering".

In the 12 months leading up to the end of May 1953, the number of British television licence holders – as opposed to television owners – rose from 1.45 million to 2.32 million, increasing further to 3.25 million by March 1954. Two years before that, diarist Nella Last had recorded: "Mrs Atkinson drew my attention to the many new TV aerials that had gone up. She knows an assistant in one of the chief TV distributing shops and said: 'There's still a long waiting list… plenty of sets but aerials are a bit slow.' Until she pointed out the fact, I'd not realised we could count over 20 from our gardens."

Some observers noted an adverse effect on community activities, with more of the population staying at home to watch shows like *The Quatermass Experiment*, the BBC's successful science fiction drama of 1953, instead of going out. This was particularly notable in the expanding 'new towns', where true local communities had yet to be fully established.[22] In Hemel Hempstead, the town's public relations officer lamented: "People get home at night and just don't seem to have any desire to join in with the social activities."

Labour MP Barbara Castle would observe in 1954 that "people are glued to their television sets and are more interested in the latest rude remark of Mr Gilbert Harding than in what is being done around them".

Clearly, radio's days as the pre-eminent broadcast medium were numbered. BBC radio in the 1950s was

. . . .

22 New towns were created in England after the Second World War to deal with housing shortages. The first wave of development, between 1946 and 1950, was concentrated mostly on the outskirts of London.

divided into three channels, reflecting the mantra of founder and former director general Lord Reith that the BBC was there to "educate, inform and entertain". In increasing order of accessibility, the Third Programme focused on the arts and culture, the Home Service featured news, talk and light drama and the Light Programme concentrated on entertainment and music. The somewhat haughty ambition of the current director general, William Haley, was that listeners who began with the Light Programme would gradually progress up the intellectual pyramid. Figures released in 1949 suggested that no such migration was occurring, with the Light Programme attracting 5.5 million listeners each evening, 3.25 million tuning into the Home Service and only 90,000 listening to the Third Programme.

By 1952, the potential of television – which amounted to 30 hours of BBC programming per week – was being recognised widely enough for the introduction of a commercial network to become a heated debating point. Lord Reith, who had left the BBC in 1938, argued that such a turn of events would be a national disaster, but Churchill countered by speaking out against the monopoly enjoyed by the BBC. The Prime Minister was merely reflecting the growing public support for sponsored programming, although many also felt that if the BBC broadened its offering then there would be no need for it. A Gallup poll in June 1953 would reveal that only 19 per cent would support commercial television if the BBC provided a wider range of viewing. Ian Coster, TV critic of the *News of the World*, summed that up by urging the BBC to "cut out the intellectual drama and put on thrillers and comedies". Eventually, a government white paper emerged from the debate allowing for the introduction of commercial television, while allowing the BBC to maintain its radio monopoly.

Radio coverage of football had taken the sport to a wider audience than ever. The first game broadcast was a

1927 First Division match between Arsenal and Sheffield United, with the *Radio Times* famously printing a diagram of a football pitch split into numbered segments. It helped the listener follow the path of the ball and, it is conjectured, brought the phrase "back to square one" into everyday use.

The drama of live sport enthralled even those with no previous interest. Novelist Winifred Holtby told the *Radio Times* in 1930: "No one could listen with cold blood or sluggish pulses to the quickening crescendo of the roar preceding the final shout of 'goal.'" The Football League, blinkered to the benefits of spreading the sport by their fears of a negative impact on attendance, responded by banning live coverage of matches in 1931. The first FA Cup Final to air was Arsenal's victory over Huddersfield in 1930, with coverage as reflective of the great English occasion the event had become as it was about the on-field contest.

Radio commentaries became more frequent during the war years and continued on the resumption of League football, although from 1951/52 the *Radio Times* was not allowed to give advance notice of which game would be broadcast.[23] *Sports Report*, the BBC's long-running Saturday evening round-up of results, reports and interviews launched in 1949 in a format that has changed little over the decades.

Televised football began tentatively with a delayed recording of a game between Arsenal and Everton in 1936. Pictures were transmitted of the 1938 FA Cup Final,[24] but it was after the war that televised sport picked up with

. . . .

23 By 1951/52, the Football League was receiving the princely sum of £2,000 to grant radio coverage to the BBC; the money being split between the benevolent funds of the FA, Football League and the players' union.

24 The Preston–Huddersfield contest was goalless after 29 minutes of extra-time, at which point BBC commentator Thomas Woodrooffe declared that if there was a goal scored he would eat his hat. Preston were promptly awarded a penalty and won the game, after which Woodrooffe kept his on-air promise.

coverage of the London Olympics in 1948, the same year that partial broadcast of the Cup Final resumed.

The football authorities were, of course, even more suspicious of television than they had been of radio. The number of TV sets in Britain had reached only 20,000 by 1947, so initially there was virtually no threat posed to live attendance – even on Cup Final day, which at the time also featured a full League programme. But the 1950 final between Arsenal and Liverpool produced a television audience of one million in London and Birmingham, the two regions served by TV, and the Football League reported a significant drop in stadium attendance in those areas. Although bad weather had also contributed to the decline, Sunderland, who stated that their final-day attendance had slumped from an expected 40,000 to 17,000, went as far as proposing a complete ban on transmission of the final, although a compromise decision was made to show only the second half of Blackpool's defeat to Newcastle in 1951.

Even then, the televised pictures proved a disincentive to stadium attendance, with crowds down 42 per cent in London and 39 per cent in Birmingham (although there was also a 34 per cent drop in areas with no TV coverage, so the fall was not solely related to television). It was enough to persuade the Football Association to allow no television coverage of the 1952 final unless it was delayed by one week, beyond the end of the League season, even though not every League team was playing on that final Saturday. Unsurprisingly, the BBC declined the offer.

Football wasn't the only sport concerned about the perceived threat of television. In January 1953, the Rugby Football Union replicated a decision of the Welsh Rugby Union not to allow live coverage of internationals for fear of the adverse effect it would have on club games.

The 1953 FA Cup Final, however, was to be put before the nation – even though there would still be some other games to be played on the same day. A fee of £1,000 was enough to secure BBC the rights. "The national interest in soccer must come first," the FA stated, although a meeting of Football League clubs two weeks before the final would become a forum for protests. League chairman Arthur Drewery conveyed some teams' anger that television coverage had been agreed after League matches had been arranged and called for the final to be given its own calendar date in future years.

Charles Buchan, meanwhile, welcomed the decision. "The FA have acted wisely, I think, in allowing the final to be televised," he wrote. "The League clubs were warned months ago that this was likely to happen and were advised not to arrange fixtures on the day. But 32 clubs decided to play on the final day. Now, most of them are rearranging games. Really, they have no cause for complaint."

The size of the Wembley television audience would finally persuade the football authorities to separate the date of the Cup Final from the climax of the League season.

The important place that the 1953 FA Cup Final occupies in English football history has much to do with it being the first game to attract a significant television audience; a factor boosted by that rush for sets caused by the Coronation. And with so many television sets being shared, it became a true community event, a collective experience. A Blackpool newspaper captured the nature of the viewing audience with a cartoon showing a man asking if he could watch his neighbour's television because he couldn't get near his own for all the visitors.

Also in Blackpool, reports recorded that "most streets were almost deserted" when television and radio coverage of the game began. The chairman of the Blackpool Tower and Winter Gardens reckoned that game cost the town £75,000 in lost business. While beer sales on the day were reported to be up, cinemas and trams did slow business. Meanwhile, one grocer anticipated spending would be down for a month because of the money people had devoted either to travelling to Wembley or purchasing television sets. The first of those points was a familiar one, raised frequently when inhabitants of northern towns emptied their coffers for their big day out.

Nella Last had recorded the effect of her local team, Barrow, reaching rugby league's Challenge Cup Final two years earlier. "I was talking to a shopkeeper today and he was a bit gloomy already about all the money taken out of Barrow already by the rugby semi-final and replay." She suggested that "if people do flock to Wembley it stands to reason something will suffer" and related a story of a couple who sold their bedroom suite for 20 shillings, spending half of it on a trip to Wembley and the remaining ten shillings as a down payment on replacement furniture. Later in 1951, she wrote: "The coal man spoke of empty coal boxes everywhere. 'That trip to Wembley is having to be paid for by many silly folks.'"

The invasion of London by fans from northern outposts was a popular theme of the overall media coverage of FA Cup Finals of the time. As reverential towards royalty and politicians as the newsreel films were, so they were patronising in tone towards the working man, especially those from the north. London-based reportage saw as vaguely quaint the spectacle of flat-capped hordes arriving wide-eyed and innocent in the smoke on one day every year.[25]

. . . .

25 Some southern journalists, though, were less kind when they saw northern men intruding more permanently on their cultural heritage. The reviewer in the *London Evening Standard* had greeted the West End appearance of George Formby in *Zip Goes a Million* by saying: "I am unable to accept the theory that a banality of catchphrases acquires wit or 'philosophy' when delivered in a north country accent." To which Formby responded: "I wish I'd have stayed in bloody Manchester."

The northern-based media, however, was clearly happy to participate and take pride in the story. The *Bolton Evening News* reported glowingly that "thousands of fans poured into London with their team favours to the fore and with rattles, bells and hooters working overtime", while the *West Lancashire Evening Gazette* ran the headline: "Lancashire takes over as London is invaded."

Media outlets all over Lancashire expressed the pride that the people of the county took in the achievements of their teams. Blackpool's triumphant train journey home would be delayed at various stations by fans waiting to see the Cup being displayed out of windows. "At Warrington the screech of local whistles deafened the cheers of people lining the platforms and the blaring 'congratulations to Blackpool' greeting broadcast over the station's loudspeakers," the *Lancashire Evening Post* reported proudly, noting a similar reception at Wigan and the 5,000 people estimated to have been waiting at Preston station.

In their 2006 study, *The 1953 FA Cup Final: Modernity and Tradition in British Culture*, authors Martin Johnes and Gavin Mellor stress that "for both towns the match was presented as an opportunity to celebrate their civic identity on a national stage". They add: "The local and national press told and retold these stories in a remarkably similar fashion every year. The towns, cities and individuals involved might vary from Cup Final to Cup Final but the messages behind them stayed the same."

Few in the country emerged from the game without images of the 'northern invasion' stuck in their minds, whether it was sun-bathed fans cavorting in the Trafalgar Square fountains or the flamboyantly dressed Atomic Boys from Blackpool delivering a stick of Blackpool rock to 10 Downing Street.

The newspapers' importance in shaping people's memories of the day cannot be underestimated. Jones and Mellor cite a Blackpool paper's story of the 79-year-old woman whose radio malfunction denied her the opportunity to follow the game live. When told the final score she "broke down and wept unashamedly". According to the authors: "Such tales were more than mere anecdotes passively reported. They represented the press consciously emphasising the broad appeal and importance of the game. In doing so they contributed to how people thought about the game." The media's portrayal of the match as a civic event – combined with the Matthews effect – encouraged those not usually bothered about football to take a great interest in the happenings at Wembley.

The sheer size of circulation numbers in the 1950s was a significant contributor. Historian David Kynaston notes: "Papers, cigarettes, drink; those were the three staples of the working class, especially male working class, way of life." At the time, the average combined circulation of the national daily newspapers exceeded 16 million, with more than seven million buying a regional paper every day and in excess of 30 million Sunday newspapers being sold. Meanwhile, *The Radio Times* boasted 20 million readers every week.

Growing interest in football was being reflected in all branches of media. Match reports and training ground gossip became increasingly prominent in the newspapers, while, as well as the regular BBC commentaries, radio listeners could tune in to the Brylcreem-sponsored *It's A Goal*, a half-hour show airing on Radio Luxembourg at 8.30pm on Wednesdays. In 1951, a new magazine, *Charles Buchan's Football Monthly*, was established, its founder's ambition being to "provide a magazine worthy of the world's greatest game and the fine sportsmen who follow it". At the beginning of the 1952/53 season, another new publication appeared, *Raich Carter's Soccer Star*, which later dropped the personality name from its masthead. Several years after launching his title, by which time the magazine was selling

350,000 copies per month, Buchan reflected: "For many years after the old *Athletic News* closed down there was no paper or magazine devoted exclusively to the game. It was in a bid to fill this gap that I started [the magazine]. It has caught on so well that it was obvious something of the kind was badly needed."

Football Monthly offered glossy photographs – albeit often crudely coloured – personality features, life stories and comment. It mostly walked an uncontroversial line, however, offering a somewhat sanitised picture of the game. Opinion pieces, of which there were plenty, focused mainly on safe on-field issues, such as tactics or team selections. The various wage disputes of the time and issues of ground safety and, later in the 1950s, declining attendance were rarely touched upon.

Local newspapers, too, tended to be more celebratory in their approach to the game and were, by their very nature, parochial in their coverage. It was the national newspapers where the digging for a story went a little deeper, burrowing into some of the less savoury aspects of the sport. Publications such as the *News of the World* were never slow to expose players whose behaviour failed to meet public expectations or directors involved in dodgy deals and unethical payments.

Author Simon Inglis notes in *League Football and the Men Who Made It*: "Professional football's reputation seemed to sink in direct proportion to the rise in newspaper circulation. Had an outsider based his assessment of the League in the mid-'50s upon the popular Sunday papers, he might have concluded that all footballers were rowdy, dishonest, greedy and corrupt, while most club chairmen and League officials were either lazy, ignorant fools or insanely ambitious profiteers."

In this regard, a pattern of journalism was being established that would eventually spawn fake sheikhs, drug stings and Premier League kiss-and-tell exposés. According to Dave Russell in *Football and the English*: "It became easier to see the 1940s and 1950s as a seedbed for a later revolution in media-football relations." Russell also suggests that such routine investigation and questioning of the football hierarchy, even in politically pro-establishment newspapers, was well in advance of any similar theme in the wider context, football being seen as a self-contained world that did not mirror society as a whole. Such reportage may even have been political insurrection by proxy. Russell ventures: "Consumption, via the media, of arguments criticizing the football establishment might have served as a substitute for radical political and industrial action; industrial and commercial elites were perhaps more easily challenged in the sporting than in the political and industrial context."

As far as the 1953 Cup Final was concerned, however, it was the presence of live television that elevated the game into an event of cultural importance. If, as has been written "live television coverage enabled the Coronation to become an intimately shared event in a way that no previous historic occasion had been", then the same could certainly be applied to the events at Wembley a month earlier. It meant that, along with the winning of the World Cup in 1966 and, later, Italia '90 and the launch of the Premier League, the match was one of the most significant landmarks in the broadening of football's fan base beyond the traditional working-class demographic.

* * * * *

THE MIDDLE-CLASS tone of Wolstenholme reflects, therefore, not just the broadcasting style of the day but the sport's expanding constituency. At times his delivery has the reverence of a commentator at a state occasion, especially when discussing the biggest names in the game. When

Bolton's star player misplaces a pass from the halfway line, he ignores that fact and focuses on his efforts to chase after it, citing it as an example of the "keenness that makes Lofthouse the great player he is".

After another pinball exchange, the ball flying back and forth across halfway without anyone able to get it under control, it is Matthews, still stationed towards the left, who brings his light touch to bear, instantly controlling and flipping the ball ahead of him. Beating Wheeler to begin a surge towards the box, he slips the ball to his left but Perry is flagged offside as he shapes to cut it back.

Taylor misdirects a crossfield ball and the stooping figure of Ralph Banks advances like Groucho Marx across halfway. After careless passes by Moir and Garrett, the ball is pushed forward by Langton to Lofthouse, whose shot from the edge of the box seems to have gone harmlessly wide, only for a corner to be awarded. Fortunately for Blackpool, Garrett heads away Holden's initial delivery into the box and when the winger is given a second chance he overshoots the far post. Lofthouse chases Shimwell out towards the corner flag, where, for his pains, he takes the clearance in the midriff, leaving him crouching in pain until Bert Sproston applies the 'magic sponge'.

When Lofthouse finds himself back in the same area of the field a few seconds later, his attempted dummy fails to beat Shimwell outright but sends him slipping to the ground, from where the defender grabs his opponent's leg rugby-style. Even in the days when it needs grievous bodily harm to force a referee to book a player, Shimwell appears lucky to escape with no more punishment than a free-kick, which is subsequently wasted. While the Bolton fans boo their disapproval, Wolstenholme offers sympathy: "I think I'd grab Nat Lofthouse's leg if he was getting away from me."

10

UP FOR THE CUP

"I loved the tournament, and so did our supporters. Every match was a sell-out and the atmosphere was electric." – Bolton full-back Tommy Banks.

FA CUP fever, that ailment much beloved of journalists looking to label the excitement contained in the promise of a Wembley appearance, had officially broken out in Bolton. The local team's achievement of reaching the quarter-finals had prompted *Evening News* writer Haydn Berry to provide the diagnosis in the days leading up to the sixth-round tie at Third Division Gateshead, the outsiders among the remaining teams.

"Not for years has the town waxed so enthusiastic about Cup football as it is doing now," he gushed. "Even when the Wanderers reached the last four in 1945/46 there was not such enthusiasm" – which was hardly surprising given that they arrived there over the bodies of 33 fans who died during the quarter-final tie.

Two days later, however, the paper's opinion pages allowed the semi-anonymous pen of JDG to expound further on what the FA Cup meant to those towns still engaged in the competition:

> Where are we? We can beat them. Is it a ticket match?"
> Thousands of comments float around in factory, shop, club
> and home. Note how the personal angle creeps in – "they"
> becoming "we".
>
> With the victory of their team normally sane men go
> crazy. The 'Boss' has a kind word for every employee,
> everyone is smiling and happy.
>
> The atmosphere of the town changes as the sixth round
> is reached; papers and books are scanned eagerly for news
> of the local teams' fitness. Pulled muscles, strained tendons
> and other soccer mishaps are luckily absent; woe betide any
> newspaper correspondent who says the locals will lose. He
> is certain to get a full mailbag from indignant fans.

In Blackpool, meanwhile, the prospect of a trip to championship-chasing Arsenal, seven days after beating them 3-2 in a league game, had fans fretting over the likelihood of gaining access to Highbury. The match had not been designated all-ticket, and the *Evening Gazette* grimly warned spectators to be at Arsenal's ground by 1pm to have any chance of getting in. "Unless ticketless visitors from Blackpool are in town at about the time the larks are rising they might as profitably go off to Madame Tussaud's as take the tube to N5," wrote Clifford Greenwood.

The stationmaster at Blackpool Central, GA Addy, announced that a special train would depart for the game at just before midnight on Friday, while the Lancashire Aircraft Corporation intended to "send off early planes for passengers without tickets". Greenwood continued: "If ever there was a case for an all-ticket match this is it. Probably without intending it, Arsenal have given London the chance to 'hog' the match – and it's just too bad for Blackpool customers."

One group of Blackpool followers assured of entry were the colourful Atomic Boys, who had been granted permission by Arsenal fans to put on a show before the match, provided they did not bring the duck that usually accompanied them. Their coach – draped in tangerine, even though Blackpool would be wearing white for this game – was booked to leave the Washington Hotel at 11pm on Friday.

Since the late 1940s, the arrival of the Atomic Boys on opposition grounds had become almost as synonymous with a game against Blackpool as the emergence of Stanley Matthews onto the playing field. Syd Bevers, a Blackpool shopkeeper, had been struck during a journey to Elland Road by the depressing greyness of the typical post-war attire among the fans. He galvanised a group of his friends to rethink their wardrobes, turning up to games in orange coats, white trousers and straw hats, which made them an eye-catching feature of the 1948 Cup Final.

From there on, the extravagance escalated into oriental robes with turbans, military fancy dress and even a spot of cross-dressing. The group would parade around the pitch before matches, their costumes further accessorised by bells, bugles and the soon-to-be-famous duck. First suggested by a fan who worked at Blackpool Pleasure Beach, the Atomic Boys' original duck was called Donald, although after Hungary's victory at Wembley in 1953 the name Puskas was adopted. "There were a number of ducks through the years," Bevers told Mike Prestage in *Blackpool: The Glory Years Remembered*. "We always put one on the centre circle before every game, home and away. The duck achieved national fame."

Early attempts to dye the duck orange were thwarted, until someone suggested trying the food colouring used to stain haddock. The process usually resulted in as much orange ending up on those attempting to apply it, and surrounding walls, as the duck itself, but it proved an effective strategy.

The Atomic Boys were tolerated in a way that would become unthinkable in the hooligan-scarred days of later decades, although Bevers admitted that he "had to do a lot of preaching" to ensure his troops conducted themselves in an orderly manner, without succumbing to excess alcohol. Expulsion from the group awaited those who failed to comply. Such was the fans' adherence to behavioural boundaries that they soon became adopted as ambassadors for the club, frequently being awarded free tickets. The likes of Matthews supported their fund-raising efforts, helping them to sell tickets for a dance at the Tower Ballroom and donating a dinner service for the raffle. Blackpool's council gave them official status as mascots for the town, entrusted with handing out promotional literature for the resort as they journeyed around the country. Bevers quickly found himself on the receiving end of requests from fans to join the inner circle as a way of ensuring easy access to matches.

One of the group's finest hours was the 1951 FA Cup Final. Having been seen off from the Town Hall by 1,000 well-wishers, including councillors drinking a toast to them, the Atomic Boys journeyed south to fulfil their secret mission. They were determined that their duck, this particular one being called Stanley, would make it on to the hallowed Wembley turf. After a Saturday morning when a single policeman had been given the impossible task of trying to keep 4,000 Blackpool supporters off the base of Nelson's Column, the Atomic Boys took up their places in the stadium. Inside a zipped-up shopping bag taken into the ground by Bevers sat Stanley. Seeing his opportunity as kick-off approached, Bevers leapt from his seat near pitchside, clambered over the low barrier, raced to the centre circle and released the duck. As the Blackpool fans roared their approval, Bevers was ushered back to his seat by sympathetic stewards who issued nothing more than a polite warning.

The innocence of the times was further reflected in the Blackpool fans having adopted, with a naive charm, *Yes! We Have No Bananas*, an old Broadway musical favourite, as their club song. As the quarter-final game at Arsenal approached, the *Gazette* printed new words, composed by a fan living in Clinton Avenue, which would duly be sung, with admirable lack of self-consciousness, on the big day:

> Yes we have some footballers
> We have some footballers today
> We've Matthews, Morty, Perry and Brown
> And they are all going to stay
> We have a nice group of supporters
> A nice team of footballers
> And yes, we'll see you at Wembley
> We'll see you at Wembley this year

While Blackpool prepared for a money-spinning game against arguably the biggest club in the country, Bolton's accountants were less enamoured with the prospect of a tie at Gateshead's ground, which held little more than 17,000 and had only one small seating area. The reality of the FA Cup coffers was presented in Blackpool's financial report of their replay at Southampton, played before a 27,543 crowd paying a ground-record £4,536. By the time £1,102 had been taken off for tax and further sums for other commitments, the two teams each received a cheque for £1,040. Bolton reckoned that once they tallied their share of the gate at Gateshead with the compensation they would have to pay to Liverpool for the postponement of their scheduled League match the club would be out of pocket by £1,000.

A suggestion was made to Gateshead that the game should be switched to a larger stadium, such as Newcastle or Sunderland, but was rejected immediately. That was hardly a surprise. As well as their fifth-round victory at Plymouth, Gateshead's victories in the season's Cup competition had included a home win against First Division Liverpool and success at Second Division Hull City. On being drawn against Bolton, club chairman Will Tulip commented: "We hoped for a home draw and we've got it. What more could we want? On our own ground we are a good team."

Even though the Third Division North side had lost only three of 15 League games at their Redheugh Park ground, the bookmakers had reacted to the pairing by shortening Bolton's odds to win the competition from 18-1 to 11-2. Even manager Bill Ridding, who immediately made plans to watch his opponents for the third time during the season, had said of the draw: "We like it. How could we say otherwise? But that doesn't mean that we count ourselves as through or that we shall treat Gateshead any differently from Arsenal."

The mood at Burnden Park as game week arrived was light, reflecting the town's relief that fuel supplies had improved, as highlighted in the Western Gas Board's advertisement stating: "Coke is Plentiful – Prices Now Reduced." Reporter Berry recorded that "training and other preparations, including their clinic treatment, have gone through quietly without setback". Ralph Banks, nursing a muscle strain and feeling the effects of flu, was the only absentee from the practice ground early in the week, while the club revealed plans to give the players a few days away after the Gateshead game, regardless of the result.

On Thursday, as the club was unveiling a broadcast box at Burnden Park to accommodate new commentaries to be fed into Bolton Royal Infirmary and Bolton General Hospital, club captain Willie Moir began complaining of flu-like symptoms. He had felt fit during the players' round of golf the previous day but was now excused the team's light training session and immediately sent home. Yet even he reported back the following morning, pictured with his colleagues – all wearing heavy, belted overcoats – and healthy enough to make the trip to the coastal resort of Whitley Bay, where Bolton would spend the night.

Nat Lofthouse arrived at Burnden Park fresh from visiting the hospital in Preston where Sheffield Wednesday striker Derek Dooley was said to be in a comfortable condition in a room full of flowers and cards following the amputation of his right leg. Dooley had also discovered that he was to be the recipient of a £3,000 gift from an insurance clerk in Battersea who had won £109,000 on the pools on the weekend of his accident.

A dual-purpose greyhound stadium, set in the industrial area of north Durham – a mile and a half from the centre of Newcastle – Gateshead's ground was well on the way to full capacity as Bolton's team bus arrived the next day. Local fans had formed a queue a mile long when 10,000 three-shilling (15p) tickets had gone on sale at the Town Hall earlier in the week. They were now joined by 5,000 fans from Bolton, about 1,000 of whom travelled on the 'dinner' and 'buffet' specials that had departed early in the morning. Two coaches on one of those trains had been reserved for club directors and the players' wives.

Joyce Barrass recalled: "The wives were like a team and we all sat together for the matches. We were all friends; not like now when they don't seem to know each other. I enjoyed being a 'wag', but we didn't wag as much as they do now! I used to go to all the games."

Gateshead were without injured centre-forward George Wilbert and would be relying heavily on centre-half Tom

Callender, whom club chairman Tulip had been talking up as good enough for the First Division. He would need to be if he was to contend with Lofthouse, although he and his colleagues were given some assistance by a narrow pitch, bumpy surface and what the Bolton players felt was a very light ball. Lofthouse would argue: "The ball did the most amazing tricks. Just when you thought you were set for a shot up it came on the bounce at the wrong angle. It almost made you afraid to have a go."

Although admitting that "the north-east is not the sort of place anyone fancies going to with a semi-final place at stake", Lofthouse also said that Bolton "weren't the kind of team to be rolled over by giant-killers". So it proved, with the First Division club's superior players proving adept enough to win the day. Lofthouse broke clear of Callender for just long enough to score the only goal of the game after 55 minutes. Running on to a delivery by Langton, the sheer force of his header was enough to beat the goalkeeper's dive, prompting the *Daily Telegraph* to write: "Few centre-forwards can head the ball more accurately than Lofthouse."

Until then it had been what the *Bolton Evening News* described as a "bustling, fidgety tie" in which Gateshead's defence impressed with its organisation and durability. Eric Bell, Malcolm Barrass and Harold Hassall displayed willingness to match the hard work and high tempo the home team attempted to impose on the game, with Hassall in particular giving the impression that he was putting in overtime in order to compensate for any lack of fitness in Moir. It was he who forced the first save out of Gateshead's long-serving keeper Bob Gray. Further back, Higgins had his hands full against the speed of Ken Smith and John Ingham on the right flank of the home attack and Smith should have done better from ten yards after hesitancy in the Bolton defence.

The second half saw Gateshead apparently running out of steam and Bolton could have had three more goals after Lofthouse's decisive effort. Moir came closest with a diving header that tested Gray, but the Wanderers captain ended the game with a bloody mouth after taking the ball full in the face 20 minutes from time. He was cut badly enough to prevent him from eating anything on the journey home.

Meanwhile, Blackpool fans had been struggling to digest the quirky regulations that required them to play a rescheduled postponed game against Charlton on the Monday before their FA Cup game while opponents Arsenal were enjoying seven clear days – even though the London club had three postponements to make up. The anomaly, it was explained, was because games called off due to the FA Cup (as in the case of the Charlton match) were treated differently to those postponed because of the weather (which applied to the whole of Arsenal's backlog). The former had to be played the week following a Cup tie; the latter could be arranged at the club's convenience. Even by those rules, Birmingham – due to face Tottenham in the last eight – should have been obliged to play against Southampton. When they didn't, even more letters arrived at the *Gazette* office complaining of inequitable treatment.

While Blackpool were losing by two goals at The Valley, Arsenal were able to digest the defeat they had suffered at Bloomfield Road against the team who would stand between them and the FA Cup semi-finals a week later. Captain Joe Mercer had poked his head into the victorious Blackpool dressing room to warn them: "Well played, you fellows, but watch out next week in the Cup."

Arsenal expected to have two injured players back, defender Lionel Smith and forward Jimmy Logie, although *Gazette* reporter Clifford Greenwood had been singularly unimpressed by the high-flying visitors, describing them as "too bad to be true" and noting that "the vaunted iron wall

Arsenal defence lost all its medals". Gunners manager Tom Whittaker saw enough to say: "It will be no walkover next Saturday, but then I never said it would be."

Three days after returning from their unwanted trip to Charlton, Blackpool's players set off for London again on Friday's 1pm train. "Every man selected is fit," said Joe Smith, who had not thought to risk Stan Mortensen even though he had been back in full training for more than a week. The manager added: "This is the team's greatest test. Win this match and Wembley will be near again."

The players spent Friday evening at the theatre watching *The Crazy Gang* and were arriving back at their Southampton Row hotel as Blackpool's followers began their own various travels to the capital. More than 250 climbed aboard the pre-midnight train, while a further 850 would leave on three morning trains that stationmaster Addy assured passengers were "nice and warm".

Others took to the road. Supporter Mel McCarthy recalled: "Me and a guy called Tommy Stanhope went down on a coach overnight. I was only 15 and I remember asking my dad if we could go and he said 'yes'. It was an eight-hour journey because there were no motorways then. We didn't have tickets. We just paid at the ground and we ended up right behind the goal."

There was a tragic turn of events for one family, however, when a car carrying Blackpool fans struck a stationary lorry – revealed later to have run out of petrol – on the Rugby to Daventry road at around 4.45am, more than six hours into its journey. A 24-year-old fan, Harry Beadsley, a former stoker in the navy who lived close to Blackpool's North Shore, died from abdominal injuries suffered in the crash shortly after being admitted to St Cross Hospital in Rugby. His father, Albert, had been due to travel with him but had changed his mind at the last minute and given his place to a friend.

The remainder of the travelling party continued their trip by coach, although well behind the bulk of the Blackpool contingent. Some of the early arrivals, confident of their place inside the ground, headed to Trafalgar Square, where newspaper photographers were, as usual, unable to resist pictures of grown men in clown hats and fezzes messing around by the fountains. Others preferred to make their way direct to Highbury, where queues began growing around 8am, four hours before the opening of the turnstiles. That allowed plenty of time for the fleet of ticket touts – all cigarette-scarred voices and pockets stuffed with bank notes – to seek out willing purchasers of their 12 shilling and sixpence (62 and a half pence) seats, which were being offered at £5. By 1pm, the five- and six-shilling entrances had closed and, 45 minutes later, the roads of terraced houses leading to the stadium were barred to all but those already in possession of a ticket.

In the meantime, the Blackpool team bus arrived, escorted by police outriders. They took the field with not just the support of their own travelling fans but with the sympathies of most of the media. This was down to more than the mere presence of Matthews. In the most recent issue of *Football Monthly* it had been stated of the Seasiders: "They favour the classic style rather than the safety-first methods so prevalent today. Even in defeat Blackpool have won admiration."

Arsenal's outside-right that day, Arthur Milton, related his extensive memories of the game almost half a century later. Despite playing for the eventual League champions and being a dual England international at football and cricket, he easily recalled the special nature of being on the same field as so many household names of the era. "For me, the west country cricketer, to be on the same field playing with and against the likes of Matthews and Mortensen and Mercer and Forbes was something in itself."

Referring to Mercer's prediction of a week earlier, he said: "Joe was wrong. Blackpool came down to us and took over where they'd left off. They just didn't allow us to get into the game. It was a team effort by them, because I don't recall [Matthews] dominating as he usually liked to when he came to London."

Arsenal's performance was as off-colour as their appearance. Wearing unfamiliar black and white stripes to comply with competition regulations requiring both teams to change in the event of a clash of kits, they were inferior to their visitors in teamwork, speed and individual skill. The *News of the World*'s Frank Butler called them "so colourless, so lacking in ideas". Farm was only infrequently called into action as the creative forces of the Arsenal team – Logie, Lishman and Holton – were stifled by what the *Gazette* called the "vice-like grip" of the Blackpool half-backs.

Meanwhile, the home team's own half-backs – Forbes, Daniel and Mercer – were led haphazardly around the field by Blackpool's attack. Those who viewed the Pathé News highlights of the game in their local cinemas saw the twitching run of Matthews take him outside two defenders to cross for Perry, who miscued his shot back across goal and well wide. While waiting for the main feature, which that month included Danny Thomas in *The Jazz Singer* or Walt Disney's *Peter Pan*, those moviegoers would also be shown Harry Johnston chesting the ball away from his goal line after Holton and Farm had challenged for a Lishman cross, the calmness of Johnston's action reflecting the assuredness of Blackpool's display.

Sitting in the dressing room at half-time with the game still scoreless, Matthews demonstrated his unselfishness by pointing out how distracted Arsenal appeared to be by his presence, which he knew could make him a valuable decoy. "I think I'll just stick to the touchline," he said. "They seem to be liking my company out there."

It was a while coming, but when the first Blackpool goal arrived at last with only ten minutes remaining, it was indeed via an attack down the less congested left wing. Brown, being watched on this day by the Scotland selectors, drew a defender towards him after receiving the ball from Ernie Taylor and played it back inside for Taylor to score with a first-time shot. Yet Arsenal fans barely had time to begin fretting over this threat to their ambition of a League and Cup double before they were level, Logie hooking into an unguarded goal when the ball dropped following Lishman's challenge on Farm.

"Blackpool had deserved to win but now it looked like a draw," Milton would recall. "More than 60,000 seemed happy to have settled for that as well. Certainly I had. I remember the dusk coming in and the great crowd in good heart, watched over by just one policeman on either touchline."

Blackpool's players were far from prepared to settle for a replay, however, and one man in particular was prepared to pay a heavy price to settle the tie at the first attempt. "I can see Blackpool's Allan Brown, who'd been the star of the game, bear down on our goalie Jack Kelsey who came out to thwart him and still kept coming," Milton remembered. Brown, who had been eager to attempt as many shots as possible and whose control and strong running had constantly intimidated the home defence, chased a pass from Mudie and poked his right leg at the ball, falling over Kelsey as he did so. As ball rolled into netting, the forward lay motionless on the goal line, causing team-mates to pull themselves up short as they arrived in readiness for robust celebrations. "It's no use," Brown told them through clenched teeth. "My leg's had it."

Half a century on from the game, the incident remained painfully lodged in Brown's memory: "My whole lifetime later I can still see that ball popped into the box... I suppose

Jack and I reckoned we were as brave as each other at a 50-50 and I managed to toe-cap it over him with my right boot as he hurled himself at me. With his momentum his hip crashed into my left leg."

Blackpool were a further step closer to the final but Brown knew instantly that, just as two years earlier, he would be no part of any Wembley engagement: "It was broken in two places. But I knew I'd scored and I knew we'd won."

The serious nature of the injury was obvious to most inside Highbury. "Everyone could hear the crack," said Milton. "We've lost, we're out of the Cup, and there was Brown flat out in the area and the stretcher-bearers running on."

Mel McCarthy was standing behind the Arsenal goal. "I can see it now. A flick inside an Arsenal defender and Allan Brown came running in and put it right in the bottom corner where we were standing. But he went over the keeper and you could tell he'd broken his leg."

At Bloomfield Road, the biggest cheer of the afternoon during Blackpool Reserves' loss to Preston was prompted by the announcement of Brown's winner, but those fans were yet to discover the story behind the goal. Johnston would comment: "If we'd have known what was about to happen to Allan in those last few minutes we would have been more than content with a replay. All the Blackpool team could have cried as Allan was carried off."

The human drama of Brown's injury overshadowed Blackpool's feat in twice taking the lead inside the final few minutes against the team destined to be champions. "All our Cup matches were very close that season, and we had some high tension, nail-biting finishes," Johnston said later. "We always kept going, right to the final whistle. We were a very fit team, and we knew it."

While Blackpool went home to celebrate and await Monday's semi-final draw, Brown was condemned to two nights in the Royal Northern Hospital before being transferred to Manchester Royal Infirmary's private patients' home. "They sent a car to the hospital to bring me home. I sat in the back with my foot up," he recalled. Before being discharged, he was visited by Arsenal manager Whittaker and former Highbury legend Alex James, a fellow-Scot, telling them: "It was just an accident. Nobody was to blame – not Kelsey or anybody. Nobody must reproach himself." Brown also received a telegram from Derek Dooley, who knew too well the danger of such injuries: "Tough luck, Allan," he wrote. "Congratulations on the goal. Hope you will be up and about soon."

The irony of Brown once again missing out on Wembley was that he was a confirmed fitness fanatic. Described by Matthews as the hardest trainer he had seen, he was adept at one-handed press-ups and a frequent winner of the team's cross-country runs. According to Jimmy Armfield: "If our trainer wanted to get any player fit he would always send them out running with Browny."

Brown, meanwhile, credited the influence of Matthews, whose disciplined fitness and training he had read about as a young boy. It even encouraged him to compete in running events at Highland Games meetings. His approach also reflected the ethos of Joe Smith, who believed that hard work could compensate for the days when players' skills were a little off. "Eleven grafters, all working, want a lot of beating," he said. Now, one of the hardest of those grafters would miss out on the greatest reward of all.

WEMBLEY CALLING

"On our day we were a match for anyone. Although we went through an indifferent spell and finished seventh in the League our attention was diverting to the FA Cup and we were determined to have a real go to see if we could go one better [than 1951]. We arrived at Villa Park quietly confident." – Blackpool's Bill Perry.

DOUG HOLDEN was going home. A semi-final at Maine Road not only meant that the Bolton winger was playing close to where he had been raised and still lived, it also meant that the biggest game of his career so far would be played on the field of his childhood dreams. "I was a Manchester City fan," he explained. "I lived right on the doorstep and my father took me to see them play because they were the big team. We won the Cup in 1934 and title in 1937. As kids, all we did was play football and everything was Manchester City. But I can't remember City ever having shown an interest in me."

Instead it was United who came knocking on the door of the youngster who had been performing well on either wing for Manchester YMCA. Yet he had no interest in becoming part of a group who would eventually be known as manager Matt Busby's "Babes". He said: "We had someone from United come around to the house, like they did in those days. They watched people playing for their local teams and had seen me playing for the YMCA. We had great facilities there – a gymnasium, swimming pool – and it was a great set-up. United were more forward looking than other clubs at that time, but all the youngsters were going there. I could have gone to Old Trafford, but I decided there would be more opportunities elsewhere.

"Bolton made some enquiries about me and a guy from there came down. I decided there would be more chance there than United. I went into the army to do National Service in about 1949 and my father did a good job for me. Bolton wanted to sign me, so he put pressure on them to pay me so much money per week while I was in the army for two years and occasionally when I was on leave I would get a game in the third team or something. When I came out of the army I signed for them. I suppose that was the pressure on Bolton; if they wanted me then give me some money while I was in the army."

Holden made his Bolton debut in 1951 and would soon establish a reputation as perhaps the best winger in the game behind the illustrious duo of Stanley Matthews and Tom Finney, eventually winning five England caps. Like his hero, he was noted more for his close control than his outright speed. "Matthews was my idol. As a child, I looked up to him and tried to base my game on him; the jinking, the tricks. But when it came to the professional game, if you tried to be funny on the ball, they'd knock you over."

A popular figure in Bolton, Holden nevertheless remained living in Manchester. "I got the bus to the games. One time I missed it and I was late arriving for a game against Arsenal and everyone was in a panic. But I played really well."

Holden was delighted when the traditional nervous wait for Monday's semi-final draw ended with news of a visit to Maine Road to face Everton, the only Second Division team left in the competition. It meant that if Bolton were to reach the final they would have done so without facing any top-flight opposition. "We like it very much," said Ridding of a tie scheduled to be played on 21st March, before adding cautiously: "We have a 50-50 chance of going to Wembley."

Similarly, Everton probably felt that fortune had favoured them in choice of opponents. Having beaten a pair of Division One teams in the previous two rounds they weren't about to fear anyone and manager Cliff Britton, an ex-England half-back, confirmed: "I feel if our boys play as well as they did against Manchester United and Aston Villa we are going to Wembley this year."

Blackpool were yet to know the identity of their semi-final opponents, but both possible options had a familiar feel. Depending on the result of the quarter-final replay, they would either face Tottenham at Villa Park, as they had five years earlier, or Birmingham City at Goodison Park, which had been their 1951 engagement. They were, however, told who the referee would be; Arthur Ellis, the man who would become known to a later generation as the avuncular adjudicator on television's *It's a Knockout*.[26]

Another issue determined on the day of the draw was that the people of Blackpool would soon be able to either celebrate victory or drown the sorrows of defeat for a little longer. The Blackpool Licensing Sessions agreed to extend

. . . .

26 In the company of presenters Stuart Hall and Eddie Waring, Ellis's typical duties might include using his ubiquitous 'dip-stick' to see how much water contestants dressed in pantomime costume had managed to deposit in a bucket while running on a greased treadmill and being attacked by opponents with giant pillows.

winter licensing hours by half an hour to 10.30pm, in line with many other towns. John Budd, applying on behalf of the Blackpool Licensed Victuallers' Association, had pointed out the anomaly of visitors coming to Blackpool for entertainment in the winter only to find the pubs closing early. "They came for the bright lights of Blackpool from the gloomy industrial background and it is extraordinary that they can get refreshments in their own town up to 10.30pm, but not in Blackpool," he argued. "It is Gilbertian[27] and bad business to boot."

Wednesday's replay in north London – played while the British press digested news of the death of Soviet president Joseph Stalin and pondered on his successor – saw Tottenham and Birmingham battle to another draw, forcing a second replay at Wolverhampton's Molineux ground the following Monday. Before that, Spurs visited Bloomfield Road to be beaten 2-0, after which full-back Alf Ramsey dismissed Blackpool as a one-man team. "It's just Matthews, Matthews, Matthews," he scoffed, prompting Clifford Greenwood to retaliate in the *Evening Gazette* by stating that Bill Perry "could give Ramsey two yards and still beat him over ten".

Wanting a closer look at their semi-final opposition, Blackpool dispatched manager Joe Smith, captain Harry Johnston and veteran players George Farm and Eddie Shimwell to see the long-running quarter-final determined at last by a single goal by Tottenham's Sonny Walters. Alf Ramsey's come-uppance was not far away.

The bad weather that had dogged earlier rounds of the Cup finally seemed to have been chased away by the spring sunshine that presided over Bolton's Tuesday training session at Burnden Park, five days before they faced Everton. Players were pictured hurdling over a bench, after which

. . . .

27 Referring to the comic style of a Gilbert and Sullivan light opera.

they dispersed for shooting and crossing practice, followed by passing drills. Full-back Ralph Banks, nursing a thigh injury, was the only absentee, although Malcolm Barrass was struggling with impaired breathing after taking a bang on his nose in the previous Saturday's win at Stoke, during which Bolton conceded only their second goal in a run of six matches.

Everton were preparing for the 12th semi-final in their history – one more than Bolton – on the back of a 3-1 defeat at West Ham, a result typical of a season in which they were destined to finish 16th in the Second Division with only a dozen wins to their name. They had been a different side in the FA Cup, dispatching Ipswich and Nottingham Forest in high-scoring games before their double success against higher division clubs.

While Everton's players were spending Wednesday afternoon playing golf, Bolton's were learning the identity of the 11 men who would contest the semi-final. Roy Hartle and George Higgins won the battle for the two full-back berths, while the rest of the team picked itself. Holden was still troubled by a groin injury, however, and Harry Webster was placed on standby for 24 hours until the winger confirmed that he was fit enough to play – which was just as well seeing that Webster proceeded to injure himself in a services game on the same day.

Everton named the same full-strength team that had upset United and Villa, which meant that left-back Jock Lindsay was healthy for the first time since the quarter-final and centre-forward Dave Hickson, who had scored the only goal in that match, was also cleared to take the field. Hickson had made a great impact on the competition, as he had on young *Leigh Guardian* reporter Gordon Brown. More than half a century later, Brown recalled standing with his father watching Everton's 2-1 victory over United: "Hickson put up the most courageous performance I have seen in football, playing on with a gashed head and nodding the winning goal with blood running down his cheek after a clash of heads with Allenby Chilton... Dave had been off the field for stitches and had returned. The cut had opened up again."

With a day to go before kick-off, headlines from Hollywood were prominent, with Gary Cooper taking the Oscar for his performance in *High Noon* and Vivien Leigh flying home to England after suffering a nervous breakdown. Bolton, meanwhile, had their own drama to focus on, although they could have done without the California-type sunshine that was beating down on Manchester. Having hoped for rain to soften the Maine Road pitch, the Wanderers players arrived at the ground for some light exercise to find that the ball was bouncing "head high from gentle lobs". Eric Bell warned: "That's going to be the trouble tomorrow, unless we get a sousing tonight: how to keep the ball down where it should be."

Reporter Haydn Berry reported that his chats with Ridding and Moir had shown manager and captain to be confident, but reluctant to talk too much about Wembley itself. He then indulged in some national stereotyping by announcing: "Everton will play five Irishmen and that should mean loads of inspiration. But it could also mean too much temperament." In Berry's world, there was no substitute for a clear and unemotional English head, especially if the pitch was going to offer the kind of troublesome baked surface upon which the national team had often come a cropper in overseas internationals.

A total of 24,000 fans had grabbed Bolton's allocation of tickets, although black market prices of £3 for a 25-shilling ticket and up to four times face value for a five-shilling ticket must have tempted at least a few to sell. One day behind their heroes, they began their journey to Manchester early on the morning of the match. Ten trains, including five football specials, set off on the short journey south, while a convoy of cars quickly filled the roads. Dress code varied from cloth caps to Sunday best. For some, like four youths boarding the train in tall black and white hats, fancy dress was the chosen attire. The quartet also sported megaphones and displayed a banner announcing: "It's Bolton's year. Let's hear that cheer."

Arriving in the big city, Bolton's followers were judged by the *Manchester Evening News*, however, to be trailing their Merseyside counterparts when it came to boisterousness. Of course, this was good news for the local police, whose spokesman commented before kick-off: "The crowd from Bolton so far has been one of the quietest and best-behaved we have had in a Cup tie for some time."

Yet they were noisy enough with their rattles and horns when their team emerged to make the Wanderers players well aware of their presence. And within a minute of Moir having won the toss and forced Everton to kick into the sun, they were almost celebrating with even more vigour.

In the classic English mode, Lofthouse played the ball out to Langton and was in position in the box to meet the winger's cross with a shot that was blocked by centre-half Tommy Jones for a corner. Langton delivered the dead ball and Lofthouse's flick with the outside of his boot beat keeper O'Neill and was cleared in desperation by Lindsay. Stan Hanson's save from a 30-yard effort by John Willie Parker went almost unnoticed among a relentless Bolton assault that brought four corners in the first six minutes. There was nothing quiet about the Wanderers fans now.

It took three Everton men to halt Hassall in full flight and it was no surprise when, after ten minutes, Bolton broke through. Holden received a pass from Lofthouse and, despite being closed down, managed to send a speculative cross in the direction of the Everton goal. The ball swerved, deceived O'Neill and landed in the corner of the net. "Dougie Holden on the touchline was very good," said

Barrass. "Teams had difficulty in getting hold of him. Bobby Langton, they clobbered him a bit more."

Holden had just scored the last of his three goals in the season and would only ever score a handful each term. "My job was basically to get the ball into the middle for Lofty, not score goals myself," he explained. "We played to him."

Hickson led Everton's attempted fightback, but Bolton's only nervous moment was eased when Higgins made up for Hanson's hesitation. No sooner had Hickson returned to the field with typical bravery after going off following a bang to the head than Bolton added a second goal. Langton and the dangerous Hassall combined from a quickly-taken throw and Moir converted a left-foot shot inside the penalty area, the ball squeezing between O'Neill and the post.

Before half-time, Bolton had doubled their lead. On 28 minutes, Lofthouse concluded a 20-yard run by firing the third, before adding another in the 41st minute. It had been a brilliant display, half-backs linking effectively with their front men and the forwards operating cohesively and incisively, with strength and skill. "Bolton's forwards were irrepressible demons dancing around with fire and intent," recorded the *Sunday Chronicle*. At the back, Barrass had continually negated the threat of Hickson. "Everton were a good team," Barrass recalled. "We read what was said about them, what a good centre-forward they had. But we were ready for them."

Had Everton pulled one back before the break it would barely have taken any gloss off Bolton's performance, but full-back Tommy Clinton ensured that the Wanderers' advantage remained intact by putting his 43rd-minute penalty a yard wide. Everton clearly needed to change something after the break. What they came up with impressed Haydn Berry enough for him to describe it as "an object lesson in tactics from Everton for the soccer theorists". In fact, it amounted to little more than playing the ball more directly into the Bolton penalty area in an attempt to by-pass their opponents' dominance in the middle of the field. There was no denying the results, however, as Everton launched into what threatened to become one of the most stunning comebacks in Cup history.

With the second half still only a minute old, the head of Parker put Everton on the board following Buckle's in-swinging corner, although Lofthouse, dominating his marker Jones, almost made it 5-1 when he drove the ball against the post. Everton scored a further two goals on 71 and 82 minutes through Peter Farrell, from a free-kick, and Parker again. "Everton hit us with everything but the kitchen sink," said Lofthouse. "Perhaps we should have gone on the defensive but that wasn't our style. In fact, it wasn't really anyone's style in those days. You rarely saw a team sitting on a lead."

Despite their scare, Bolton were adjudged by most observers to be worth their win in what Lofthouse called "one of the most remarkable Cup battles of them all". Yet their passage to Wembley – free from First Division opposition and containing various close-fought battles – did not appear likely to convince the majority of their potential to upset favourites Blackpool at Wembley. Ironically, Blackpool had taken a similar route in 1948, playing only lower division sides.

"Many people have been saying that Bolton are lucky; that we are not a great side," Lofthouse commented. "My response is that we have 11 good players and that we have improved as we have played each round. I thought that in the first half of the semi-final against Everton we played some fine football to get a four-goal lead, although maybe with a margin like that we slackened in the second half. I think the half-back line of Wheeler, Barrass and Bell has proved to be the real reason for our appearance in the final."

* * * * *

TEN MINUTES have been played since half-time and Bolton's wounded heroes still lead 2-1. In fact, far from capitalising on their superiority in terms of fitness, Blackpool are about to suffer another setback. Bolton win a throw on the right and Johnny Wheeler propels it at Holden, who beats Cyril Robinson on the outside. With the half-back floundering on one knee, Holden hits a dangerous cross towards the six-yard box. The injured Eric Bell may be unable to run, but somehow he manages to leap above right-back Eddie Shimwell to send a header past George Farm, who dives in vain to his left.

According to Robinson: "I think Eddie said: 'Well, he's injured; he is not going to head it,' so he didn't bother to jump."

As Bell hops and hobbles away in celebration, Langton holds out a warning arm to team-mates, ensuring they don't risk worsening his injury in their eagerness to celebrate with him. As the players disperse, taking up their positions for kick-off, Lofthouse can't resist grabbing the scorer's face in both hands and planting him with a big kiss.

Eyes are cast towards Matthews, the central character in the narrative of the game. "It looked pretty grim. I couldn't believe it," he admits later, although he receives immediate reassurance from the body language of his colleagues. "All my team-mates, far from being despondent and throwing in the towel, were still buzzing."

When play restarts, Jackie Mudie misdirects a pass, but the ball eventually finds its way to Matthews. "Come on, Stanley. You've got a lot of work to do," remarks Kenneth Wolstenholme. "Everyone, even the Bolton supporters, would love to see him get a Cup winner's medal." Almost with a sigh, he adds: "Probably the greatest footballer of all time."

After some harmless exchanges of possession, Robinson tries his most adventurous move of the game, beating one man but then running the ball out of touch. "Joe [Smith] wanted me to play defence, but I liked to go up," he explained, his withdrawn role meaning that Blackpool were effectively employing a back four. "If you scored a goal Joe used to bollock you because you shouldn't have been there to score it. In the final, Jonty was always shouting at me to come back. I wasn't in the game a lot. If Matthews could pass to Taylor or Morty and I was there too, then he would pass to them. They didn't want me to go up beyond the halfway line."

A series of misplaced passes cause Wolstenholme, with justification, to observe: "Blackpool have fallen away very badly." Seemingly by way of emphasis, Ernie Taylor, having beaten Harold Hassall, hesitates as he approaches the box, uncertain of his course of action. He is easily dispossessed. Lofthouse is bolder when he receives the ball with his back to goal 30 yards out. Yet he is too rash, launching a shot that is easily blocked when he had plenty of time to be more considered.

It has been a while since Blackpool posed any kind of threat, but Mortensen angles a pass to Matthews on the wing and, in what will prove to be a portent of the game's climax, the winger leaves Barrass sprawling on the grass and pulls the ball back behind his centre-forward. Perry follows up at the back post and shoots across goal. Proving he can often find the right words, Wolstenholme quips: "I wonder if Banks and Barrass went down in prayer then."

The commentator then reports: "We've just received confirmation from the Bolton dressing room that Willie Moir scored the second goal. He must have touched it with his head."

As the game moves to the hour mark, Robinson invites the wrath of his bosses by advancing over the halfway line once more, but clips the ball beyond the straining Mortensen. Matthews also over-hits a pass intended for his centre-forward. Wolstenholme allows the moment to pass without comment, "the great Stanley" being apparently beyond criticism, although when a team-mate misdirects a pass up the left touchline a few moments later, he is less forgiving. "A dreadful pass from Garrett," he mutters.

* * * * *

BLACKPOOL HAD reached the 1948 final by beating Tottenham, then in the Second Division, by the only goal of the game four minutes from time. Since then, the Seasiders' past and forthcoming semi-final opponents had won the Second Division title and lifted the First Division crown at their first attempt in 1950/51. It was their method – the 'push and run' system, encouraging players to move into space when they didn't have possession – that made as big an impact as their meteoric rise.

Manager Arthur Rowe explained something of his philosophy in the *FA Bulletin*. "One of the slogans which partly describes our game is push and run, the application being to push the ball to a colleague and run into position for the immediate return pass. A simple progression on the favourite schoolboy trick of pushing the ball against a wall and moving forward to get the angled return beyond the opposition."

According to Ron Reynolds, a goalkeeper on Tottenham's books at the time, Rowe felt that "football was far too stereotyped in this county, that far too many teams played what we still have as the traditional English game, all about power and strength and running". In *The Life of a 1950s Journeyman Footballer*, Reynolds told authors Dave Bowler and David Reynolds that "Tottenham players had a licence to do what they thought was right". It meant, for example, that right-back Ramsey had the freedom to go forward and join his winger in attack. Players were encouraged to break free of the traditional positional rigidity of the English game if they saw an opportunity, while team-mates were drilled to become aware enough to cover for them. "It was about intelligence and movement," Reynolds explained.

Tottenham had many fans among neutral observers of the game. At the start of the 1952/53 season, Charles Buchan had written: "Spurs and Manchester United have proved that destructive defensive methods are out-dated. Attack brings victories, irrespective of the number of goals conceded."

Buchan may have been somewhat premature. Tottenham's style would not exactly revolutionise English football. After finishing second in the table in 1951/52 they were on their way to tenth place during this current season. Rowe's team would grow old and slip from the top of the game, leaving Stan Cullis's Wolverhampton Wanderers to win the championship three times in the 1950s – either side of the peak of the Busby Babes' power. Wolves achieved success with a direct approach that made use of long passes, quick wingers, a strong centre-forward and outstanding fitness throughout the side. Athletics was placed ahead of aesthetics, and in that regard they were no different to most teams of the time; simply more effective.

Like their semi-final opponents, Blackpool had been forced by their inconsistent form to accept that the FA Cup was their one chance of success in this particular season. The win against Tottenham two weeks before their Cup contest was only their fourth in 11 League games since Christmas, but confidence remained high in the sudden-death environment.

The optimism within the Blackpool team was reflective of the feel-good atmosphere that had been pervading the town, a jolly enough place at the worst of times, over the previous few weeks. Not only were the FA Cup exploits of the players attracting column inches in places as far away as Canada and China, but Blackpool was enjoying more than its fair share of profiling in the limited television timetable. The exposure offered by the BBC's televising of live Saturday evening boxing from Blackpool Tower Circus was considered to have enormous value, as was the screening of the Northern Counties Amateur Snooker Championship from the same venue a few days earlier.

Four days before the Tottenham game, more than 100,000 were estimated to have gathered on Blackpool's beach and promenade to watch the skies as pilot Neville Duke attempted to break the sound barrier above the town in his Hunter jet fighter. In the end, a thick mist meant that the crowd could see nothing, although they did clearly hear two loud bangs from an easterly direction as Duke soared above them in excess of 700mph. Three days later, the beach was the focal point once again as Blackpool Tower Circus launched its summer season by parading its three elephants along the sand at a somewhat more sedate pace.

Blackpool Corporation were determined to make the most of the town's fortunes, with the publicity committee discussing a campaign led by publicity director Harry Porter. He won approval for a plan that, if Blackpool beat Spurs, would "take advantage of the nationwide interest in the resort through the exploits of its eleven ambassadors". His activities were to include a display in Regent Street and the distribution of folders showcasing the best of Blackpool.

The die-hard fans of the team were less concerned about the PR spin-offs for their home town than about their prospects of returning to Wembley for what they felt was unfinished business. They were buoyed by Stan Mortensen's successful appearance in a pair of reserve team games and happy to endure the usual long Sunday morning queuing process to secure tickets for the semi-final. The top-priced seats were priced at 25 shillings, prompting Clifford Greenwood to declare that he and "nearly everybody else in this part of the football world" thought it was too expensive, even though it represented a rise of only four shillings on the same ticket in 1948. The first arrivals for the distribution of ground tickets – costing two shillings and sixpence – were outside Bloomfield Road at 8pm on the Saturday before the following morning's sale. Three married women by the names of Doris Williams, Molly Johnson and Winifred Miller turned up with camping stools and torches and happily played cards throughout the night.

They duly took up their places among a crowd of 68,221 at Villa Park, producing record semi-final receipts of £20,084. Messages urging people not to travel to the game without tickets appeared to have had an effect, certainly according to the black-marketeers who ended up handing spare tickets to the turnstile operators at kick-off time. "I have never known anything like it," said one tout. "I cannot even give them away."

Blackpool's followers had made their usual journey via road and rail, with one fan, Jack Knighton of Cleveleys, proudly brandishing his piano accordion as he boarded his train and announcing: "I thought it was as good a way of passing the time as any." The train's dining carts offered ham, tongue and pressed beef salad on the way to Birmingham and roast chicken, with sausage and bread sauce on the way back. Stationmaster Addy this time assured everyone that he had inspected every carriage personally and stated: "No one can complain they were not heated, cleaned or serviced properly."

The most disappointed traveller of the day had been Pat Hallaghan, who had intended to journey to Blackpool to sell team colours and 'favours' to fans before they headed south. However, he missed his train and arrived in Blackpool only when most of the Birmingham trains had already disappeared down the track. "I haven't sold much," he complained. "No other team uses their tangerine colours so I can't flog them anywhere else."

There was, of course, plenty of colour among the Atomic Boys, but their attempt to parade around the Villa Park pitch before kick-off, as they had five years earlier, was denied on this occasion. As they attempted to climb out of the paddock area to the cinder track around the playing area, they were repelled by stewards, who warned that they would be removed from the ground if they encroached further. It was not enough to deter one of their number, however. Harry Richards, a dwarf entertainer who had toured with comedian Charlie Chester and the Crazy Gang, ran on to the pitch shortly before the teams emerged. Making for the penalty area, he knelt as if in Arabic prayer before being caught by a policeman and returned to the terraces. A familiar figure to the Blackpool team, he appeared again as they warmed up and the players seemed indulgent of his efforts to fire the ball into the net. The authorities were less amused and this time he was escorted to the gates and deposited on the street outside the ground. "Whether they were entitled to do it, I don't know, for I'd paid to go in and watch the match," he said later. It was his luck to be recognised by a group of late-arriving Blackpool fans, who offered him their spare ticket, and he was back inside in time for kick-off.

The game he witnessed saw Tottenham – outside of the first and final ten-minute periods – emerge as the greater attacking force, despite Blackpool taking an early lead. Only seven minutes had been played when Matthews's corner was met by Perry's close-range header as he made a run from the edge of the penalty area, an accomplished finish that made Matthews wonder why he didn't aim for him more often.

From then on, the slippery pitch – watered shortly before kick-off and characterised by Joe Smith as "grease and slime" – seemed to suit Spurs better. Mortensen looked ineffective on his return in the inside-left position, although he was much more threatening after his late switch to centre-forward, which also freed Jackie Mudie from the stifling attention of centre-half Harry Clarke. Blackpool appeared to rely too heavily on Matthews, who was able to display occasional flashes of his brilliance but, in the main, was well handled by Charlie Withers. The Spurs left-back tackled well, intercepted at key moments and kept the impact of his illustrious opponent to manageable levels. On the other flank of the Tottenham defence, Ramsey was similarly unflustered under pressure, strong in his challenges and acutely aware of situations developing around him. He frequently instigated attacks with thoughtful passes out of defence to his wing-halves and inside-forwards.

Blackpool's defence was almost as impressive, Johnston proving himself, according to one report, as "one of the best and one of the fastest centre-halves in the country". He and Garrett broke up numerous Spurs attacks and, when they didn't, Farm was on hand with some important saves.

Tottenham outside-left Sid McClellan was a consistent threat and it was his good run and cross-shot that Garrett managed to turn away for a corner, with Spurs claiming the defender had handled. McClellan brought a save out of Farm, and it was he who was at the business end of a sweeping move out of defence at the end of the first half. Bill Nicholson swapped passes with Ramsey and the ball went via Len Duquemin to McClellan, who ran on and shot just wide from 15 yards. Two minutes later, Eddie Baily headed against the bar from a free-kick; then Farm scrambled away a shot from the same player as Spurs again appealed for handball in the area.

Spurs' continued dominance was rewarded five minutes after the break when Baily sent Les Bennett away on the right wing. He carried the ball to the goal line, centred low and saw Walters wrong-foot the defence by letting the ball run on for Duquemin to score from three yards.

They came closest to taking the lead when McClellan went through and beat Farm with a shot that hit the post, but as the final ten minutes rolled around it was Blackpool who were pressing and Ted Ditchburn who was forced to save from Matthews and Mortensen. Then Matthews conjured up a cross for Perry, who had space to measure a shot with Ditchburn out of position, only for Ramsey to hurl himself across goal and, two feet above the ground, head the ball off the line. As well as being confronted by Ramsey in top form, Perry had been playing most of the game with a badly twisted ankle, swollen horribly by the time he squeezed his boot off at the end of the match. "How he kept going I don't know," Joe Smith would comment later. "It must have taken a lot of pluck to do it."

Ramsey's performance throughout the game made the nature of Blackpool's winning goal particularly cruel. It resulted initially from Arthur Ellis accepting his linesman's signal that Baily had handled. The Spurs and England player was still arguing that he had used his chest when Taylor slipped a quick free-kick to Perry to launch an attack. Ramsey appeared to deal with the danger just outside the Spurs box, turning to play the ball back to the safety of Ditchburn. At the crucial moment, though, Ramsey slipped, the ball bouncing off his knee and giving Mudie the opportunity to steal it away and send a left-foot shot under the desperate lunge of the keeper. There was not even enough time for the ball to leave the centre circle after the restart before the final whistle confirmed Blackpool's place at Wembley.

Ramsey, the man who would eventually lead English football out of the wasteland into which it would be banished later in the year, was inconsolable. Having given one of the finest performances of his career, he now attracted this description in the *Sunday Dispatch*: "A mud-spattered figure in a white shirt turned and walked alone towards the dressing room, his head down in dejection."

Ramsey, who privately felt his team-mates were equally culpable for giving away the free-kick and then being unprepared to contend with it, told reporters: "Football is my craft and as a craftsman I am paid not to make mistakes. I miskicked it. There it is. I can only say I am terribly sorry."

Blackpool captain Johnston recognised that Ramsey had come unstuck by opting not to simply bang the ball as far away from danger as possible. "It was a cruel blow to a man trying to use the ball constructively," he said. "The idea was good even if in this case it didn't come off."

Others felt less inclined to sympathise. "There was both relief and elation in our dressing room," said Perry, while Matthews would describe "the glorious feeling of achievement when you have cleared the semi-final hurdle".

12

THE LONGEST DAYS

"Reaching the FA Cup Final has become a form of torture because of the length of time which elapses between the semi-final ties and the final itself." – Wales international John Charles.

IF KENNETH Wolstenholme's commentary was a battle to balance his affection for Bolton with his admiration for Stanley Matthews, then that conflict was merely a reflection of the delicate matters of civic diplomacy that came into play once the identity of the two FA Cup Finalists was known.

Having seen his team triumph in their semi-final, Bolton chairman Jim Entwhistle was delighted to receive this message, via the *Queen Mary* in mid-Atlantic, from Field Marshal Viscount Montgomery: "My Dear Chairman – I have just heard on the ship's radio that you beat Everton today and will now go to Wembley. As an Honorary Freeman of Bolton, I would like to say how very glad I am. Please congratulate the team from me and say I shall look forward to seeing the Cup in Bolton on my next visit."

When Entwhistle proudly informed the press of such an endorsement from one of the nation's most-loved war heroes, the council chambers in Blackpool shook with umbrage. Apparently Monty had forgotten that he was similarly affiliated to their town. Mayor Peter Fairhurst wasted no time in firing off a telegram to the Field Marshal: "Understand you have promised to support Bolton Wanderers at Cup Final. May I express the hope that, as an honorary Freeman of Blackpool, we can have your undivided loyalty to both clubs if you are present."

Ignoring the fact that if loyalty was to be shared between teams it would, by definition, be divided, Fairhurst also sent a message to Prime Minister Winston Churchill: "May we expect you, as Blackpool's most distinguished Freeman, to be shouting for Blackpool?" The *Bolton Evening News*, however, was dismissive of the apparent upset caused to a rival town, suggesting that "perhaps it is just Blackpool's publicity flair".

Entwhistle, meanwhile, responded: "I think they have put a wrong construction on what Lord Montgomery said. He did not say he was going to support Bolton in the Cup Final but merely congratulated the club and said he hoped to see the Cup in Bolton next time he visited the town. We accepted it as a friendly gesture and an honour to the club and that, I believe, is all he ever intended."

Most observers saw this as harmless skirmishing that added to the fun of the final. Of far greater import to the fans was the possibility of getting their hands on a ticket for Wembley after the announcement that each team would get an allocation of 12,500, which covered only a fraction of the competing teams' home attendances. Underlying the Football Association's policy was the feeling that it was simply unwilling to have its national event dominated by the working-class masses that typically made up most clubs' fan base, especially those from the north. Far better to allow in the lords and colonels who dominated the committee rooms of the amateur game.

Barely had the follow-up stories to the semi-finals hit the streets – with Blackpool's match-winner, Leading Aircraftman Jackie Mudie, pictured back on duty 24 hours later at RAF Weeton – than supporters of both teams were contacting their clubs in the hope of grabbing whatever tickets were on offer. Both Bolton and Blackpool had to remind fans that it was too early to request tickets and began returning applications. People were wasting their time by sending money without knowing the prices and other arrangements, the clubs explained. The *Evening Gazette*, having been sent money by hopeful Blackpool fans, reminded readers that they had no supply of tickets in their office.

It was a further week before Wanderers were able to announce the acceptance of postal applications for tickets, explaining that they could not sell in person via the box office because FA regulations demanded that clubs had a record of who had purchased tickets as a safeguard against the black market. Specifying the need for applications to include the correct money and stamped, addressed envelopes, the club stressed that season ticket holders would have first priority. Those with seats in the Centre Stand and Burnden Stand would be eligible for one Wembley seat per season ticket; Burnden and Manchester Road paddock season ticket holders could apply for one terrace ticket; while ground season ticket holders also qualified for one terrace ticket. Applications from non-season ticket holders would be dealt with "as far as possible" after allocation to season ticket holders. Prices at Wembley were £2 10s, £1 5s and 15 shillings for the stands, 10s 6d for seated tickets on the terracing and 3s 6d to stand on the ground level.

With so few tickets to distribute, it was clear that demand would be nowhere close to satisfied, leading the club to decide not to consider applications from those who lived outside the town and the immediate surrounding villages. The *Evening News* published only one letter of complaint and reporter Haydn Berry spoke for both participating teams when he wrote: "Pity the club that has to dispense its miserable pittance of tickets and face the fury of its own people."

The ticket allocation seemed designed to feed the black market, taking tickets out of the hands of those who really wanted them and awarding too many to those around the nation's clubs and associations who would be happy to exploit their windfall. Fully aware of this potential, the FA felt that a statement of warning would be more effective than a re-think of their distribution policy, although its threat was hardly likely to strike fear into those thinking of cashing in.

> The committee had always been aware of the importance of distributing Cup Final tickets fairly through authorised channels and of preventing them from falling into the hands of the profiteers. Any club or person proved to have sold a ticket at enhanced price will be debarred from receiving a ticket for at least five years.

Bolton received several thousand letters in each of the first and second posts on the day after the announcement of ticketing arrangements. By the time the local newspaper's photographer arrived at Burnden Park to take a picture of manager Bill Ridding helping to sort envelopes, an estimated 10,000 had been delivered and the club's letter box was overflowing. Some envelopes had been stolen from the box and the money taken.

The 85 sub-post offices in the Bolton area were planning to stay open longer to deal with the extra demand on their services. Tom Eccles, who owned the post office shop across the road from the stadium, said: "I've seen nothing like it in 33 years. Some folk who don't believe in wasting time are buying a postal order, a sheet of notepaper and two envelopes and rushing across to the ground with them. Everything would have worked smoother if the football people had told the postal authorities beforehand. This rush for 3s 6d [postal] orders was a shock – one that could have been avoided."

Not everyone, however, was organised enough to follow the required procedures. The club reported that some people were applying multiple times; others were sending coins instead of a cheque, postal order or notes. Incorrect or incomplete applications were piled into tea chests to be dealt with later. When the number of requests reached 40,000 inside two days, anyone who was not a season ticket holder was told not to bother.

Requests were arriving from all corners of the world; from Australia to Africa. One letter asked for tickets for members of the Sudanese government working in London. It was at a time like this that the players noticed more than ever the familiarity with which they were viewed by the fans, who were often living in the same street. Joyce Barrass explained: "Malcolm was a very popular player. We didn't have big posh houses like they do today, but the club paid the rent for us. It made the fans feel closer." Even the biggest star of all, Lofthouse, commented: "We didn't really see ourselves as celebrities around the town. More part of the community."

With that closeness went the feeling that fans could approach their heroes for tickets. Inside a week of reaching Wembley, Lofthouse had counted 97 ticket requests dropping through his front door. With a personal allocation of only 12 tickets to juggle with, he was forced to have a 'regrets' letter printed for him to sign and send back, a tactic also adopted by Bill Ridding. "I never knew I had so many friends," said Lofthouse, who also recalled: "I lost count of the number of times I was hailed in the street with: 'Don't bother coming home if you don't bring the Cup with you, Lofty.'"

Such was the frenzy around the whole allocation process that the *Bolton Evening News* printed a headline saying "THE TICKETS ARE HERE" to mark the Football Association's delivery to Burnden Park. The paper was denied permission to photograph them, however, because the club wanted no disturbance to the start of the distribution process.

Meanwhile, the *Evening News* took receipt of letters from fans complaining that some households had multiple tickets. "People have got them who never go to a match," wrote an anonymous reader under the name "Disgusted", adding: "One young man at a dance on Saturday night offered to sell me a 3s 6d ticket for 30 shillings. He had three!"

Another supporter reported that his application was returned with the information that a claim had already been made on his name and season tickets. He suggested that in future the club should require actual books to be sent in to support applications.

In Blackpool, the situation was no less frantic. Within two weeks of beating Tottenham, 40,000 applications for Wembley tickets had arrived at Bloomfield Road. The *Evening Gazette* ran a statement from the club telling fans that no more should be sent. More than £10,000 would eventually be returned to those who missed out. "Is it worth the while getting to the final when you have to disappoint so many loyal supporters?" pondered Joe Smith.

The physical arrival of the tickets in Blackpool proved somewhat farcical. The FA gave the club details of the tickets' arrival at Blackpool North station. The train duly arrived without any tickets on board, prompting panic calls to London and local paper headlines about "The Great Cup

Final Ticket Mystery". The FA sent revised instructions. The tickets would turn up the following day at Blackpool Central. When they did, the photographers were waiting, following a bemused-looking porter down the platform as he pushed his trolley bearing a priceless brown paper package.

As in Bolton, the locals assumed that more of those precious pieces of paper would find their ways into the hands of players with no one in particular to give them to. Refreshingly, Matthews found that the begging letters were outnumbered by the messages from well-wishers with no thought of attempting to blag a ticket. "People who'd never seen me play, or in fact never even seen a football match, sent me their good wishes. I received hundreds of mascots and thousands of letters," he told biographer David Miller. "Complete strangers called at my home to wish me well. It was good to feel that I had so many people behind me."

Meanwhile, even Blackpool's town officials were made to sweat over their prospects of seeing the final in person. The club gave ten tickets to the Blackpool Corporation and the names of the lucky councillors were drawn out of a hat by the Mayor. The *Evening Gazette* was rebuffed when it tried to find out the names of the recipients.

Television retailers in Blackpool and Bolton were quick to attempt to capitalise on the disappointment suffered by the thousands unable to secure a place at Wembley. "Don't be downhearted because you didn't get a ticket. Take advantage of this offer and have the finest viewpoint possible," read an *Evening News* advertisement for Proffits in Knowsley Street, Bolton, where a Phillips 12-inch set was on offer for an £11 down payment followed by weekly amounts of 16s 8d. The store even offered to stage evening demonstrations for those uncertain of the benefits or workings of this new technology. In fact, the whole industry was excitedly bracing itself for the biggest month in the history of the medium in Britain. The Radio and Television Retailers Association went as far as urging car owners to fit radio interference suppressors to their engines to ensure better nationwide reception for the Cup Final and Coronation broadcasts.

In the towns of the competing teams, the final dominated like no other topic. Stories such as the death of the Queen's grandmother, Queen Mary, and the forecast of the end of sugar rationing came and went, but the build-up to Wembley remained and intensified. No civic event in Blackpool or Bolton could pass without a toast to the fortunes of their respective teams, from council meetings to the annual dinner of the Fylde Amateur Billiards and Snooker League at the Winter Gardens.

Any quirky Wembley-related story was guaranteed prominent placement in the local newspaper. The *Evening Gazette* reported on 22-year-old toolmaker Eddie Drew, who had emigrated to Toronto from his home on the North Shore two years earlier, but was spending all his savings on returning home for the game, even though he had no ticket. The next day it was reported that an anonymous Blackpool man had called Drew's aunt's house with an offer of a spare ticket. "He said that for personal reasons he was unable to attend the final and refused any offer of payment," said the delighted traveller. "My 3,000-mile journey has not been in vain."

Not so lucky was Frank Hesketh, a Blackpool fan from Carleton, who lost his ticket early in the week of the final and advertised – naively and in vain – for its safe return. A year earlier his one-year-old daughter had tossed his season ticket on the fire and, having no record of its number, he had been forced to pay to go to each individual match. Hesketh said he planned to go to Wembley regardless, yet a Mr G Ramsbottom of Fleetwood would not even get that close to seeing the game. Having been unable to use his ticket for the final in 1951 after going into hospital, the same thing had happened again two years later. "This case of mine must be a record," he said from his sickbed.

The *Evening Gazette*'s attempts to stir up an argument over train arrangements to London were quickly dismissed, however. According to the paper, some fans were complaining that if they took certain early-morning trains on the day of the final they would be required to pay a compulsory charge of 17 shillings to cover meals, in addition to the 47 shillings return fare. British Railways quickly refuted the claim, pointing out that it applied only to the one specifically designated dining-car train, with passengers perfectly entitled to choose whether or not they partook of the meals on offer on all other trains.

Meanwhile, the RAC helpfully issued suggested routes for those planning to drive to the game from Lancashire. Looking back from the current era of direct motorway connections, the tortuous journey suggested for Blackpool fans seems designed to keep people at home: Kirkham by-Pass, Ashton-on-Ribble, Euxton, Wigan, Ashton-in-Makerfield, Newton-in-Makerfield, Warrington Stretton, Tarporley, Nantwich, Stapeley, Blackbrook, Meaford Stone, Weston-upon-Trent, Rudeley, Lichfield, Atherstone, Kilsby, Towcester, Stony Stratford, Hockcliffe, Dunstable, St Albans, Radlett, Elstree, Harrow, followed by the A409 through Wealdstone, turning left at Carlton Avenue and proceeding to Forty Lane, finally turning right into Wembley Park.

Around the editorial space being devoted to the game, advertisers wasted no time in wishing their local team good luck – even if their product had nothing to do with football – while anyone who felt they had a stake in the game was quick to make that fact known. "Again! Matthews reaches Cup Final in C-W-S Football Boots – available from Blackpool Cooperative Society," read a typical *Evening Gazette* ad.

Yet commercial opportunities for the Cup Final participants were nothing compared to the more lucrative agent-led 'player pools' that would become the norm in future years, when every interview, appearance and photo opportunity added valuable pounds to the pot. The Blackpool team had to be content with whatever their organising committee, under Johnston's chairmanship, could come up with. This included an FA Cup Final celebration dance, held in the middle of April at the Tower Ballroom, where 3,000 people paid four shillings per head for the chance to brush shoulders with the players, enjoy comedy by George Formby, Frank Randle, Richard "Stinker" Murdoch and Norman Evans, and dance to Reginald Dixon and the Tower Band, who were decked out in tangerine and white. Johnston also negotiated an unseasonal deal for overcoats with King's menswear shop, the result of which was some sweaty and uncomfortable-looking players being photographed when leaving and returning to the town in the sunshine of early May. One year later, Preston North End's finalists were estimated to have shared the princely sum of £550 from such activities.

Players of neither side would be getting rich on bonuses offered by their clubs. Bolton's players had been promised £25 for bringing back the Cup, £5 more than their Blackpool counterparts. "We got 20 quid bonus because we won," recalled Cyril Robinson. "I don't know what we'd have got if we lost. It was up to the club and they didn't say. Their attitude was: 'Think yourself lucky. Look at all the pros that play and never get anywhere near the final.'"

The Bolton Wanderers annual general meeting, staged three days before the final, reported a profit of £4,000 in the previous financial year, giving the club a balance of £17,000 – of which only £500 would be distributed to the players in the event of Wembley victory, even if as many as 20 men were rewarded. Without any worries about the employees taking too much money from the vaults, it was a predictably upbeat meeting. Manager Bill Ridding was commended for his achievements with the team and the value of reaching the final to the town as a twhole was emphasised. The only concern expressed by chairman Entwhistle was the "very great difficulty" the club had experienced in satisfying demand with its meagre allocation of final tickets.

While Blackpool's squad were preparing to model their new overcoats, it had been revealed that Bolton would be setting a new fashion with their Cup Final jerseys. Each player would take the field in a "silvery shirt of rayon satin with ashen, such as Wembley has never seen before" it was announced a month before the game. Their navy shorts would have the same rayon satin finish. Bolton trader T Thompson, of Albert Ward Ltd, had written to the club offering to supply the new kit as a gift, as he had done for the Wanderers' three Wembley appearances in the 1920s. Players and club officials were allowed a say in the selection of the material while, with the help of the Bolton School of Art, a new badge was designed for the occasion, incorporating the red rose of Lancashire, the town of Bolton's coat of arms and the club colours.

Two weeks later, the team were photographed for the first time in their new uniforms, which had been made at a factory in Wilmslow. The kit was then placed on display in a shop window. Public opinion was divided on the satin finish and some fans were unhappy that the shorts were navy blue, the official club colour, rather than the black that was more commonly worn by the team.

A few days on, the Bolton squad was on display again, this time posing in their Wembley blazers. "This Cup Final has cured any possible camera shyness on the players' part," noted a sardonic Haydn Berry in the *Evening News*.

While smiling their way through such preliminaries and scratching their heads over the task of getting hold of enough tickets for families and friends, the biggest concern for the players of both teams in the six weeks between semi-finals and final was giving their all to the season's remaining League games while avoiding an injury that would keep them out of the biggest match of their careers. It was "the worst period of the season" according to Harry Johnston, who added: "I think we tended to play things a bit carefully in the six weeks before the final. The match immediately before the final was agony because of the thought that there was only one more match to play, and a chance that one of us might get hurt."

In 1948, Blackpool felt they had played themselves out of form between the semi-final and final – a somewhat convenient excuse for the losing team – but three years later, both Joe Smith and Newcastle manager Stan Seymour complained about a seven-week hiatus before Wembley. Newcastle even left leading forward Jackie Milburn out of one match before the final because, they said, he was suffering from "a bad attack of Wembley jitters". Smith argued that year: "It is cruelty to the players. They get edgy and nervous. We want this to be the last time any player is exposed to this miserable spell of anticipation." It wasn't – and memories of Smith's dissatisfaction can't have done anything to instil a positive attitude in his players when faced with the same situation before the 1953 final.

With neither Blackpool nor Bolton in serious contention for the League title, the players took the field each week with a feeling of obligation to the paying public rather with any great relish for the contest at hand. Results reflected this situation, Blackpool winning only four of the nine League games they played in the build-up to Wembley. In their last match before the final they conceded five at Manchester City, just as they had at Middlesbrough two weeks earlier. In the end, only five of the Wembley team played in both of the final two First Division games as Smith looked to nurse his men towards their big day. Matthews played only four matches during that time, and none of the final three, as he looked after a troublesome knee. Bolton had ten League games to complete after their semi-final, winning only three. Success in the season finale against Newcastle brought to an end a run of six matches without victory.

Inevitably, someone was going to suffer the fate that every player dreaded. Two weeks before Wembley, during the final home game of the season against Liverpool, Blackpool left-half Hugh Kelly injured his right ankle. Kelly, who had won his solitary Scotland cap a year earlier, was found to have suffered a fracture.

Robinson didn't know it yet, but he would be the player to benefit from his colleague's misfortune. "The reserves were playing away and as we were coming back they were saying on the radio that Hughie Kelly was injured. The Cup Final was two weeks away, but I didn't think any more about it. Eric Hayward, who used to play centre-half for us, said: 'You might have a chance, Cec,' but I thought Joe Smith would probably move somebody over because I'd not had a lot of experience."

Just as Allan Brown's second Wembley disappointment was discussed sympathetically in the media, so was the injury to Kelly, a popular, hard-working player of whom Clifford Greenwood of the *Evening Gazette* said: "If there is a wing-half stronger in the tackle than [him], giving 20 shillings in the pound in every game, I have not yet met him."

Upon Kelly's death in 2009, the youngest of his three daughters, Jayne, explained: "Naturally he regretted missing the final, but not as much as others did for him. Dad didn't want to focus on the things he missed out on. He genuinely felt that football had given him a wonderful life. He was a team man and thought it was wonderful that Blackpool had won. He took satisfaction from playing in all the games up to Wembley."

Kelly himself said during his latter years: "I lived a great journey to Wembley. That's what fascinated me. And it was a privilege to know such a good crowd of players. They were lovely. Even though we'd lost the other two [finals], it was great to have played on the sacred turf at Wembley and I have fond memories."

The two candidates for Kelly's place, Robinson and centre-half Johnny Crosland, played in the last League game at Manchester City, where Robinson was said to have mistimed tackles but attempted to make intelligent use of the ball. A further scare was suffered when Tommy Garrett went up for a header and landed with a broken nose. Two days later the left-back was pictured as he emerged from Victoria Hospital after having the broken bone reset. Despite looking like an early Hannibal Lecter, his eyes peering out from massive bandages across his forehead and cheeks, he announced: "Miss Wembley? Not on your life." He explained: "It was my ball. I had headed it away as Bill Spurdel went up for it too. I met him as I was coming down and he was going up." He would, he insisted, be training on the Tuesday, although with instructions not to head the ball.

While the players enjoyed a day off, Smith gave a strong indication that he had made up his mind about the number six shirt, saying that Robinson was "probable" to play. After practice on Wednesday, the decision was confirmed. "We were training at Stanley Park and he told me I was playing," Robinson recalled.

Crosland, who had played in the 1948 final as a late replacement for injured full-back Ron Suart – at which time he was a part-time footballer and trainee accountant – would join Jackie Wright as a travelling reserve. Smith explained: "I have chosen the first reserve for the position. Why not? Why make a shuffle of the entire line when there's only one vacancy? That would not have been good football tactics." It was a remarkable opportunity for a player who had earlier been so unconsidered that he had not even been invited to the pre-season photoshoot, meaning that publications printing Blackpool team pictures in the week of the final had to insert his face in a box.

"The alternative to putting me in was to put Crossy in at centre-half and moving Harry Johnston to wing-half," Robinson remembered. "But Joe knew that Harry would handle Lofthouse better than Crossy would. I mean, Crossy was OK but Jonty was a better player. Joe said: 'Why change your centre-half as well? Just put your reserve in.' He should have said that a few times before."

Over in Bolton, manager Bill Ridding also entered the week of the match with some doubts about team selection. The intrigue centred on the full-back positions, where Johnny Ball, Ralph Banks, Roy Hartle and George Higgins were vying for the two places. The fact that Ball had not yet been issued with a blazer was considered a clue by some, although it turned out to be a red herring. Having begun the season as club captain and regular right-back until being injured at Christmas, Ball was considered fit enough to play at Wembley after appearing in four games since recovering from a thigh injury. It meant disappointment for Hartle, who had played in every earlier round but had to be content with being named as the official 12th man. His time would come five years later in partnership with Tommy Banks, the young reserve player whose older brother Ralph was preferred over Higgins – a participant in the previous three rounds – as the man to face Stanley Matthews.

Elsewhere, Willie Moir and Harold Hassall were recovering quickly from cuts and bruises, while Higgins, wing-half Tommy Neill and Ray Parry were confirmed to be joining Hartle as non-playing members of the official travelling party.

When the players were not worrying about injury and selection, there had been more than the usual discussion about the opposition, a natural consequence of having so long to ponder what awaited them in the final. "We talked a lot among ourselves before the 1953 final," said Johnston. "We'd played Bolton so many times; we knew them and they knew us. You get to know footballers as you go through season after season."

Johnston's memories, however, suggest that those talks did not extend to detailed plans to combat opposition strengths – certainly not at the risk of changing their own team's usual playing patterns. "We had to watch certain players, such as Willie Moir, their inside-right, and Hassall, their inside-left. I had the job of watching Lofthouse. We all had these special jobs to do. We were told to do them, but not to the detriment of our own game." The summary was: "We'll mark these men and then, when we get the ball, it's their turn to find us."

Things were no more scientific at Burnden Park. "We had made no special plans to deal with the threat of Matthews," said Lofthouse later. "We were happy with our ability to deal with him. And for 66 minutes you couldn't argue with that."

Ralph Banks told Matthews biographer David Miller: "Bill Ridding wanted us to play our normal game. I'd only had one previous match against Stan, at Blackpool that season. He was all right if you could stand on him. With Stan you had to stop the ball getting to him and even if it was 50-50 he wouldn't really go for it. I wasn't worried about the final."

To be fair to Bolton, neutralising their opponents' attacking options did extend a little way beyond the hope that they could stifle Matthews. The days of Blackpool being considered lop-sided, with Mortensen, Matthews, Johnston and Shimwell providing a purely right-flank threat, had long since passed with the move of Mortensen and Johnston into central positions and the emergence of Perry on the left wing.

Malcolm Barrass recalled his own combat plans: "With Morty playing I couldn't spend too much time looking to go out and cover Matthews. Morty was good so I was just intent on stopping him. He was going to get a belting. Everyone wanted Blackpool to win and Bill Ridding said: 'Clobber anybody if you catch them.' We were going to have a good go at them. We trained in our usual positions and that was about it.

"We weren't a brilliant side by any means but we made up for it in effort and we never gave up. Consequently we could run better than them and we were confident we could win the game."

The unique nature of the Wembley pitch appeared to be of far greater concern to both teams than the opposition. Before their two previous Wembley visits, Blackpool had spent the week training on the grassy promenade at Lytham in an attempt to replicate the thick, clinging surface they would find at the national stadium. On this occasion, Smith opted for Stanley Park "because the turf is fairly thick. At Bloomfield Road after a season's football everything's parched or bare and the pace of the ball is faster than it will be at the stadium". The team did head for Lytham on the Tuesday afternoon, however, to partake of brine baths, although Johnston would later recall a "hard week of training". For once, Eddie Shimwell was working out with his team-mates rather than with Chesterfield after taking a full week away from his Derbyshire pub.

Interest in viewing the Cup Final teams' preparations proved to be modest, with the *Evening Gazette* reporting that Blackpool were watched by "a couple of dozen men, two women, four press photographers and a dog". Meanwhile, Bolton ran laps of the cricket field and practised their passing on the playing fields of Bolton School, in front of pupils who braved the rain on their morning break. Again, the field conditions had been the motivation for the venue and coach George Taylor announced that "the experiment was worthwhile".

Bolton were the first team to venture south, making a low-key departure by train on Thursday morning for the Hendon Hall Hotel, in north-west London. Barely a dozen fans were at the station to see them off. "We know it's going to be a very hard game," said captain Willie Moir. "We are hoping that the best team will win – and the team will be ours. We know we've got what it takes to win."

Blackpool staged their final full training session later that day, concluding with a six-a-side game played without goalkeepers. The scenes that confronted them at Central Station the following morning were in chaotic contrast to Bolton's peaceful exit. Approximately 2,000 fans were estimated to have shown up, lining the entrance to the platform and clambering upon seats and barriers in order to get a better look at the players as they arrived individually to board the train. Matthews and Johnston were the first arrivals, their happy demeanours reflecting the brightness of the morning as they signed autographs and posed for pictures. Officers from the British Transport Commission police had to clear their path to the train as palms slapped them on the back and rattles swirled close to their heads. "It's been a hard journey," Johnston told reporters before he departed. "No club reaches the final without a struggle. Now that we're there, rest assured, we'll give it everything we've got."

Before Mortensen and Farm became the last men to board the train there had been a sympathetic welcome for the injured Kelly and Allan Brown. While Brown looked somewhat sombre, Kelly was all smiles, but he was to find that being a part of the official squad when unable to play in the game was a stressful experience. In *Blackpool: The*

Glory Years Remembered he would describe it as a "long, drawn-out affair" and said that both he and Brown would have preferred to have travelled on their own on the day of the game. They felt removed from the players, even embarrassed at their own presence in the inner sanctum. "I wouldn't recommend any player to go through it," he said.

While the players settled themselves alongside the directors in the train's front carriage, their wives and girlfriends – bound for a separate hotel in London – were allowed to travel in the next car back. Once everyone was on board, the police gave up their attempts to protect the barriers, opening them up to allow an excited surge of fans desperate to reach the front of the platform for a last glimpse of the players as they waved their farewells. As the crowds dispersed, a 40-year-old opportunist from Dublin was arrested, along with his 16-year-old companion, for causing an obstruction as he attempted to sell souvenirs. Grateful for the peace of their private compartment, the players enjoyed lunch as they journeyed and arrived in London at 3.15pm. Met by a coach, they were taken to the Edgwarebury Country Club in rural south Hertfordshire, a converted Elizabethan manor house that offered, according to the newspapers, a "secluded retreat".

While Blackpool prepared for a quiet Friday evening at the cinema in nearby Elstree, Bolton's players were tea guests of the town's two Members of Parliament at the House of Commons before heading to Highbury to watch Arsenal play Burnley in the decisive game of the First Division title race. Joe Smith had already stated that his Blackpool team would stay away from the match, arguing that "the less they think of football the better".

The early-evening game witnessed by the Bolton men provided a thrilling contribution to what would end up as one of the most dramatic final weekends of any English season. Needing victory to beat Preston North End to the title on goal average, the Gunners fell behind in the ninth minute, fought back on a heavy pitch to lead 3-1 and then suffered a scare when Burnley pulled a goal back 15 minutes from time. The championship secured, followers of the London team were able to join the rest of the country in hoping for Blackpool to fulfil Matthews's dream, a result that would at least mean that their own Wembley ambitions had been denied by the eventual winners. Blackpool South MP J Roland Robinson awoke the next morning to find he had been sent a gift by Arsenal fans; a small bag made from tangerine cloth, containing a silver cup and a note saying: "Any team that can beat us must win the Cup."

Bolton's busy day contained one final appointment, the presentation of the Footballer of the Year award to Nat Lofthouse at the Football Writers' Association dinner. Having led the First Division with 30 goals, scored in every round of the FA Cup and added eight in international matches, plus six in a single game for the Football League, there were few arguments about Lofthouse's right to be the recipient.

* * * * *

CUP FINAL morning found the players drifting down for cooked breakfasts in their respective hotels, Matthews after a fitful and sweat-laden night's sleep. Few were surprised to find the dining rooms already occupied by team-mates who were similarly unable to sleep late on the most exciting day in any English professional footballer's life. Eggs and bacon consumed, the players took a gentle walk in the hotel grounds.

Blackpool manager Joe Smith collared trainer John Lynas and suggested an early visit to Wembley, where they found a pitch that, to their relief, was "not too gluey". When he returned to his team's headquarters in late morning, Smith discovered his players attempting to pass the time and soothe nerves. Cyril Robinson recalled: "Come Saturday morning it was a good hot day and we moped around – I think we had a game of cricket." Some played snooker; others sat in the sun reading the various match previews.

Charles Buchan had already published in his monthly magazine the prediction of a memorable final. "Though not among the glamour boys of the day, they are teams in every sense of the word," he wrote. "Blackpool, of course, have caught the imagination with their all-round play. It can be a classic final. For many years we have been promised the 'Match of the Century'. I believe this final will satisfy us all with a clean, bright display of the arts and crafts."

The morning newspaper sports pages gave prominence to the day's events at Wembley over reports of Arsenal's League triumph. It was a sign of the pre-eminence of the FA Cup in football's narrative hierarchy in the early 1950s, especially when it had a central character like Stanley Matthews at the heart of its story-telling and a new monarch in attendance.

"QUEEN AT WEMBLEY TODAY" was the headline above the match preview in *The Times*, demonstrating the reverence in which the young Elizabeth was held and the way in which her presence elevated football's biggest day. Matthews, of course, was the main subject of the report, which stated that "his presence in a victorious side at Wembley is as eagerly awaited by the man in the street as Gordon Richards' first win in the Derby".

A *Daily Mirror* headline predicted "ONE MAN CAN MAKE IT GREATEST FINAL", while Derek Dooley, signed up by the paper as a columnist for the game, cited Matthews as the reason why he would choose to play for Blackpool over Bolton if given the choice. "It will be no more than he deserves if he gains that Cup winner's medal at last," he stated. "He has given millions of people many hours of entertainment."

The *Manchester Guardian* asked "WILL MATTHEWS GET HIS WINNER'S MEDAL AT LAST?" and felt that, even though the loss of Allan Brown and Hugh Kelly might make Bolton the stronger team overall, "Matthews would always be running rings round Banks".

The *Daily Express* was happy to answer the *Guardian*'s question. "STAN SHOULD WIN THAT MEDAL" was the headline above a preview by Desmond Hackett, who looked beyond Matthews's contribution to cite the Johnston–Lofthouse battle as one of the game's most important elements and warned Blackpool of the threat of Moir, whom he described as "the brain boy of the forwards".

Other than Hackett's typewriter, the respective team dressing rooms were perhaps the only places in the country where talk about the game did not revolve around Matthews and his bid for the elusive winner's medal. It is hard to see Matthews's comment later that "I never realised that... there were so many people who wanted me to win an FA Cup winner's medal" as anything other than false modesty. "We kind of ignored it," said team-mate Robinson. "There wasn't that thought amongst us players. We just wanted to win. There was that much publicity about Stan, but it wasn't a distraction. He took it all in and I don't think it bothered him. He had travelled to different countries and they had even made him a chief in Africa so one game didn't affect him."

Meanwhile, those morning papers had been helping fans pass the time after arriving in London before dawn had broken. While some of those who disembarked the overnight trains at Euston at 4am headed straight for the West End, others handed their change to newspaper vendors and sat in the station waiting for the cafes to open. "I went with my dad," said Mel McCarthy, "but I can't remember how we got the tickets. We got there very early in the morning and there were plenty of places where you could get breakfast. Then we went round the shops in the West End. London was the glamour place so we made the most of it."

The opportunity to walk the route of the Coronation parade proved irresistible for some fans of both teams, while the *Lancashire Evening Post* would note: "Among the many women who travelled to London were some who will spend the day shopping while their husbands watch the final."

Blackpool's Atomic Boys were more intent on handing over a souvenir to one of London's most prominent residents rather than hunting for bargains themselves. They strode purposefully towards Downing Street in their garish array of outfits, one of their member sporting a sign around his neck that promised: "Morty will em-Barrass Bolton." Ringleader Syd Bevers approached the country's most famous front door clutching 7lb of pure sugar in the form of a giant stick of Blackpool rock. To his companions' surprise, the door opened and he was invited inside. "I was conducted into an ante-room and a secretary came and said: 'Sir Winston is out for an hour,'" Bevers reported. Accepting the confectionary, which had "Sir Winston" stamped through it, the aide assured Bevers it would be delivered to the Prime Minister. Approximately seven minutes after he had entered Number 10, Bevers rejoined his companions and the group set off for Trafalgar Square, where 5,000 Seasiders were reckoned to have assembled, chanting for their team and enjoying the antics of the infamous Little Harry at the foot of Nelson's Column.

It was clear to the Blackpool fans where the sympathies of the Londoners lay. "We had beaten the Arsenal and Tottenham," said McCarthy. "We were going in places like Swan and Edgars [store] on Piccadilly, and people were saying: 'You are going to win today,' or 'Matthews is going to do it.'"

Those travelling in support of Bolton were given the same message, although Joyce Barrass remembered: "We walked through the city and you could hear people saying 'Stanley is going to win today', and we said: 'Yes he is. Stan Hanson.'"

The Wanderers fans, seven trainloads of whom had made the overnight journey, were just as committed, if somewhat less eye-catching, than their counterparts – although one, Peter Powell, impressed onlookers with a massive FA Cup hat and a silver chain comprising 11 miniature cups, one for each player, slung around his neck.

As the stadium opening time of 12.45pm approached, the crowds dispersed. But wherever they ventured, the touts trotted along behind. What tickets they could acquire were easily sold, with 50-shilling seats fetching as much as £6, but the supply lines were being strangled by the determination of the people of Blackpool and Bolton to witness their teams in action. "The boys from the north have brought no spares with them this time and they part with their own tickets for gold," said one disgruntled entrepreneur.

Those left behind in the competing towns were feeling the excitement of the day almost as keenly as those who, like an army on manoeuvres, were heading south to create their own tales of the battlefield. Driver Tom Begley and his conductress, Flo, arrived at work at 6am in order to decorate the front of their number 9A bus with a giant tangerine and white rosette. "It brings us some smiling passengers," said Flo later in the day. "All the small boys in town seem to be trying to get on our bus."

Many of the town's shops were adorned with "Up The Pool" signs, as was the Infectious Diseases Hospital in Talbot Road. Thousands of those without television sets grabbed their radios and went to claim their sun-kissed places on the beach and promenade. They would, however, have to settle for only second-half commentary on BBC's

Light Programme after the corporation failed in its late bid to persuade the Football Association to permit them to mirror television's coverage of the entire game.

Those with other business to attend to on this day of possibilities were left cursing their lack of foresight. One convention organiser, congratulated by a passer-by with a cheery: 'You've certainly chosen a beautiful day for it,' issued a curt reply: "We've chosen a bloody silly one."

As kick-off approached, the streets emptied. Former Blackpool resident Tom Alder recalled: "The town was always such a busy place, but that day I took my son, John, for his very first haircut and there was hardly a soul about."

Understanding its readers' desperation to see the FA Cup brought to the Fylde coast for the first time, the *Evening Gazette* offered various omens of victory. Blackpool pianists were reported to have won more prizes than anyone else in the Morecambe Musical Festival, while young cinemagoers at The Odeon were said to have cheered loudly when the Children's Cinema Club's showing of the Will Hay film *Windbag The Sailor* reached the part where a radio announcer, reading the football scores, said: "Blackpool 3" – the din drowning out the remainder of the fictional result.

Back on the outskirts of London, the teams ate a light lunch and boarded their coaches for the short journey to Wembley, both scheduling their arrival for little more than an hour before kick-off. As the players undertook their traditional pre-game walkabout on the pitch – while the bands of the Scots and Irish guards played *She's A Lassie From Lancashire* – Mortensen turned to Matthews and remarked: "Thanks heavens we didn't have to wear the raincoats today."

Matthews was in no mood for jokes, however. For a start, his habitual nerves were intensified by the memory of the promise he had made to his father. And, even though he wore a red, white and blue good luck charm given to him by a fan, he would be taking the field in an hour's time in the hope that orthopaedic expertise, rather than superstition, would see him through his afternoon's work. Unknown to anyone outside the team, Matthews had been concerned about a strain in his thigh since the final practice game of the week two days earlier and requested that the team doctor give him a pain-killing injection on the morning of the final, in the hope it would alleviate any pain that might make him slower into his stride. "I never felt anything," he would report. "I did feel a bit sore about a day later, but nothing much."

It was to prove one of the most significant pieces of medical intervention in the history of the FA Cup.

* * * * *

A FEW hours later, Barrass plays the ball forward to Moir, who steps away from a tentative challenge by Robinson and hits a right-foot shot from outside the box. Farm deals with it comfortably, almost sucking the ball into the safety of his stomach. At the other end, Matthews, his thigh injury long forgotten, passes inside to Taylor, who feeds the ball into the box for Mortensen to chase. From the resulting corner, taken by Matthews, Mortensen can't get any power behind his header.

Further intelligence from the Bolton sideline reaches Wolstenholme – and this in the days before the likes of Sky Sports' Geoff Shreeves stalking the dug-outs for tittle-tattle. Bell's injury, it is revealed, is a recurrence of that which had made him miss five late-season games. More problems loom for Bolton when Lofthouse is seen doubled over in the centre circle holding his side as the ball is booted into the Blackpool half. "It's the old injury when he stopped the ball a few minutes ago," Wolstenholme suggests as Bert Sproston rubs the right side of the centre-forward's torso.

Meanwhile, Bill Ridding puts his physiotherapist's training to use by attempting to work some life back into Bell's left thigh.

When play resumes, Taylor slides effortlessly past a white shirt and frees Matthews close to the by-line, only for his cross to be cleared to safety. Langton hits the ball long into the Blackpool half, but Lofthouse is able to make only a token effort at chasing Johnston for possession. Taylor continues his prompting, playing towards Perry in a central area – a positional move that fails to get Wolstenholme as excited as whenever Matthews strays from the touchline. In any case, Perry is beaten to the ball. Barrass takes a free-kick from inside his own half, knocking it short to Wheeler, who advances unopposed as Blackpool players back away to the edge of the box. Holden is unable to capitalise when given the ball, delivering his cross behind the goal.

Twenty minutes of the second half have been played and the twist in the plotline of the 1953 FA Cup Final is about to be revealed. The months of matches in earlier rounds; the mounting anticipation and excitement surrounding two teams and two towns; the growing sense of drama in a changing nation eager to embrace an iconic event and its hero; all have led towards this. Twenty-five minutes of football that will endure for all time.

13

COMEBACK

"There was only one Stan Matthews. We'll never see anyone like him again. Unique. I freely admit that if I'd had a gun at the end of the 1953 final I would have shot him." – Nat Lofthouse.

P RINCESS MARGARET saw it coming. Seated in the Royal Box, Blackpool chairman Harry Evans had greeted Bolton's third goal by slumping forward with his head in his hands, only for the Queen's younger sister, not noted for her football punditry, to lean across and assure him: "Don't worry. You'll win."

On the field, her optimism was not reflected by everyone in a Blackpool shirt. Some were unable to suppress their worst fears. "It looked hopeless then," Cyril Robinson recalled of the moment Bolton gained a two-goal advantage. "I was thinking to myself: 'At least I've been to Wembley.'"

Bill Perry always maintained that his most deeply ingrained memory of the game was not the decisive contribution he was to make later on, but the sinking feeling of Bolton's third goal: "The thing I remember most about the final was this moment because I was really dejected and had the feeling that we would walk off the pitch having lost again." On the bench, Allan Brown felt similar emotions. "I thought Blackpool had had it when Bolton popped the third one," he admitted.

So Harry Johnston appears to have been mistaken when he said: "I don't think any of us had given up hope." His own optimism came from his perception of his team's superior physical condition. "It helped us tremendously to see that we were looking fitter than they, even though we were 3-1 down."

Among the Blackpool fans being forced to face up to likely disappointment was a watery-eyed Mel McCarthy. "I was there a week before watching St Helens lose [to Huddersfield] in the rugby league Challenge Cup Final. I was in tears and people were saying: 'You should be here next week.' I was, and with 20 minutes to go I was in tears again. I know you are optimistic when you are a young lad, but not that much."

Back home, not even the novelty of being able to watch the entire game could persuade seven-year-old Graham Kelly, who would sit at many Wembley finals as secretary and chief executive of the Football Association, to stick around until the end. "Watching the match on television at a friend's house," he remembered, "we decided it was a lost cause at 3-1 down and went out to play on our bikes – oblivious to the great comeback."

All over the country, those who were Blackpool fans for the day out of loyalty to Stanley Matthews were beginning to despair as well. Diarist Nella Last was listening on the car radio after taking a drive in the countryside around her home in Barrow. Her husband had suggested that there was still a chance of a victory for their hero. "But we agreed it was that of a snowball in a hot stove," she noted.

There were barely 25 minutes to play and Blackpool were still trailing 3-1. Something had to be done, Johnston decided, and as captain he had the authority to make a change. Radically altering the tactics and formation that ran through his team like the town name through a stick of rock might have been beyond him, but he recognised that the extreme pace of Perry could be better utilised. Believing that he could be more threatening to Bolton's defence if coming from a deeper, more central position, he ordered Perry to swap positions with inside-left Jackie Mudie, who had been struggling all afternoon with a troublesome boot.

No sooner had the change been made on the left, Blackpool attacked on the right, Matthews taking a pass from Ernie Taylor and knocking it into space behind Ralph Banks. Johnny Wheeler was neither quick enough nor near enough to close down Matthews after he raced past the full-back. "Look at the speed of that man," gasped Kenneth Wolstenholme. Matthews clipped over a cross, explaining later that he intended to stretch the keeper. But he appeared to have over-hit it harmlessly to the far post, where Stan Hanson was under no pressure. "I grimaced when I saw Hanson in the Bolton goal reach up," Matthews admitted.

Yet the Bolton keeper seemed reluctant to lift his feet off the ground and merely pawed at the cross like a kitten after a ball of string. Matthews suggested that he must have taken his eye off the ball for a moment, while Banks would recall shouting at Hanson to allow it to go out of play. The ball flopped near the feet of Stan Mortensen, who had followed up with his usual optimism, and the striker slid between two defenders to steer it the yard or two it needed to travel across the line. "I caught it with my studs and it just crept in," he explained. Hanson turned and, to complete his embarrassment, stumbled over the prone body of Mortensen.

Taylor tossed Hanson's limbs aside so he could get to his goalscoring team-mate, while Malcolm Barrass put his arms on the keeper's shoulder and bent down to speak words of encouragement in his ear before patting him on the leg and kicking the ball away. Barrass had been as surprised as anyone at Hanson's lapse: "He was a very useful goalkeeper. He had a good pair of hands and we had a lot of confidence in him. I covered him and if he missed the ball he used to clobber me."

Wolstenholme's only word during this crucial passage of action was a somewhat disinterested "Mortensen" after the ball was nestling in the net. But as the scorer limped away and referee Mervyn Griffith first checked on his welfare and then called John Lynas on to the field to look at his left thigh, the commentator added: "Mortensen has scored twice now." This was the first suggestion to television viewers that the first Blackpool goal was being awarded to Mortensen. Two minutes later, though, Wolstenholme corrected himself and reminded viewers that Harold Hassall's earlier deflection meant that Mortensen had scored only one.

It is still not entirely clear at which point that first goal became generally credited to Mortensen. A more pertinent fact appeared obvious to Nat Lofthouse at that time, even with a quarter of the match still to play. "The tide had turned," he said. "We knew it. Blackpool knew it."

While Mortensen was receiving treatment, Matthews went to Ewan Fenton and urged his half-back to deliver the ball down the right wing at every opportunity. "They're rattled. Come on. Give it to me." Fenton nodded wearily in reply.

As the game restarted, Johnston made a couple of interceptions and Perry, from his more central position, got the weight wrong on a pass to the right. After the ball was banged back and forth a few times, Taylor clipped a short half-volley to Matthews just inside his own half. He dragged the ball back and inside the attempted sliding tackle of Banks, who offered a somewhat gentle effort. Matthews set off on a run, looking typically well-balanced, but then slid the ball too far ahead of Taylor. There had been signs, though, in the last few minutes of the great man stepping further towards the front of stage.

According to Perry: "Stan was causing the Bolton defenders trouble every time he was in possession. They were so tired and Stan still had plenty of energy in those old legs of his."

Perry switched to the right but failed to get past Hassall, who attracted boos from the Blackpool fans by booting the ball into the crowd when they felt it was already out of play. Matthews quickly dispatched his colleague back to his own side of the field. Fenton threw to Shimwell and, with Blackpool committed to attack, Doug Holden had room for a long-striding run into their half on the counter attack. Matthews would recall that "we poured forward, sometimes leaving alarming gaps at the back". On this occasion Holden played the ball to Lofthouse but there was no one around to challenge Farm when the centre-forward crossed into the box.

Robinson misplaced a couple of passes, allowing Bobby Langton to link with Eric Bell, who was able to give up his comedy limp long enough to lift the ball towards the far post, where Lofthouse was left rolling on the floor after an aerial battle with Garrett. The Blackpool man walked away and then dropped to his knees, blood colouring his shirt from a cut above his eye, while Willie Moir and Bert Sproston hauled Lofthouse to his feet. Having had a sponge squeezed over his head, Lofthouse staggered back to the centre circle like a man trying to shake off one too many on the morning after. Meanwhile Banks, the man whose responsibility it was to mark Matthews, had gone to the bench and was getting his right thigh rubbed. Bolton were down to eight fit men and the game was becoming more feisty.

When Fenton impeded Moir on his way towards the edge of the box, Langton lined up the free-kick, but

Wolstenholme warned that "he might pull a fast one". He was right. Langton ran over the ball in exaggerated style and Wheeler followed up to shoot straight into the wall. Hassall was bundled off the loose ball and Perry was quickly dispossessed in another robust challenge. Lofthouse appeared to be feeling the effect of his injuries when he was unable to react quickly enough to a pass from the advancing Wheeler.

Bolton still had 20 minutes to hold out with their depleted forces. "We never stopped running," said Barrass. "We had the game won but then it started to get away from us. But we gave a great effort and had a go."

Johnston knocked the ball ahead for Taylor, who chipped into the box in the direction of Perry. He was challenged in the air by Ball and the ball fell to Mudie on the left of the box. His tentatively poked shot was deflected for a corner. Now it was Ball's turn to receive treatment after he stood up holding his head, Wheeler whirling his arm to wave Sproston to the field. Ball recovered quickly enough to clear Mudie's corner away from the near post. By now, Bolton were happy to scramble the ball clear by any means but Langton was still looking to play football, attempting to steer a pass to Lofthouse. Again, the delivery was a yard or two astray, allowing Johnston to tidy up.

An increasing state of Matthews-induced panic saw Bolton allow another Blackpool opening. Receiving the ball in his customary position near the touchline, Matthews had time to retreat a couple of yards away from Banks and then stand still, with barely a shimmy of his toes, in front of the frozen full-back for a good couple of seconds. Instead of taking him on, Matthews slid the ball forward into the penalty area, where Wheeler and Barrass were still looking at each other as Perry's touch put the ball at the feet of Mortensen. His first-time shot from just outside the six-yard area was blocked at close range by

Hanson, who felt justified in aiming words of retribution at Wheeler.

Matthews might have been guilty of becoming a little caught up in the myth of 'his' final over the years, especially when he recalled that "I was playing the game of my life, pulling out every trick I knew", but he was clearly enjoying a spell of dominance over his opponents. After the stumbling Bell lost possession to Shimwell the ball was quickly back on the right touchline via a pass by Fenton. Matthews cut inside Banks, only to see his left-footed cross cleared. But then Robinson headed towards the Bolton end and Matthews comfortably beat Bell to the loose ball. Breezing past his stricken rival and accelerating outside Moir, he crossed deep into the box towards the unmarked Perry and Mudie. Together they headed the ball towards Mortensen and saw it bounce back to Mudie, whose toe-ender was grasped by Hanson.

Bolton had barely been out of their half for the past few minutes and Johnston now fired a diagonal ball to find Matthews yet again. He cut inside, played it short and took a return pass from Taylor, before pulling the ball back from the line. Wheeler blocked this particular cross for a corner and, with Banks receiving further treatment behind the goal, Hanson punched the ball clear. When the referee ruled he had been fouled by Mudie, Bolton at last had a chance to breathe.

"We were working the ball down the right from defence," observed Hugh Kelly from his sideline vantage point. "On through to Taylor, then to Matthews and that was the danger for Bolton and I could see them start to get rattled."

According to Robinson: "It looked bad, but then Stan started putting it together and the play was all on that side. Taylor was supplying the passes and I could see that once we equalised we would win. We had them."

Matthews, despite some of his wanderings earlier in the game, was never one to go looking too far for the ball. If he could stand on the touchline all day and have it delivered to his feet then that suited him just fine. In Ernie Taylor, he had the man to give him exactly the service he craved and it is no coincidence that Matthews's influence on the 1953 final grew as Blackpool's inside-right became more involved in proceedings.

"Once Ernie started to turn it on we all felt that things were clicking," Johnston would write. "The little man with genius in his boots suddenly found his magic touch. He kept giving Matthews the ball as though it was his mission in life. They were irresistible."

Taylor, a man whose name seemingly could never be written without inclusion of the epithet 'little', had already played a major role in the history of the FA Cup – and would do so again in tragic circumstances five years later.

Standing at 5ft 4ins and wearing size four boots, he was one of the architects of Blackpool's defeat in the 1951 FA Cup Final at the hands of Newcastle, the club for whom he had signed from Hylton Colliery in 1942, despite being born on the doorstep of rivals Sunderland. His back-heel had helped set up Jackie Milburn's decisive second goal at Wembley.

Five months later, he joined Blackpool – supposedly as a result of Matthews's urging to manager Joe Smith – taking the number eight shirt and allowing Mortensen to move to centre-forward.

A player who was able to create space among the heaviest congestion with a feint or intricate ball-work, he made the game appear effortless, with instinct rather than deep thought guiding him. Goals, even shots on goal, were a rarity but there was no lack of appreciation of his ability among his team-mates. Matthews could be gushing about him, describing him as a "cheeky, confident player" and characterising his game as "joyous, effective artistry". He told author Robin Daniels: "It was a gift with [Ernie] that whenever you were in trouble and wherever you looked up, he was always there."

While Mortensen was getting the goals against Bolton and Matthews the glory, Taylor might have been playing the finest game of his own career. When *The Times* marked the 50th anniversary of the game by commissioning modern football statisticians Opta to run a full analysis of the game, using the marking system they apply to modern Premier League games,[28] Taylor came out ahead of Matthews and behind only Mortensen as Blackpool's most effective player.

It went a long way towards earning him England selection in the ill-fated Hungary game later in the year, his only appearance for his country. Yet he would be back in the headlines early in 1958, the first player signed by Manchester United as they looked to rebuild a side ravaged by the disaster in Munich. It was his influence and experience that was as responsible as anything or anyone in getting their makeshift team to Wembley, where he suffered his first Cup Final defeat.

Bolton Wanderers were the victors that day, but with 80 minutes played against Blackpool they had the look of a losing team, even as they held on to their 3-2 advantage. Unable to contemplate launching the kind of attack that might have capitalised on Blackpool's adventure, they resorted to knocking the ball aimlessly into their opponents' half, from where the likes of Johnston and Shimwell were quick to return it. When they did get time to build something, Moir's pass to the left gave poor old Bell no chance of keeping it in play.

Bell was an even more pitiful sight when Mudie misdirected a crossfield pass for Matthews. Even though the ball ended up barely a yard from the Bolton man, Matthews

. . . .

28 Opta calculates a final ranking for each player by awarding points on a sliding scale for each contribution to the game.

still had time to drop back and take it away from him. Banks returned to the field but was unable to resume immediately at left-back, causing Hassall to drop back even further to swap positions. So Matthews was now confronted by a forward-playing left-back, supported further forward by two crippled colleagues. Still there was no apparent thought of calling for reinforcements from another area of the field. Surely there was a case for bringing Wheeler over from the right?

Banks, the man in the eye of the storm, was acutely aware of the need for assistance. Feeling that Hassall was proving ineffective in his makeshift position of left-half, he shouted at Langton to drop deeper to offer support. He also pleaded with captain Moir to assign someone specifically to the task of marking Taylor. "Moir did nothing," Banks recalled. "He thought we had it won."

Further troubled – as he had feared – by aching shins, Banks even suggested that he and Ball swap their full-back positions in the face of Matthews's onslaught. "It was impossible to do anything with him once he had the ball," said Banks, adding: "I couldn't feel my legs." But even Ball was, according to his team-mate, "hopping about" with his own injury. "We were in a right state," Banks concluded.

Matthews's next touch was in a central position, where Wheeler snapped at his heels and robbed him, before being penalised for a foul, a decision with which Moir was clearly unhappy. Bolton's first notable attack for what seemed like an age resulted from a horribly aimless pass by Fenton followed by a daydreaming Shimwell playing Lofthouse onside when the ball was banged downfield by Barrass. Lofthouse did well to hold it up as he drifted right and then attempted to switch it to the left. Had it not been for Johnston sticking out a telescopic leg, a fast-arriving Langton could have been through with only Farm to beat.

There were less than eight minutes of normal time to go when Perry and Taylor combined and the ball was suddenly at the feet of Matthews once more. He skipped past Banks with his usual lean to the inside and burst to the outside, leaving the restored left-back on his knees again. Hassall covered in time to put the ball behind for a corner. The ball was played short again – an apparently aimless rather than designed move – and when it was cleared out to Shimwell his long-range effort deflected harmlessly into Hanson's arms. Barrass, who had blocked the ball and player almost simultaneously, lay sprawled on his stomach.

Peter Dimmock, the head of BBC's outside broadcasts – which would include that year's Coronation – had been logging the game's injuries and informed Wolstenholme that four minutes had been lost to stoppages so far in the half. Bolton were going to have to hold out for a little longer yet.

With four minutes to play, it appeared that they might do so as Blackpool had not threatened for a couple of minutes. When Perry, moving gracefully across the ground, attempted to link with Taylor to work the ball into the box it was cleared once more. Robinson sent it back and his pass was laid off first time by Mudie to Perry, but the move was broken up. Robinson, understandably more adventurous now than at any time in the match, again advanced and played low to Perry, who was once more careless in his approach towards the box.

Even with the clock ticking, Blackpool needed to find time for a little more thought. Fenton failed to do so when he received the ball from Johnston and knocked it hurriedly into the heart of the box, where three Bolton defenders were the only ones waiting.

Despite the enduring myth that Blackpool did nothing but give the ball to Matthews in the second half, it had now been some minutes since they looked his way. When the ball did reach the right flank again Shimwell hoisted it harmlessly into the box rather than use his winger. Barrass headed away to the edge of the area before the ball was ushered back into Hanson's possession. However, as the keeper prepared to clear, referee Griffiths stood signalling for a Blackpool free-kick, having apparently penalised what was only the merest brush by Holden on Mudie on the left edge of the penalty area. Even in these more intolerant modern times it would have been the harshest of decisions. A group of four Bolton players stood momentarily with hands on hips, looking quizzically at the official – the closest the era ever came to a Premier League-style surrounding of the referee.

The clock was approaching 88 minutes as Mortensen grabbed the ball. Blackpool had no repertoire of set moves to choose from, Smith preferring to trust his players to make the correct decisions on the spur of the moment. Taylor volunteered to chip the ball into the box and Johnston urged Shimwell forward in anticipation of such a move. But Mortensen insisted: "I am going to have a go."

"There's no gap," Taylor argued, before eventually nodding his head in acceptance and retreating with the warning: "You'll never do it."

Mortensen viewed the defensive barrier spreading in front of him. He couldn't even see the goalposts. He retreated four paces and, without hesitation, turned and approached the ball. Shimwell's advance had made him question whether to follow Taylor's tactical advice after all, but as he began his run-up one post appeared beyond the last player in the Bolton wall. His mind was made up. "Now I could see the left post. This convinced me I should have a belt." Matthews recalled a hush as his team-mate advanced, then heard a "bass-like thud" as he made contact.

"The moment I struck the ball I knew it was in," said Mortensen, who simply blasted a shot past the wall and inside the left post; a phenomenal effort with the heavy ball and the tiredness in his legs. "I could have tried that kick a million times and the ball would have gone anywhere but in the net," he confessed.

It was as much as Hanson could do to turn his head to his right to see his goal being breached. Blackpool were level at 3-3 – and who says they didn't celebrate goals in the 1950s? Mortensen ran to Johnston and jumped into his arms, legs straddling him in the manner of an ice-dancing move. Then he collapsed at the bottom of a heap as his team-mates piled on top. Shimwell would describe it as the finest goal Mortensen ever scored, while Robinson recalled: "That was one of the best free-kicks I have ever seen. If you watch the recording, you can't see the ball. He caught it perfectly. If anyone had got in the way of that it would have injured them."

Throughout the mayhem, Wolstenholme sat in silence in the commentary box. For once, it was golden as the cheers of the crowd toppled out of television sets into crowded living rooms and parlours across the country. There was no need for words. Everyone knew they had witnessed a stunning goal and could see what it meant to the Blackpool players. "Morty has scored many magnificent goals," said Johnston later. "I don't think he has scored a better one than that dramatic equaliser."

The impact on Bolton's team was no less emphatic. "We couldn't believe what had happened," said Lofthouse. "How can you control a game for so long and see it suddenly go wrong? I know I had gone a bit. We all had. The rest was inevitable." In a later account, he said: "I had no sense of panic, only tiredness… In that final spell [Matthews] could do it, and he knew he could do it."

In the Wanderers family section, Malcolm Barrass's wife, Joyce, had already seen enough. "I remember that we were sitting a long way down the side and when we'd looked over at the Blackpool wives they were all nearer the middle, so they obviously had better tickets. I said: 'They'll be seeing everything and we'll be craning our necks.' I had a funny feeling as the game went on and I said to May Hanson: 'Could I just pass you to get out?' She said: 'You're not going out now, are you? You'll miss them getting the Cup.' I said: 'They are not going to get it.' I didn't see the end of the game, I was down underneath the stand."

Nat Lofthouse's mother also missed the game's denouement, having declared with half an hour remaining: "I can't watch another minute."

Nella Last remembered being "gripped by the intense excitement" as she heard Blackpool draw level, but that was nothing compared to the drama in the section where the Matthews family sat. Having already fainted once, when Mortensen scored the second goal, Matthews's mother-in-law did so again when the equaliser went in. Betty Matthews recalled everyone around her crying and someone offering her mother a reviving swig of brandy.

"It was a terrible ordeal for me," she explained. "I sat through the whole game with my fingers crossed. At times I thought I would have heart failure." Sat next to her was seven-year-old son Stanley junior, of whom she said: "It was his first Cup Final and he danced with joy every time he saw his father on the ball. Both of us had tears in our eyes when Blackpool scored."

14

THE WINNER

"Matthews on the edge of the Bolton penalty area, dribbling right in, past his man. Two yards out, squares it. Hit it, somebody! Yes! It's there. It's there. Perry has scored. Perry has scored number four; laid on by Stanley Matthews. Blackpool have scored number four." – BBC radio commentator Raymond Glendenning.

BILL PERRY might not have spent his childhood nights in Johannesburg dreaming of being a Wembley hero, but the FA Cup Final had made a deep impression on him. "Everybody used to look forward to Cup Final day in South Africa," he explained. "We used to listen to the match commentary on the radio." Now it was his name that would be leaping out of transistors across the home of his birth.

Brought up playing rugby, football had only become a major part of Perry's life when, at the age of 14, he moved to Queen's Junior High School, where the round ball game was all that was offered. Facing the end of his aspirations as a loose forward, he quickly resolved to cement a place in the school team via the only vacant position, outside-left. Naturally right-footed, he was driven through fear of his sports master to work on his left in order to earn continued selection. His training tools were those favoured by so many schoolboy players in England; a tennis ball and a brick wall.

Having joined the Johannesburg Rangers club after he left school to take up an apprenticeship in a car parts factory, he played on either wing with sufficient expertise to earn a place in the Transvaal provincial team. He also came to the attention of Charlton Athletic manager Jimmy Seed, whose regular scouting trips to South Africa would, in the space of a few years, take players such as forwards Eddie Firmani and Stuart Leary, defender John Hewie and future South African Test cricketer Sid O'Linn to The Valley. Perry might have arrived in south London in 1948 had it not been for the far-reaching influence of Blackpool manager Joe Smith.

"It was a great opportunity for [South African] players because all we wanted as a guarantee was our return fare if we did not make the grade," Perry explained. "It was like a working holiday."

But on this occasion Rangers coach Billy Butler, a team-mate of Smith's in the 1923 Bolton FA Cup Final side, cautioned him to wait for a better offer. Butler had already fired Perry's imagination about the greatest occasion in English football. "He often told us what it was like to play at Wembley with the crowd and atmosphere, so the competition was something special to me," he explained. Now, a few months later, Butler was reporting that Smith was interested in seeing if Perry's speed and skill would be a good fit at Blackpool. "Charlton were not a bad team," said Perry. "But Stan Matthews was at Blackpool and everyone knew what a great player he was. My fate was sealed."

Labelled "Champagne Perry" by his manager and local press, he would become yet another Blackpool signee who fell in love with the town enough to settle there for the rest of his life, even though the harsh winter weather and the 4pm sunsets took some getting used to after the climate of his homeland. Homesickness was conquered quickly enough, however, for him to force his way into the first team against Manchester United in March 1950 – only three months after his arrival in England – following a handful of games in the A and reserve sides.

Coming from a place where games were postponed if it rained heavily, Perry had to work hard to maintain his speed on the heavy pitches he now encountered. His success in doing so, allied to his strength on the ball and his instinct for goal, made him the perfect foil for his famous counterpart on the right flank, even though Matthews recalled that "we carried him when he first came into the team". Perry said: "Speed was my asset on the left wing. I was faster than Stan and played more of a direct game. Stan would get on the ball and then work his way slowly up the wing… I was looking for a lot of through balls from the inside-forwards and wing-halves."

With not much more than a minute of normal time to play in the FA Cup Final of 1953, the fates of Matthews and Perry were about to become inextricably linked. "Now we have a chance," Perry told himself after Mortensen's equaliser, "providing the final whistle doesn't go." He would speak later of the "renewed enthusiasm" that the goal injected into his team-mates, especially in the knowledge that Bolton were suffering physically.

Having been lured to England partly by romantic tales of the FA Cup, it was apt that the tournament should be providing the defining moments of his career. His goal in the semi-final against Birmingham at Goodison Park in 1951 had convinced him that the decision to move to England had been the correct one. Yet the subsequent loss in the final against Newcastle had scarred him deeply: "There's nothing worse than losing at Wembley, worse than a semi-final. I've never felt so bad."

In *Blackpool: The Glory Years Remembered* he described the "demoralising feeling" at the end of that game. "The winning team are doing their lap of honour and we were standing there with our heads bowed, waiting for it to end. It was a depressing experience." For the likes of Matthews, Mortensen and Johnston, he added, there was the added sense of a last opportunity having been missed.

Surely it was going to be different this time? With their lead taken away from them, it was hard to see from where Bolton could pull enough resources to prevent the momentum taking the Cup to Blackpool, even if the game was forced into extra-time. "The whole thing felt like a whirlwind," Perry would recall. "One minute we were down and out, 3-1 behind with barely any time left to play. The next we were level again and pressing back a Bolton smitten by injuries and reeling from the storm of attacks we'd subjected them to."

As the game entered its final moments, Harold Hassall's ball forward to the struggling Nat Lofthouse was cleared into touch, but Eric Bell's throw was headed by Eddie Shimwell to Matthews just inside his own half. Faced by Ralph Banks and Hassall, he played the ball inside to Taylor, who helped it first time to Stan Mortensen. He needed only one touch to return it to Matthews, who was by now clear of the two men who had earlier barred his way. He shaped to cut inside Barrass, went instead to the outside with an effortless glide and sent over a cross that was diverted clumsily by Stan Hanson in the direction of Jackie Mudie at the far post. To Bolton's relief, Mudie was unable to prevent the ball bouncing behind off his shins.

Kenneth Wolstenholme's match summary was on the money. "Some people might say this hasn't been the greatest final," he offered, "but there can't have been a more exciting one and a more terrific struggle against the odds than we've seen from Bolton."

Hanson's goal kick went directly out of play on Blackpool's right, prompting the question of why on earth he was kicking towards the flank where Matthews was lurking and Bolton's defences were depleted. Joe Smith grabbed the ball on the sideline and tossed it excitedly to Ewan Fenton.

Having been on the field for the first two of Bolton's FA Cup triumphs in the 1920s, the Blackpool manager could not overcome the urge to become as involved as possible. "I was so excited that in the last three minutes I was fielding the ball when it went into touch," he said. What was proving much easier was putting aside his love of the club he had skippered with such distinction. "I have a sentimental attachment to the Wanderers but I know the team I want to win and it wears the tangerine jersey," he had said before the game. When he left Bolton in 1927, he had departed with a sincere letter to the club thanking them "most heartily for the splendid treatment I have received during my 19 years' connection with the club, the consideration and many kindnesses that I have had". He had, however, diplomatically declined his recent invitation to a dinner for all the Bolton players who had played in their previous finals.

Smith had begun Cup Final week by referring to Blackpool's late winners in four of their earlier ties and saying: "If we win this time, nobody will be able to say we haven't earned it – and earned it the hard way."

Events at Wembley were certainly bearing that out. Receiving the ball from his manager, Fenton threw it down the line to Matthews. Taking possession in five yards of space, he decided not to run at Banks but played a diagonal cross to the far post, where the shaky Hanson caught the ball. The 90 minutes were up.

An additional minute had been played when Bolton, out of nowhere, mounted an attack. Bobby Langton squeezed inside Fenton and found Lofthouse on the left of the Blackpool box, but with Johnston closing him down the ball squirted away to George Farm. The keeper bowled out to Taylor, who drifted inside a tired challenge from Langton and played it right to Matthews on the halfway line. Again, Banks stood off, allowing Matthews to flick it inside to Fenton off the toe of his boot. Fenton was only half stopped by Johnny Wheeler, and Taylor played the loose ball first time back to the right, bisecting two white shirts.

The body language of the Bolton players screamed panic as Matthews advanced into the penalty area, his diagonal progress making it unclear if he intended to cut inside or make for the by-line. He opted to go outside the struggling Banks. "Out of the corner of my eye I noticed Barrass coming in quick for the kill," Matthews would record. "As his footing gave way beneath him, I slid the ball back across goal. As I fell, my heart and hopes fell also."

As he had tumbled, Matthews had pulled the ball back to the kind of central area where Mortensen had been lurking hundreds of times during the previous six years of their partnership. On this occasion, however, the England striker had advanced into the six-yard box in the direction of the far post, while Hanson waved at his defenders to cover him. "This is our last chance; what is he doing?" flashed through Matthews's mind in a split-second of abstract thought.

However, the ball was delivered – intentionally or otherwise – perfectly into the space behind Mortensen, where Perry ran in to fire a right-footed shot into the goal, with none of the five Bolton bodies in the six-yard area able to keep it out of the net.

"It's there! Perry! Perry!" exclaimed Wolstenholme as most of the Blackpool team, after a cursory acknowledge-ment of the scorer, went to embrace the goal's creator. "I was rather lucky in getting that ball across for Bill Perry to score," said Matthews. "A split second after I made my pass I slipped over. Had I fallen a moment sooner the pass would have gone wrong."

Perry explained: "Stan slipped slightly as he centred it, so Morty over-ran it and it was left to me to bang it sweetly in through a scrum of Bolton players. It was a marvellous moment." Relieved that his shot had not been deflected by the crowd of defenders, Perry's pleasure was heightened further by the feeling that he'd been struggling to contribute against the tough opposition of Ball.

Robinson added: "I have got to laugh about the last one. Matthews crossed it and Morty says: 'I could have got that but I knew Bill was behind me.' I thought: 'Morty, you liar.' Can you imagine him leaving it to someone else? He got ribbed about that quite a bit."

Matthews, meanwhile, was only vaguely aware of the detail of what had happened. He was conscious of the explosion of excitement among his team-mates, yet all he could hear was a "low droning buzz" that muffled the detonation of noise on the terraces. Later, he attributed his temporary deafness to the act of swallowing hard to get some saliva into his dry mouth because when he swallowed a second time his ears were assaulted by "the loudest and most resounding roar I'd ever experienced in a football stadium".

Players converged on him, Perry swinging his head manically from side to side and Taylor punching the air. So overwhelming was the excitement in the stadium that the scoreboard operators in charge of each team's goal tally both put up the figure 4. BBC cameras focused on Matthews making his way back to the centre line for the kick-off. There was no doubting what the story was on this day – never mind Bolton's injury-hit heroics, Mortensen's goals or Perry's winner.

On the Blackpool bench, preparations for extra-time were swiftly being abandoned. "After the equaliser I went to get some lemons," said Jackie Wright. "But shortly after returning we got the winner so I threw them up in the air."

In the press box, reporters gave up on any pretence of neutrality when the winning goal went in. Geoffrey Green, covering the game for *The Times* recalled: "Pens, pencils, notebooks, writing paper and even typewriters went flying. Journalists were standing on their chairs cheering, some even with tears in their eyes."

Around the country, scenes described by Nella Last were being replicated in the vicinity of television and radio sets everywhere. "I laughed aloud at sober working men who had been listening in, and near parked cars, doing a kind of little jig," she recorded.

Matthews had created his fairytale ending, although the detail of the winning goal would soon become the subject of myth and mis-recollection. Only a couple of years later, Harry Johnston's account in his autobiography would have Matthews beating Hassall and Banks, racing down the touchline and breezing past Barrass before he "casually almost, flicked the ball neatly back". Matthews got it wrong too, describing in print how Taylor got a long throw from Farm and beat Langton before laying the ball to him to run at goal. Perry would say of Taylor: "He didn't get the credit, but he was the main man." Everyone seems to have forgotten the intricate pass inside that Matthews himself played to set things in motion, not to mention Fenton's important role in the move.

From the kick-off, Holden chased the ball through the middle of the Blackpool defence and into the penalty area but Farm was quick off his line and sure-handed enough to snuff out any brief hint of danger, despite an excited shriek from Wolstenholme, for which he apologised. "Peter Dimmock and I are going as mad as everyone else in the stadium," he said in mitigation.

Moir took a throw-in on the right, hurling it towards the advanced figure of Barrass, but the ball was cleared deep into the Bolton half. Referee Griffiths had seen enough. As Banks gathered the ball and launched it forward, the final whistle signalled the end of the game – and the beginning of a legend.

Blackpool arms went up in the air, mirrored by the hats and scarves in the stands and on the terraces. Mayor Peter Fairhurst was among the first to leap up, although he was fearful that by throwing his hat in the air he had breached the etiquette of the Royal Box. "I could not restrain myself," he explained. "I just stood up and shouted: 'We've won!' Princess Margaret turned round when she heard me and gave me a wonderful smile."

Journalist and author David Miller offered this description of the scenes at the end of a game he had attended as a young fan: "The stadium is in pandemonium. People lose hats, scarves, umbrellas, and probably some of their children, in an ecstasy of celebration. Thousands are in tears, tens of thousands are limp with emotional exhaustion. Such an event could not have been achieved by design for Coronation Year."

On the field, two Bolton players were the first to congratulate Matthews, who was then quickly surrounded by five team-mates. "There's the man, Matthews. At long last he's done it," said Wolstenholme as the cameras remained fixed on the drama's leading character. The suited figure of Smith appeared at his right shoulder, turning him towards him and grabbing him. "I just jumped out of my seat and ran across to Stanley Matthews to shake his hand," said Smith, before adding: "The players did a grand job."

As if worried that by relinquishing contact with his talisman he would break whatever magic spell had made this moment possible, Smith was reluctant to let go as he ushered Matthews towards the sideline for the presentations. Intent on keeping him at his side, Smith seemed happy to ignore almost every other player. When he finally shook the hand of his captain Johnston, it appeared a mere afterthought. Matthews was happy to share his moment with his manager and saw the symbolism of Smith's attachment to him. It was he, Matthews acknowledged, who had continued to believe in a player in his late 30s and who had "persuaded me to stay and live out his dream".

The line to go and collect the Cup formed with such speed that Johnston was almost caught in what, for him, would have been an embarrassing situation. As he looked into the stands in the hope of seeing his wife and father he suddenly remembered he had not reclaimed his false teeth. "Quick, Johnny," he called to John Crosland. "My teeth, my teeth. I've got to meet the Queen."

Johnston and Farm finally squeezed ahead of Shimwell at the front of the procession as they trotted towards the steps leading up into the stands. Behind that trio came Matthews. As the players neared the Royal Box, FA secretary Stanley Rous leaned across the Duke of Edinburgh to his right and reminded the Queen of her duties. She shuffled past her husband, exchanging places just in time to greet the winning team.

There was a brief awkward pause as the new monarch worked out the best way to hand over the trophy, telling Johnston: "Well done. It was a tremendous game," as she did so. Clutching the famous piece of silverware designed and made for the FA by a Bradford jeweller and in use since 1911, Johnston took his medal in his right hand and moved quickly towards the end of the presentation row. As if suddenly remembering the script, he raised the Cup briefly in the direction of the Blackpool fans opposite the tunnel end of the stadium before disappearing down the stairs. Perhaps he just wanted to vacate the stage for Matthews.

The cheer when the crowd saw the back of the number seven jersey accepting his box from the Queen was bigger than that when Johnston had offered the Cup to them. "Well done, Mr Matthews," she told him. "It was very exciting."

Matthews gave a brief wave to either end of the ground and was swiftly down the steps. The rest of his team followed in a brisk manner, eager not to miss out on any of the celebrations below. Perry opened his precious box to snatch a glance at his medal almost as soon as he had it in his hands. Matthews did likewise as he descended the steps, giving a quiet word of thanks as his eyes feasted upon the small piece of gold that had held such huge significance for him and millions of others. As he reached the field, he took it in his hand and held it up to the sky. "There it is, Dad," he said with quiet pride.

Behind the Blackpool players, the cheerful features and unruly hair of Moir led the Bolton team through their presentation procession. Once the last player had departed, the Queen picked up her handbag, her afternoon's work done. Directed to look down to the field, she saw Johnston standing behind an upright microphone and being introduced to the crowd. Reading from a piece of card held in front of him, the FA Cup under his right arm, he ventured: "Your Royal Highnesses, ladies and gentlemen, on behalf of the players of both teams I call for three cheers for Her Majesty the Queen."

Matthews would later write about Johnston having stunned the authorities by impulsively grabbing a microphone and instigating the show of appreciation for Elizabeth. This was nonsense. A more formal, less spontaneous scene would have been hard to imagine. Johnston seemed relieved to have got through it without fluffing his lines.

As photographers swarmed around the winning team, Johnston was lifted up on the shoulders of team-mates.

Then Mudie and Mortensen similarly hoisted Matthews, a generous gesture that demonstrated their awareness of the game's most powerful storyline and their lack of resentment at the fact. Even the Bolton players and fans were quick to realise the significance of the moment. One Wanderers fan would be quoted as saying: "If it had been another side I might have been more upset. We still went back and celebrated and when we opened the champagne we toasted Stanley Matthews."

In their home town, Blackpool fans were busy celebrating on their own behalf, not just for their hero. Happy to leave the confined and increasingly sweaty living rooms into which they had squeezed and strained as they watched the television coverage, they ran into the streets and congratulated each other as though each had played their part in the victory. Tom Begley had jumped out of the cab of his colourful number 9A bus to dance in front of its giant rosette. Some wondered how he had managed to discover the result so quickly, but one glance at the happy waves of humanity hitting the streets was all the evidence it required.

Such was the excitement of the occasion, especially for those of a more fragile disposition – which in the media's eyes usually meant women – that one *Evening Gazette* writer noted that he "heard of several cases" of female fans passing out in front of the television, with one even needing "a nip of brandy" to ensure her revival.

No one was staying by their screen in expectation of seeing their team parade the trophy around the pitch because that tradition was only just about to be launched by the happy Blackpool players. From his position on his team-mates' shoulders, Matthews noticed the shattered Bolton players treading despondently towards the tunnel. Malcolm Barrass even tossed his loser's medal away as he left the stadium. "I had just got back in," said his wife Joyce, "and I remember seeing Malcolm throw the box with his medal up in the air and it flying open. They were all on the floor looking for it and they eventually found it in the sand behind the goalmouth."

Matthews hopped down to the ground and joined his colleagues as they lifted their trophy towards the masses. His ears might have cleared since setting up the winning goal but his head and his senses were still being assailed by the surreal quality of the moment. "I still did not fully realise, as in the heat of the moment one never does, the true enormity and magnitude of our victory."

Once the players had waved their final farewells to the fans and returned to the corridors leading back to the dressing room, the relative quiet struck them almost as much as that first blast of noise had done a couple of hours earlier. These were the days before invasive television cameras lurked in corners or a PR man arrived to drag off players and managers to stand in front of a sponsor board. The occasional favoured photographer or club director were the only intruders as the players enjoyed what Matthews called a "haven from the tumultuous noise". The silence between the dressing room walls was filled by the shouts and cheers of every player as he entered, before each sat and enjoyed a moment of quiet reflection.

Bottles of champagne appeared and were quickly emptied into Blackpool's prized trophy. The foaming mixture was passed around the room, although Matthews, slumped on the bench above which his street clothes hung, preferred to sip tea. He was content to sit and watch the antics of his colleagues as he attempted to "bring some tranquillity to my fuddled brain".

Remembering their opponents, Blackpool's players drifted across the corridor in ones and twos and entered the Bolton dressing room, where Banks described the mood as "terrible". Barrass added: "We had it won. It was so disappointing. All my family were there to see us win the

Cup." For the Bolton centre-half, that last statement carried extra poignancy. It was to be the last time he saw his father alive.

Seeing some of his players in tears, manager Bill Ridding had been unable to find words with which to ease their pain. It was almost a relief when Mortensen appeared and broke the silence with his commiserations. "We know how you're feeling," he told the Wanderers players. As further Blackpool players entered, Matthews made a point of shaking the hand of Banks, the man he had tormented and whom he would praise in interviews for not resorting to attempts to kick him off the field.

Willie Moir responded on behalf of his team to Blackpool's gestures of sympathy: "If we had to lose there's no team we would have preferred to lose to. It was a terrific effort."

At the distance of six decades, it all seems somewhat twee and disingenuous. Yet it was nothing of the sort. There was no false, or forced, graciousness in Moir's words. When Johnston said that "in a way, the Bolton boys were glad to see the maestro get his Cup medal" he wasn't guilty of over-sentimentalising.

The camaraderie that existed among men with a shared background, the same lifestyle, commonly held dreams – and who, in many cases, had together experienced the hardships of more meaningful conflict less than a decade earlier – was genuine. For all its injustice, football's maximum wage created a bond between its professionals. For all their horror, the years of warfare had forged a spirit of benevolence among the people of Britain that was yet to be eroded by the passing of time and the arrival of new social disruption; a mood that was reflected on its playing fields and in its dressing rooms.

Besides, there was no one at Wembley who could fail to realise the history in which they had participated.

15

AFTER THE PARTY

"This reception is the best any team in any country has ever received." – skipper Harry Johnston to the Blackpool fans after the 1953 final.

THEY HAD come to be close to their heroes. Still wearing their tangerine scarves and rosettes, hundreds of them gathered outside the Café Royal in Regent Street, straining their necks in the hope of seeing beyond the commissionaires guarding the doors and catching a glimpse of one of the Blackpool players. Their good humour reflected the joyous events of earlier in the day and even when the police attempted to move them along they soon returned with their laughter and songs. This was where the Cup Final celebrations were being held and no one was going to deny them the opportunity to be close to the men who had made their third visit to Wembley so worthwhile, so memorable.

Those already on their way home in their cars, buses or trains were having no less a good time, singing and chanting, swapping memories of the day and, in the case of one fan, losing his teeth. As his train pulled out of Preston, he leant his head out of the window and yelled: "Up the Pool!" – only for his dentures to fall out.[29]

Inside the Café Royal, where both teams had booked ballrooms for their post-match banquets, Blackpool's gathering was naturally the more lively. The key ingredient was the FA Cup itself, which was passed from table to table, being replenished with champagne along the way. Local dignitaries, many of them a mixture of self-importance and starry-eyed worship, took the opportunity of rubbing shoulders with the men who had ensured the presence of the trophy in their midst.

No one wanted to miss an opportunity to add their congratulations and enjoy a little reflected glory, with Blackpool South MP J Roland Robinson attributing the victory to "guts, courage and endurance". When club chairman Harry Evans got up to speak, his desire to acknowledge the efforts of his team was strangely at odds with his unwillingness to offer significant financial reward for their accomplishments. "We can acclaim these lads now – tonight it's so easy," he began. "But we ought to concern ourselves seriously with their future when their playing days are over." As puzzled looks flickered between the players, he went on: "Our job should be to go on encouraging them when they're winning no more glory." More than one player was unable to resist the thought that a little more tangible encouragement right now would not be such a bad thing.

There was also a little historical revisionism at play when Football League president Arthur Drewery addressed the diners. The man who had argued against the live broadcast of the final for fear of damaging attendance at League games asserted: "The televising of such a match as we have seen

. . . .

29 He went back the following day and, with the help of railway officials, was able to identify the section of line where his mishap had occurred. After a brief search of the area – and a quick clean – his teeth were restored.

today at Wembley can bring nothing but the greatest credit on the game itself and on the 22 players who were in it." He had seen the light.

While champagne was being drunk and humble pie eaten in the Café Royal, newspaper offices in Fleet Street and Manchester – amid a flurry of tea cups and hastily-grabbed sandwiches – were putting the finishing touches to the pages that, in the morning, would bring the events at Wembley to the breakfast tables of the nation. If anyone was in any doubt about the way the game would be remembered in years to come, that was erased by what they read over their cornflakes. As presented to the reading public, the 1953 FA Cup Final was one in which Stanley Matthews had beaten Bolton on his own.

The *News of the World* led its front page with the tale of Matthews at last winning his FA Cup medal, adding the sub-heading: "That Old Matthews Magic Delighted the Queen", before reporting that "Stanley Matthews played the greatest game of his life". The last two Blackpool goals were attributed clearly to his influence, even though he had not been involved in Mortensen's equaliser. On its back page, the hyperbole was no less evident, with "STAN MATTHEWS INSPIRES THRILLING CUP VICTORY" as its headline. The *Guardian* – "Matthews Undermines Bolton" – ignored Bill Perry's scoring of the winning goal completely with an intro that read: "A footballing genius called Stanley Matthews won the FA Cup for Blackpool when his centre two minutes from time enabled his side to take the lead for the first time against Bolton Wanderers."

The *Sunday Chronicle* – "MAGNIFICENT MAT-THEWS" – went even further toward the altar of hero worship. "Matthews 4, Bolton 3 is more correctly the result of this pulsating, mistake-stricken, most sensational match ever staged at Wembley Stadium," it gushed.

In the modern day of tabloid reporting, where the events of a game are frequently prioritised in order to fit around the newspapers' chosen storyline, such side-stepping of objectivity is commonplace. In 1953, predetermining of the narrative was rare. And, to be sure, it was predetermined. As long as a week before the game the *News of the World*'s Frank Butler was using the title that would forever be attached to the game. "If they do win," he wrote of Blackpool, "it will go down in soccer history as the Stanley Matthews final. Never have so many wished so much for one man to get a winner's medal."

How much the public's desire for that outcome was being created – or at least fortified – by what they were reading on a daily basis is an interesting question. Fortunately for posterity, Matthews played well enough and contributed decisively enough to allow this distortion of the absolute truth to pass unnoticed by a public happy to buy into the myth. In Coronation year, with the surge of national pride that came along with it, they wanted their hero as much as the newspaper offices.

In future years Matthews would consistently repeat comments such as "to be honest, I found the whole thing one big embarrassment", and "every time I hear the words [Matthews Final] I cringe with embarrassment because quite simply it's not true". But, by and large, it was.

When looking back six decades on the game and making judgements on the appropriateness of the title "The Matthews Final" it is easy to fall into the trap of assuming that the name was applied purely because of what happened on the field – in which case it is easy to feel sympathy for the overlooked Stan Mortensen and Bill Perry. When Mortensen died in 1991, there were even sarcastic questions – born of sympathy for Mortensen's plight in 1953 – about whether his memorial service would be known as "The Matthews Funeral".

Yet firstly it should be noted that by the time the presses rolled on Sunday's publications, Mortensen was still only being credited in most newspapers with having scored two goals, his first attributed to the unfortunate Harold Hassall as an own goal. More importantly, when Hugh Kelly said of the "Matthews Final" label: "I thought it was all wrong for it to be described in that way; there were others in the team that had been to Wembley twice before," he missed the point that it referred not just to events on the pitch – or to fairness – but to the way that the public had anticipated and would forever recall the game. One could argue that had it been Bolton who scored the late winner, the label could still reasonably have been applied.

The title affixed to the match by the media projected this reality rather than creating the association. Even the actions of Matthews's team-mates in carrying him on their shoulders after the final whistle could be seen as an early acceptance of this, a reflection of the mood of the nation.

Indeed, if Prime Minister Winston Churchill had hoped that the tradition and sentimentalism attached to the Coronation would provide a further anchor for his people in times of change and uncertainty, then he must have nodded silent approval as he watched the 1953 FA Cup Final, and the reporting of it, achieve some of that a month ahead of time.

The Opta report of the action commissioned by *The Times* to celebrate the 50th anniversary of the game is interesting as it highlights the individual contributions of the players, ranking the performance of Matthews behind, in descending order, Mortensen, Moir, Wheeler, Taylor and Perry. But the conclusion that the newspaper drew – "Put simply, the Matthews Final is a myth" – is based purely on a statistical breakdown of the action and ignores the environment in which it took place. It is a verdict as flawed as that of the reporters who, in their excitement, sought to credit Matthews with single-handedly winning the game.

* * * * *

THE NEWSPAPER reports having been digested, Sunday afternoon found the Blackpool players taking a stroll outside their hotel and even joining in an impromptu kickabout in a nearby park. While a disbelieving group of boys enjoyed their unique engagement with the Cup winners, the rest of the nation – those with television access anyway – had to be content with that evening's edition of *What's My Line?*

The BBC game show hosted by Eamonn Andrews invited a group of celebrities to guess the occupation of various members of the public through a series of yes or no questions, although once a week the panel donned blindfolds to identify a well-known public figure. On this particular day there was no one in the country with greater fame than Stanley Matthews, but his appearance on the programme came with the condition that his colleagues appear alongside him. Andrews would explain that Matthews had insisted on this because victory at Wembley had been achieved through teamwork, not the efforts of any individual – although anyone whose only knowledge of the game had been their reading of the Sunday papers would have been hard pushed to agree. The show's pre-eminent participant, Gilbert Harding, correctly identified Matthews within two questions.

The BBC weren't the only ones keen to honour the heroes of the hour. On Monday, Blackpool FC received a telegram from Winston Churchill offering "hearty congratulations" on the team's achievement. "I am delighted that Blackpool has won the FA Cup," he said. "As a freeman of Blackpool I can share in the pleasure it will give to all citizens."

As the message from the Prime Minister was being pinned on the Bloomfield Road notice board, the team were leaving London for home, the trophy stowed precariously on the luggage rack in their first-class train compartment. While some chatted excitedly about the welcome that awaited them, captain Harry Johnston sat in silent meditation, his bowed head staring at his winner's medal. Others left him alone to his thoughts, and Matthews couldn't help wondering if he was thinking about his mother – just as he himself had spent so long since the final whistle contemplating his fulfilled promise to his father.

The party disembarked from their train at Preston at 3.20pm, boarding an open-topped Blackpool Seagull bus with its dark panel and seagull crest along the side. This was the vehicle that would take them on a triumphant final journey into Blackpool. By 4.15pm, they would be on the outskirts of town at Squires Gate, as the *Evening Gazette* had announced earlier, outlining the planned milestones on the route to the Town Hall in Talbot Square, where the team would arrive at 5.30pm. Crowds had begun to gather at the various vantage points from noon onwards, jostling for position with the various news cameras determined to record the emotional homecoming. By the end of the day 300,000 would be estimated to have turned out to see the FA Cup's first-ever journey to this part of the world, with 15,000 of them crowded into Talbot Square itself.

Stan Mortensen's shop had been decorated with ribbons and streamers and the *Gazette* described the scenes as "colourful, bewildering and certainly most moving". People hung from trees, clung to rooftops and leaned out of high windows. Tangerine confetti filled the air as buses and cars engaged in a concerto of honked horns.

As the team bus progressed along its 35-mile journey, the density of the tangerine-clad crowds grew, reaching five deep inside the boundaries of the borough. Cyclists battled to lead the bus into the town centre. Fans threw sticks of rock and chocolate footballs towards the players as they looked down from their elevated positions; Johnston front and centre with the orange and white-ribboned Cup secure in his grasp.

Blackpool fan Tom Alder reminisced for the *Stoke Sentinel* years later that "the day the Blackpool team toured the streets with the FA Cup was the busiest ever". He recalled: "My wife, Thelma, took our children to see them. She had the two youngest in a pushchair and the two other daughters holding on tightly to the pram so they wouldn't get lost in the crowds."

At the Town Hall, the players climbed down and gathered on the steps, in front of many of those same people who would have been standing there in Talbot Square in the first minutes of this historic year. For one player there was a special welcome. "Tommy, you're a father," a friend yelled at Tommy Garrett. His wife Moira had just given birth in a local nursing home to Paula, a sister for the couple's one-year-old son, Nigel. "Everything seems to have happened this weekend," the full-back remarked.

Robed and chained, Mayor Peter Fairhurst stood proudly between Johnston and Matthews. "Welcome home," he began, turning to look at each man in turn. "The reception you have just received now and your tour of the town is some proof of the tremendous admiration we all have for your magnificent effort at Wembley. It was a very great display and, although you gave us all a nasty shock at one time, I was always certain that you would win."

Johnston, whose promise on those very same steps two years earlier had been discharged, paid tribute to the town's response to their team, before Mortensen revealed that it had "brought a tear to our eyes". But it was Matthews from whom the throng wanted to hear, chanting for him to step forward. Somewhat shyly, he stood before the microphone, Johnston on his left holding the Cup at head level. "I do want to say what a wonderful reception you have given us. I also want to say I am told by one or two people that I was the match-winner, but I don't believe that for the simple reason that we have here 11 match-winners."

Cheers ricocheted around the square and the barriers strained to keep the crowd at a safe distance. The players were led inside the Town Hall to receive cigarette lighters bearing Blackpool's coat of arms. The memories of the reception they had received would last longer, and be of considerably greater value.

As the crowd dispersed, similar scenes were taking shape a few miles away in Bolton, with the obvious absence of the Cup and the lighters. Having arrived in Manchester shortly after 5pm, the beaten team departed an hour or so later in two buses. At five minutes before seven they took the cheers of the crowds outside Burnden Park. Over the next half-hour, they progressed slowly between packed pavements to the Town Hall, where the official welcome was given by Mayor James Vickers.

"The reception they got when they went back, you would have thought they had won," Joyce Barrass explained. "We went for a meal at the Town Hall and it was absolutely packed. You couldn't have got another person in there."

* * * * *

ONE MONTH later, much of the nation took to the streets again as the Coronation of Queen Elizabeth II turned out to be everything her people had hoped it would be. Not even a grey, showery day could dampen the enthusiasm of a public who watched in their millions, lined the procession routes in their hundreds of thousands and ravenously scoffed cream teas in street parties up and down the country.

As the day had approached, so the frenzy of anticipation had grown. The *Daily Sketch* even invited its readers to vote on "the best picture of the great events", offering anyone participating the chance to win "£1 a week for life". Norman Hartnell, designer of the Coronation gown, was in demand as keeper of the greatest secret in the land, just as he had been six years earlier after creating Elizabeth's wedding dress. Those who camped out in London for as long as three days in advance of the big day had to be content with the merest glance as the Queen passed by, but those inside Westminster Abbey or watching on television were able to feast their eyes on the full glory of his creation. A couple of hundred children and VIP guests inside Great Ormond Street Hospital were even able to see it in colour as part of an experimental broadcast.

Guests arrived at the Abbey from 8.30am, two hours before the Queen left Buckingham Palace for a ceremony that lasted more than three and a half hours, a severe test of patience and concentration for three-year-old Prince Charles, who managed just over an hour of proceedings. At the moment of crowning, relayed to those outside via hundreds of speakers, cheers of "God Save the Queen" resonated through the streets. For those gathered in The Mall, their reward came when the Queen returned to Buckingham Palace, six hours after departure, and emerged on the balcony to wave to her subjects. After an evening broadcast to the nation, the day was completed by a firework spectacular along the Thames, again delivered into the homes of millions of new television viewers. Britain had rarely felt so happy and glorious.

Football had celebrated the event early by staging the Coronation Cup at Hampden Park, Glasgow, in late May, Celtic beating Hibernian in front of 117,000 in the final of an eight-team knockout tournament that also featured

Arsenal, Manchester United, Newcastle, Tottenham, Aberdeen and Rangers.

There was little worthy of honouring a new monarch, however, in the first post-Coronation visit of a national team to Wembley. England, who had sandwiched a 4-4 draw against a Rest of Europe team between victories over Wales and Northern Ireland in their early-season games, were totally unprepared for the events of 25th November. The 6-3 victory of Hungary's 'Mighty Magyars' set in progress an evolutionary chain that moved through initial uproar to, in some places, a gradual and meaningful re-evaluation of the English game and, in less enlightened quarters, a further burying of heads in ever-deepening sand.

The impact of Blackpool's success in May contributed to the presence of three of their players, Matthews, Johnston and Ernie Taylor, in England's humiliated team. Neither Johnston, totally flummoxed in his tenth international by the positional versatility of centre-forward Nándor Hidegkuti, nor debutant Taylor would wear the England shirt again. Matthews would survive the scars of this momentous defeat sufficiently to play a further 18 games over the next six years. Yet the status of wingers as the most indispensable members of any English team, the conductors through which all the attacking energy was channelled, was already coming to an end. So much so that this book could even have been called *The Last English Final*, given that May 1953 marked the ultimate hurrah for a distinct – more innocent – era in the English game.

Tom Finney, who said the Hungary defeat left him "wondering what we had been doing all those years", went on to recall: "It was a shock to some people to find we were not only not the best team in the world, we weren't even the best team in Europe. We started questioning the 2-3-5 formation, which we'd always taken for granted." It was more than mere symbolism that when England finally reclaimed their place at the pinnacle of world football at the same stadium 13 years later, they did so in the wake of Alf Ramsey's decision to jettison the traditional wingers in his squad in favour of a narrower 4-1-3-2 formation.[30]

In the first wave of post-Hungary outcry, led by a press who could hardly be said to have foreseen events at Wembley, the Football Association set up technical committees to examine English methods and compare with other nations. Men such as Matt Busby, Stan Cullis, Arthur Rowe and Joe Mercer, as well as England manager Walter Winterbottom, were called upon to voice their opinions. There was no overnight revolution, England failing to make much of an impression on the 1954 and 1958 World Cups. It was more a case of gradual evolution, with the likes of Malcolm Allison, Alan Brown and Ron Greenwood continuing to work for a change in English methods long after the initial furore had died down.

The fortunes of the national team might not have been responsible for a drop in crowds at Football League games, but it was not until the aftermath of the 1966 World Cup that the steady decline of the second half of the 1950s and early 1960s was temporarily halted. One of the critical factors in falling attendance was the increasing spending power of working men, more of whom were moving away from urban areas into out-of-town estates. An improved home environment made them more likely to spend time in it, especially when faced with stagnating stadia with lack of cover, poor sanitation and inadequate catering facilities.

Stanley Matthews, of course, could still pack them in, as he would do right through to his retirement as a 50-year-

. . . .

30 Orthodox wide men John Connelly, Terry Paine and Ian Callaghan played one game each in the group stage of the 1966 World Cup before Ramsey settled on the pairing of Alan Ball and Martin Peters on the right and left of midfield.

old in 1965, four years after rejoining Stoke City. His skills, and the esteem in which he was held by those who covered the game, remained sufficiently undiminished for him to be named as the football writers' Footballer of the Year for the second time in 1962/63 as he helped his team win the Second Division title.

Even though he never added to his one England cap, Matthews's right-flank colleague, Taylor, would return to Wembley for a third FA Cup Final as part of the rebuilt Manchester United team of 1958. Johnston, meanwhile, left Blackpool in November 1955 to become player-manager of Reading, the club where Joe Smith had first taken charge of a team. His achievements as a manager, however, never measured up to the reputation he had earned as a captain, failing to get them out of the Third Division.

The season of Johnston's departure saw Blackpool, now under the captaincy of Hugh Kelly, achieve their highest-ever placing in the First Division, runners-up – albeit by some distance – to Manchester United. Following fourth and seventh place finishes over the next two seasons, Joe Smith finally brought his long run as club manager to an end in May 1958. Over the next nine unremarkable seasons the club was guided by former player Ron Suart, whose tenure was ended with the club's slide towards relegation during 1966/67.

That paved the way for the return of Stan Mortensen, who had left the club around the same time as Johnston for spells at Hull City, Southport, Bath and then Lancaster City. He had finally devoted himself to his business interests in his home town, where he became a Conservative councillor, but the offer of managing his beloved club tempted him back into football in February 1967. Among his first acts was to bring back Johnston as chief scout, but Mortensen lasted only two years in his job, narrowly missing out on a return to the First Division.

Promotion in 1969/70 to the First Division – where they lasted only one season – and a famous victory under Bob Stokoe's management in the 1971 Anglo-Italian Cup, beating Bologna on their own turf in a final shown live on BBC, were the club's last steps in the glorious path trodden by their predecessors of the 1950s. For almost 40 years the club skipped around the lower divisions, twice being managed by their unlucky forward Allan Brown, whose two stints combined lasted less than three years. Only when they made their unlikely, romantic return to the top flight under Ian Holloway at the end of the new millennium's first decade were they back in the spotlight created by the likes of Matthews and Mortensen.

Bill Perry and Cyril Robinson, close friends who remained living in Blackpool, were regular visitors to the club during those disappointing years, Perry having played for the club until 1962 – making three England appearances – before winding down his career at Southport, Hereford and in Australia. When he died in 2007, aged 77, it left Robinson as the last survivor of the victorious 1953 team. Robinson never was able to command a regular first-team place at Blackpool, playing only 21 games before going on to Northwich Victoria, Bradford Park Avenue and Southport and completing his playing career with a series of minor non-league teams and a couple in Australia.

The fortunes of Bolton Wanderers remained a little more robust than their rivals over the ensuing decades, although after winning the FA Cup in 1958 they slipped out of the First Division in 1964. They regained top-flight status for a couple of seasons at the end of the 1970s under manager Ian Greaves and spearheaded briefly by the flamboyant Frank Worthington, the antithesis of the direct and robust style of centre-forward play favoured by Lofthouse. They fell to the depths of the Fourth Division before twice climbing into the Premier League in the 1990s, under Bruce Rioch and then

Colin Todd. On both occasions, they lasted only one season but further promotion under Sam Allardyce began a run in the top flight that, in 2011/12, ended after 11 seasons.

The abolition of the maximum wage for players in 1960/61 contributed to the difficulty small-town clubs such as Blackpool and Bolton would have in competing with the richer clubs from Manchester, Merseyside and London. It also made obsolete stories such as those of Finney and Lofthouse, who remained fixtures at their local clubs because they knew there was no additional money to be made anywhere else.

Lofthouse remains a constant presence at Bolton, having had a stand named after him when Wanderers left Burnden Park to move into their new home at the Reebok Stadium in 1997. His playing career was ended by a knee injury in 1960, by which time he had scored more than 250 goals for his club and 30 in 33 games for England. He remained at Bolton as, at various times, assistant trainer, chief coach, manager, chief scout, executive manager and caretaker manager before being made president in 1986. When he died early in 2011, it brought to an end a 70-year association with his home town club.

His close friend Malcolm Barrass left in 1956 for Sheffield United, whose manager Joe Mercer fulfilled a promise he had made earlier that "if ever you become available, I'll come after you". The skipper of the 1953 team, Willie Moir, had departed for Stockport a year earlier after scoring 118 goals in his Bolton career, while injured Wembley hero Eric Bell remained at the club until 1958, any hopes of forcing his way into the England team having been dashed by the emergence of a remarkable young left-half called Duncan Edwards at nearby Manchester United.

By the time Bolton reached the 1958 final, against the remnants of that tragic United side, only Doug Holden remained alongside Lofthouse from the 1953 team (although two squad members, Roy Hartle and Tommy Banks, had been elevated in the full-back positions). Holden would play five times for England before leaving Burnden Park in 1962 for Preston North End, where he scored a goal in a losing effort against West Ham in the 1964 FA Cup Final.

Commentating on that game was Kenneth Wolstenholme, who would continue behind the microphone for the BBC until 1971, losing his status as the corporation's leading man to David Coleman and spending several years in the ITV network on Tyne Tees Television. Just when we thought it was all over, he reappeared in the 1990s as an announcer on Channel 4's Italian football coverage.

And as for Queen Elizabeth II, well, at the time of writing she appears destined to reign over us for a while longer, even if her football activities have been curtailed. With age making an afternoon at Wembley Stadium a less appealing prospect, her duties in handing over English football's most famous trophy to the winning team have been passed on most frequently to her grandson, Prince William, the president of the Football Association.

In the early years of her reign she became a regular attendee at FA Cup Finals, presenting the Cup to illustrious captains such as Joe Harvey, Roy Paul, Danny Blanchflower, Noel Cantwell, Ron Yeats and Billy Bremner among others. She has witnessed Bert Trautmann's broken-neck heroics, Manchester United's first post-Munich triumph, Jeff Astle's thunderbolt winner for West Bromwich Albion and Second Division Southampton's finest hour.

But never has she witnessed an FA Cup Final to match the on-field thrills, human drama and historic symbolism of the match played in her Coronation year, 1953. It's doubtful that anyone ever will.

APPENDIX

FOOTBALL LEAGUE FIRST DIVISION 1952/53

	P	W	D	L	F	A	GA	Pts
Arsenal	42	21	12	9	97	64	1.516	54
Preston North End	42	21	12	9	85	60	1.417	54
Wolverhampton Wanderers	42	19	13	10	86	63	1.365	51
West Bromwich Albion	42	21	8	13	66	60	1.100	50
Charlton Athletic	42	19	11	12	77	63	1.222	49
Burnley	42	18	12	12	67	52	1.288	48
Blackpool	**42**	**19**	**9**	**14**	**71**	**70**	**1.014**	**47**
Manchester United	42	18	10	14	69	72	0.958	46
Sunderland	42	15	13	14	68	82	0.829	43
Tottenham Hotspur	42	15	11	16	78	69	1.130	41
Aston Villa	42	14	13	15	63	61	1.033	41
Cardiff City	42	14	12	16	54	46	1.174	40
Middlesbrough	42	14	11	17	70	77	0.909	39
Bolton Wanderers	**42**	**15**	**9**	**18**	**61**	**69**	**0.884**	**39**
Portsmouth	42	14	10	18	74	83	0.892	38
Newcastle United	42	14	9	19	59	70	0.843	37
Liverpool	42	14	8	20	61	82	0.744	36
Sheffield Wednesday	42	12	11	19	62	72	0.861	35
Chelsea	42	12	11	19	56	66	0.848	35
Manchester City	42	14	7	21	72	87	0.828	35
Stoke City	42	12	10	20	53	66	0.803	34
Derby County	42	11	10	21	59	74	0.797	32

FOOTBALL ASSOCIATION CUP 1952/53

Third round
Bolton 3 (Holden, Moir, Lofthouse) Fulham 1 (Mitten). Burnden Park: 32,235.
Bolton: Hanson, Hartle, Higgins, Wheeler, Barrass, Bell, Holden, Moir, Lofthouse, Parry, Langton.

Sheffield Wednesday 1 (Sewell) Blackpool 2 (Matthews, Taylor). Hillsborough: 60,199.
Blackpool: Farm, Shimwell, Garrett, McKnight, Johnston, Fenton, Matthews, Mudie, Brown, Taylor, Perry.

Fourth round
Blackpool 1 (Garrett) Huddersfield 0. Bloomfield Road: 29,293.
Blackpool: Farm, Shimwell, Garrett, Johnston, Crosland, Fenton, Matthews, Mudie, Brown, Taylor, Perry.

Bolton 1 (Lofthouse) Notts County 1 (McPherson). Burnden Park: 40,048.
Bolton: Hanson, Hartle, R Banks, Wheeler, Barrass, Bell, Holden, Moir, Lofthouse, Hassall, Langton.

Notts County 2 (Jackson, McPherson) Bolton 2 (Moir 2), after extra time. Meadow Lane: 33,668.
Bolton: Hanson, Hartle, R Banks, Wheeler, Barrass, Bell, Holden, Moir, Lofthouse, Hassall, Langton.

Bolton 1 (Lofthouse) Notts County 0. Hillsborough: 23,171.
Bolton: Hanson, Hartle, R Banks, Wheeler, Barrass, Bell, Holden, Moir, Lofthouse, Hassall, Langton.

Fifth round
Blackpool 1 (Perry) Southampton 1 (Horton). Bloomfield Road: 27,543.
Blackpool: Farm, Shimwell, Garrett, Johnston, Crosland, Kelly, Matthews, Mudie, Brown, Taylor, Perry.

Southampton 1 (Walker) Blackpool 2 (Horton own goal, Brown). The Dell: 29,223.
Blackpool: Farm, Shimwell, Garrett, Johnston, Crosland, Fenton, Matthews, Mudie, Brown, Taylor, Perry.

Luton 0 Bolton 1 (Lofthouse). Kenilworth Road: 23,735.
Bolton: Hanson, Hartle, Higgins, Wheeler, Barrass, Bell, Holden, Moir, Lofthouse, Hassall, Langton.

Sixth round

Arsenal 1 (Logie) Blackpool 2 (Taylor, Brown). Highbury: 69,158.

Blackpool: Farm, Shimwell, Garrett, Fenton, Johnston, Kelly, Matthews, Taylor, Mudie, Brown, Perry.

Gateshead 0 Bolton 1 (Lofthouse). Redheugh Park: 17,692.

Bolton: Hanson, Hartle, Higgins, Wheeler, Barrass, Bell, Holden, Moir, Lofthouse, Hassall, Langton.

Semi-finals

Blackpool 2 (Perry, Mudie) Tottenham 1 (Duquemin). Villa Park: 68,221.

Blackpool: Farm, Shimwell, Garrett, Fenton, Johnston, Kelly, Matthews, Taylor, Mudie, Mortensen, Perry.

Bolton 4 (Holden, Moir, Lofthouse 2) Everton 3 (Parker 2, Farrell). Maine Road: 75,213.

Bolton: Hanson, Hartle, Higgins, Wheeler, Barrass, Bell, Holden, Moir, Lofthouse, Hassall, Langton.

Final

Blackpool 4 (Mortensen 3, Perry) Bolton 3 (Lofthouse, Moir, Bell). Wembley Stadium: 100,000.

Blackpool: Farm, Shimwell, Garrett, Fenton, Johnston, Robinson, Matthews, Taylor, Mortensen, Mudie, Perry.
Bolton: Hanson, Ball, R Banks, Wheeler, Barrass, Bell, Holden, Moir, Lofthouse, Hassall, Langton.

BIBLIOGRAPHY

Adamson, Richard *Bogota Bandit: The Outlaw Life of Charlie Mitten: Manchester United's Penalty King* (Mainstream, 1996)

Armfield, Jimmy *Right Back to the Beginning: The Autobiography* (Headline, 2004)

Barnes, Walley *Captain of Wales* (Stanley Paul, 1953)

Bowler, Dave and David Reynolds *Ron Reynolds: The Life of a 1950s Footballer* (Orion, 2003)

Buchan, Charles *A Lifetime in Football* (Mainstream Publishing, 2010)

Chapman, Herbert *Herbert Chapman on Football* (Garrick Publishing, 1934)

Daniels, Robin *Blackpool Football: The Official Club History* (Robert Hale, 1972)

Docherty, Tommy *Soccer From The Shoulder* (Soccer Book Club, 1960)

Elborough, Travis *Wish You Were Here: England on Sea* (Sceptre, 2010)

Finney, Tom *My Autobiography* (Headline, 2003)

Giles, John *A Football Man: The Autobiography* (Hodder & Stoughton, 2010)

Goldblatt, David *The Ball Is Round: A Global History of Football* (Viking, 2006)

Green, Geoffrey *Pardon Me for Living* (George Allan & Unwin, 1985)

Green, Geoffrey *Soccer In The Fifties* (Ian Allan, 1974)

Hayes, Dean *Britain in Old Photographs: Bolton Wanderers* (Sutton Publishing, 1999)

Hennessey, Peter *Having It So Good: Britain in the Fifties* (Allen Lane, 2006)

Hopcraft, Arthur *The Football Man: People and Passions in Soccer* (Collins, 1968)

Hugman, Barry (editor) *Football League Players' Records 1946-92* (Tony Williams Publications, 1992)

Inglis, Simon *League Football and the Men Who Made it* (Willow Books, 1998)

Inglis, Simon *The Football Grounds of England and Wales* (Collins Willow, 1983)

Jeffs, Peter *The Golden Age of Football* (Breedon Books, 1991)

Johnes, Martin and Gavin Mellor *The 1953 FA Cup Final: Modernity and Tradition in British Culture* (Taylor and Francis, 2006)

Johnston, Harry *Rocky Road to Wembley* (The Sportsman's Book Club, 1957)

Kynaston, David *Family Britain 1951-57* (Bloomsbury, 2009)

Lewis, Peter *The Fifties* (William Heinemann, 1978)

Lofthouse, Nat *The Lion of Vienna* (Sportsprint Publishing, 1989)

Malcolmson, Patricia and Robert (editors) *Nella Last in the 1950s* (Profile Books, 2010)

Marland, Simon *Bolton Wanderers: One Hundred Years at Burnden Park* (Breedon Books, 1995)

Matthews, Stanley *Feet First Again* (Nicholas Kaye, 1952)

Matthews, Stanley *The Way It Was: My Autobiography* (Headline, 2000)

McIlroy, Jimmy *Right Inside Soccer* (Nicholas Kaye, 1960)

McKinstry, Leo *Sir Alf: A Major Reappraisal of the Life and Times of England's Greatest Football Manager* (Harper Sport, 2006)

Miller, David *Stanley Matthews* (Pavilion Books, 1989)

Mitten, Andy *United! United! Old Trafford in the '70s* (Vision Sports Publishing, 2011)

Mortensen, Stanley *Football Is My Game* (Sampson Lowe, 1949)

Ponting, Ivan and Barry Hugman *The Concise Post-war History of Bolton Wanderers* (Repvern Publishing, 1994)

Prestage, Mike *Blackpool: The Glory Years Remembered* (Breedon Books, 2000)

Russell, Dave *Football and The English* (Carnegie Publishing, 1997)

Saffer, David (editor) *Match of My Life: FA Cup Finals 1953-1969* (Know The Score, 2007)

Sandbrook, Dominic *State of Emergency: The Way We Were: Britain, 1970-74* (Allen Lane, 2010)

Theroux, Paul *The Kingdom By The Sea* (Hamish Hamilton, 1983)

Tossell, David *Big Mal: The High Life and Hard Times of Malcolm Allison, Football Legend* (Mainstream, 2008)

Tossell, David *In Sunshine Or in Shadow: A Journey Through the Life of Derek Dougan* (Pitch Publishing, 2012)

Ward, Andrew and John Williams *Football Nation: Sixty Years of the Beautiful Game* (Bloomsbury, 2009)

Wilson, Jonathan *Inverting the Pyramid: A History of Football Tactics* (Orion, 2008)

Wilson, Jonathan *The Anatomy of England: A History in Ten Matches* (Orion, 2010)

Wolstenholme, Gerry *Cup Kings: Blackpool 1953* (The Bluecoat Press, 1998)

Wolstenholme, Kenneth *50 Sporting Years... And It's Still Not All Over* (Robson Books, 1999)

Young, Percy *Bolton Wanderers* (Stanley Paul, 1961)

The following newspapers, periodicals, annuals and websites have also been vital to my research: Bolton Evening News, Daily Express, Daily Mail, Daily Mirror, Daily Sketch, Daily Telegraph, Independent, Lancashire Post, Manchester Evening News, Manchester Guardian, Stoke Sentinel, Sunday Chronicle, Sunday Telegraph, The Times, West Lancashire Evening Gazette, Charles Buchan's Football Monthly, FA Yearbook (various years), Playfair Football Annual (various years), www.BlackpoolFC.co.uk, www.Blackpool-mad.co.uk, www.BoltonRevisited.org.uk, www.BWFC.co.uk, www.soccerbase.com